Quick Steps

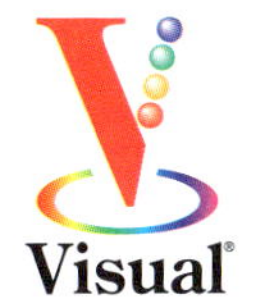

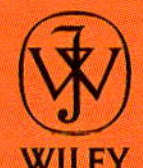

John Wiley & Sons, Inc.

Digital Photography Visual™ Quick Steps

Published by
John Wiley & Sons, Inc.
10475 Crosspoint Boulevard
Indianapolis, IN 46256

www.wiley.com

Published simultaneously in Canada

ISBN: 978-1-118-33879-7

Trademark Acknowledgments

Manufactured in the United States of America

10 9 8 7 6 5 4 3 2 1

Contact Us

For general information on our other products and services please contact our Customer Care Department within the U.S. at 877-762-2974, outside the U.S. at 317-572-3993 or fax 317-572-4002.

For technical support please visit www.wiley.com/techsupport.

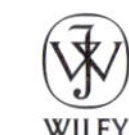

John Wiley & Sons, Inc.

Sales

Contact Wiley
at (877) 762-2974 or
fax (317) 572-4002.

Credits

Acquisitions Editor
Aaron Black

Sr. Project Editor
Sarah Hellert

Technical Editor
Dennis R. Cohen

Copy Editor
Scott Tullis

Editorial Director
Robyn Siesky

Business Manager
Amy Knies

Sr. Marketing Manager
Sandy Smith

Vice President and Executive Group Publisher
Richard Swadley

Vice President and Executive Publisher
Barry Pruett

Sr. Project Coordinator
Kristie Rees

Graphics and Production Specialists
Jennifer Henry
Andrea Hornberger
Jennifer Mayberry

Quality Control Technician
Rob Springer

Proofreader
Penny Stuart

Screen Artist
Jill A. Proll

Illustrators
Ronda David-Burroughs
Cheryl Grubbs

Table of Contents

chapter 1 Understanding Digital Photography

Why Go Digital? 4
Discover Digital Cameras 6
From Start to Finish: The Digital Workflow 8

chapter 2 What You Need to Get Started

Choose a Digital Camera 14
Consider Digital Camera Accessories 16
Build a Digital Darkroom 20
Choose a Photo Printer 22

chapter 3 Controlling Exposure and Focal Length

Learn About ISO 26
Learn About Aperture 27
Control Depth of Field 28
Understanding Shutter Speed 29
Discover Exposure Modes 30
Learn About Focal Length 32
Use a Wide-Angle Lens 33
Use a Telephoto Lens 34
Use a Zoom Lens 35
Learn About Digital Camera Lenses 36

chapter 4 Understanding Light

Learn About the Color of Light 42
Measure and Correct Light for Color 44
Learn About Light Quality 46
Use a Flash 50

chapter 5 Learning About Focus

Understanding Focus Systems 54
Focus on an Off-Center Subject 56
Use Focus Modes 58
Discover Focus Techniques 59

chapter 6 Composing Pictures like a Pro

Visualize Composition 62
Consider Design Principles 64
Discover Rules of Composition 66
Learn to Control Composition 68

chapter 7 Putting It All Together

Experiment with Depth of Field 72
Mix and Match Settings 74
Change Shutter Speed for Effect 76
Focus Selectively 77
Compose Creatively 78
Explore Different Lighting Options 80
Try Creative Techniques 82

Table of Contents

chapter 8 Taking Your First Digital Photos

Set Up a Digital Camera 86
Take Test Pictures 88
Troubleshoot Problems 90
Transfer Pictures to Your Computer 92
Evaluate Your Photos 94
Fine-Tune Camera Settings 96

chapter 9 Taking Advantage of Your Camera's Settings

Match the Scene to the Setting 100
Be Aware of In-Camera Settings 101
How Do the Scene Settings Change the Images? 102
Use the Settings Creatively 104
Evaluate Your Photos 106
Better to Change Things Later? 107

chapter 10 Avoiding Digital Photography Pitfalls

Avoid Taking Unfixable Pictures 110
What Is a Histogram? 111
Use a Histogram as You Take Pictures 112
Compensate for Shutter Lag 114
Avoid Blowouts 115
Keep Your Camera Steady 116
Avoid Undesirable Colorcasts 117
Never Use Digital Zoom 118
Reduce Digital Noise 119

Capturing Unique Photo Opportunities

Photograph Products to Sell on eBay . . . 122

Take Great Close-Up Photos . . . 124

Take Photos at Night without a Flash . . . 126

Capture Firework Displays . . . 127

chapter 12 Organizing Your Photos

Why Use Image Editing Programs? . . . 130

What Is a Digital Editing Workflow? . . . 132

Photo Editing Options . . . 134

Understanding Metadata in Your Photos . . . 136

What Are RAW Digital Photos? . . . 137

Import Photos to Your Browser . . . 138

Review, Sort, and Tag Your Photos . . . 140

Tag Photos . . . 142

Find Images Using Tags . . . 146

Use Tags to Sort . . . 148

Chapter 1

Understanding Digital Photography

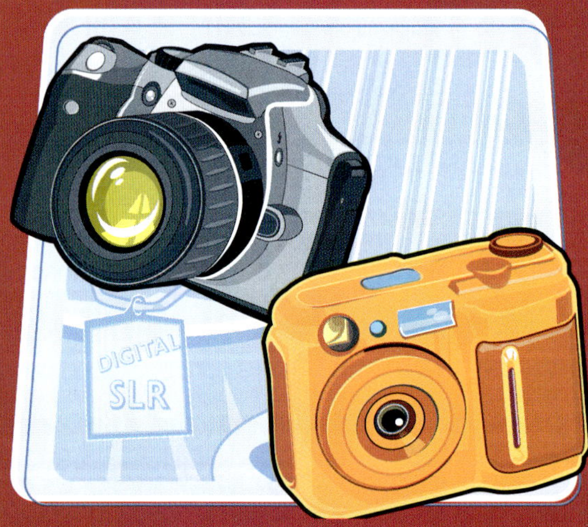

Are you confused about how digital photography works? This chapter introduces you to the advantages of digital photography, the different types of digital, and how easy it is to work with and use digital pictures.

Quick Steps

Why Go Digital? 4
Discover Digital Cameras 6
From Start to Finish: The Digital Workflow 8

Why Go Digital?

With digital photography, you can do more than take snapshots for your family album. You can use a digital camera to quickly and significantly improve your photography skills. You can e-mail your digital pictures to family and friends, share your photos on social networking sites, or create interesting Web pages about your hobbies, family, or even home business. You can also simplify everyday tasks, or take part in documenting your family history with a digital scrapbook.

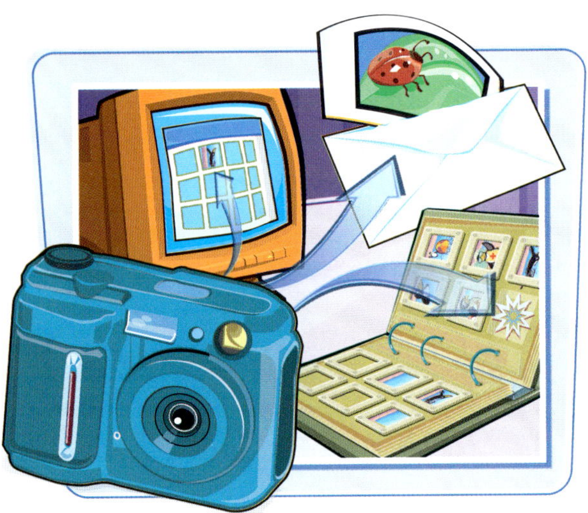

Improve Your Photography Skills

Because digital pictures do not require film and processing, you can experiment with lighting, composition, camera modes, and creative techniques at no cost. Because you see images immediately, you can modify your setting or approach, and try new things, then evaluate all your images when you get home. The best way to become a better photographer is to take many pictures.

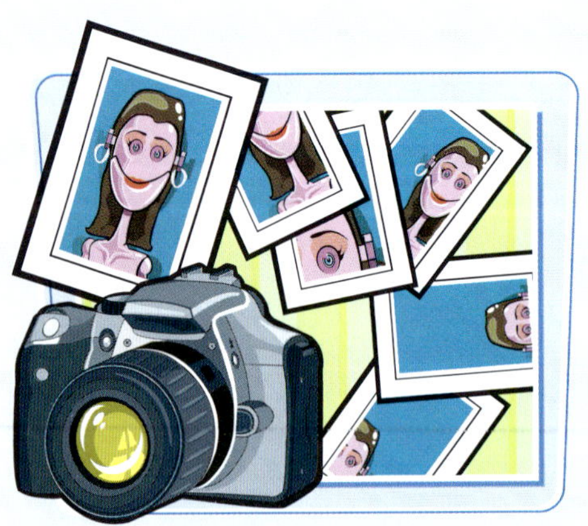

Simplify Everyday Tasks

A digital camera allows you to share and convey information easily. For example, you can capture special moments such as birthdays and anniversaries and almost immediately send the pictures to your friends in an e-mail message, or share them on a Web site. You can also take digital pictures of club members for a visual directory. Other tasks include creating a home inventory for insurance records, and photographing items you are selling online.

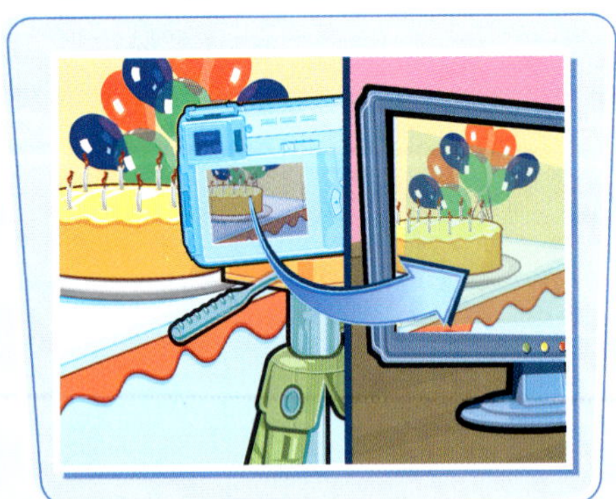

Share Pictures Online and in E-mail

Within minutes of taking a picture, you can share it in an e-mail message, or upload it to an online photo site to share with family and friends. By doing it this way, those loved ones who want prints of the photos can buy them online and receive the prints in the mail. There are countless online options for sharing photos and having prints made quickly.

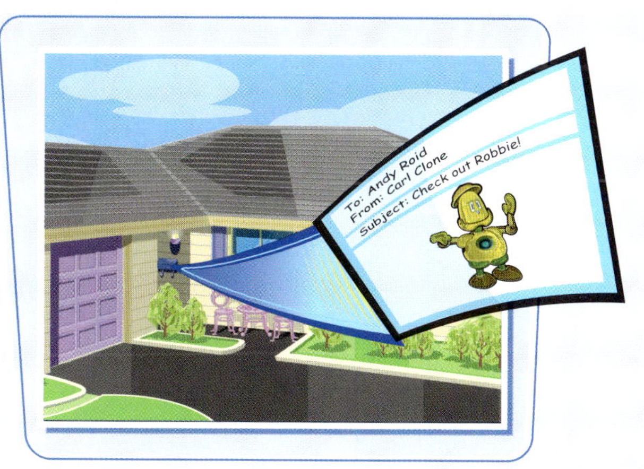

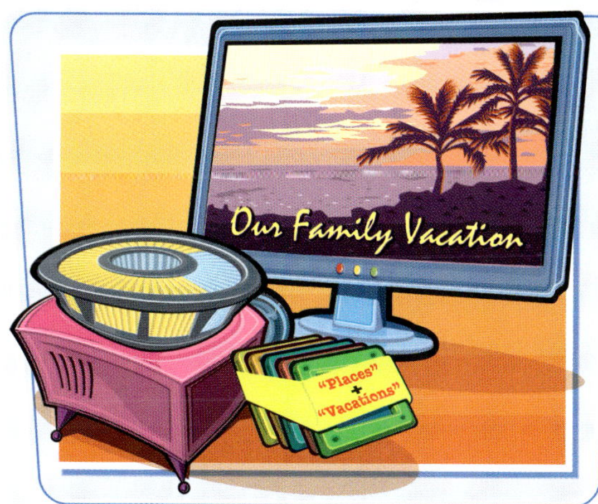

Create Photo Slide Shows on CDs or DVDs

You can use programs such as iPhoto, Windows Live Photo Gallery, and Photoshop Elements to create digital image slide shows on recordable CDs and DVDs. Then you can add voice narration, captions, music, digital movie clips, and transitions to finish the slide show. Photoshop Elements and iPhoto also let you organize your digital images by assigning each photo a keyword. If you want, you can even add a rating, color, or flag to help select your favorites. You can use these keywords or ratings to find and select a particular photo for your slide show or just see all your best photos with a click of a button.

Discover Digital Cameras

When you understand how digital cameras work, you can take that knowledge and make an informed decision when it comes time to purchase your first digital camera or to upgrade your existing one. Knowing how digital cameras work also enables you to get better images from your camera.

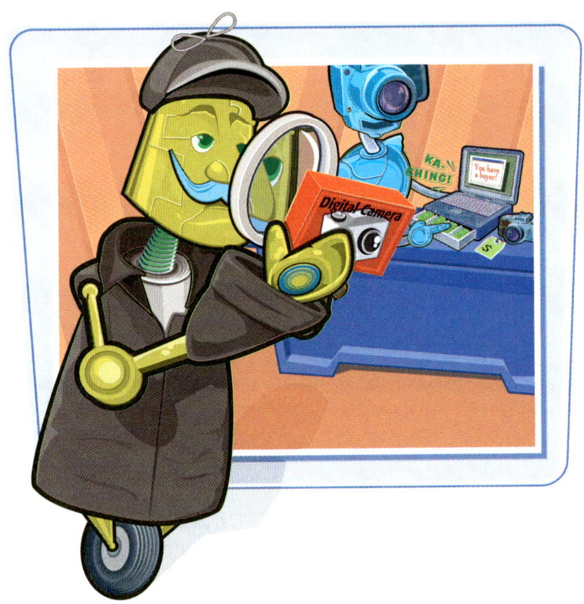

How Digital Cameras Record Pictures

Digital cameras record pictures using an *image sensor array* — a grid composed of millions of light-sensitive pixels. The term *pixel* describes a picture element. The pixels are the building blocks of all digital images. A red, green, or blue filter covers each pixel on the sensor so that it responds to only one of the primary colors of light. Each pixel reads the brightness and color in a scene to produce an electrical signal. The signal is then converted to a digital number that represents the color and brightness of the pixel. The camera's onboard computer processes the information to build a final image before storing it in memory.

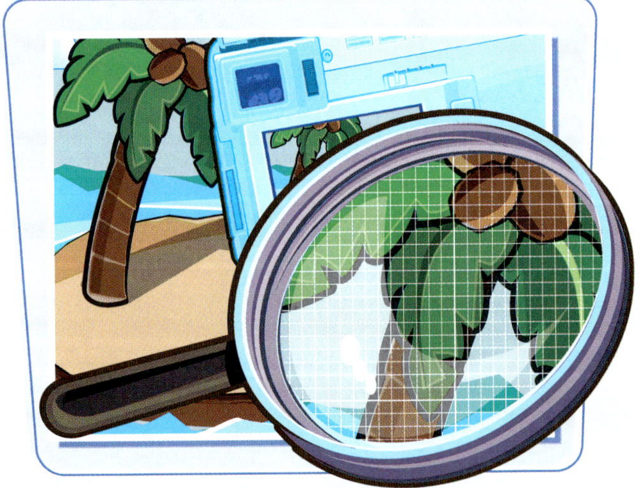

Types of Image Sensors

Most digital cameras use one of two types of image sensors: a charge-coupled device (CCD) or a complementary metal-oxide semiconductor (CMOS). Although each type of sensor has technical differences in how the light energy is transferred into electronic signals, both produce high-quality images.

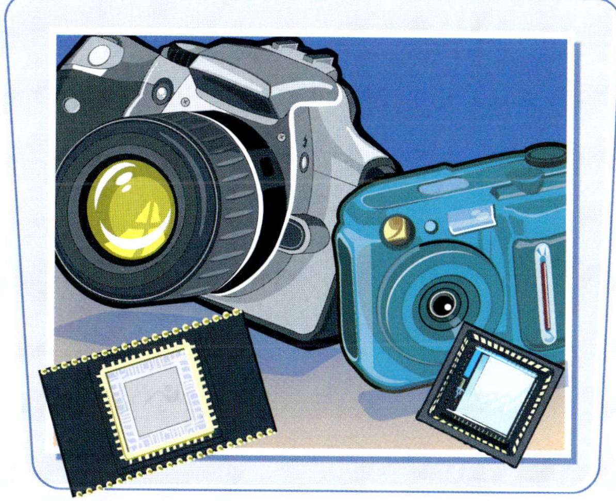

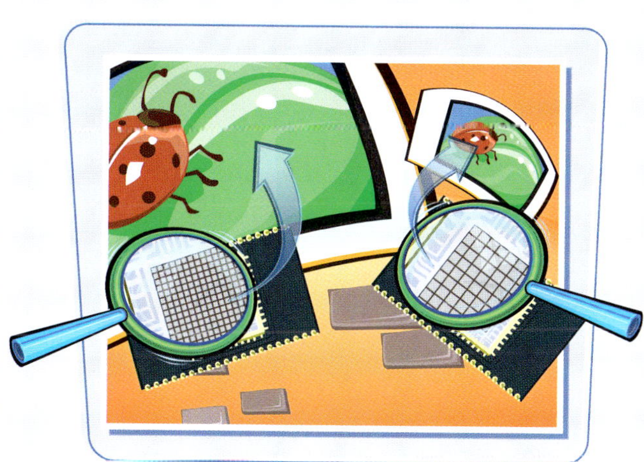

Resolution and Image Quality

Resolution is a measure of pixel density; higher-resolution images have more pixels per inch and the possibility of greater detail. On a digital camera, the greater the number of pixels on the image sensor, the larger you can print the photo. There are consumer cameras with sensor resolutions of up to 15 megapixels. Digital cameras with 6 to 8 megapixels offer excellent image quality for prints larger than 8×10 and can be very affordable. Cameras with higher resolution allow for more creative cropping and often come with more advanced features.

From Start to Finish: The Digital Workflow

A digital workflow is a step-by-step process that helps you get the best digital images and also manages your collection of images. The workflow includes taking, editing, sharing, organizing, and storing digital pictures. You can use the digital workflow described here as an introduction to and ongoing guide for working with your digital images.

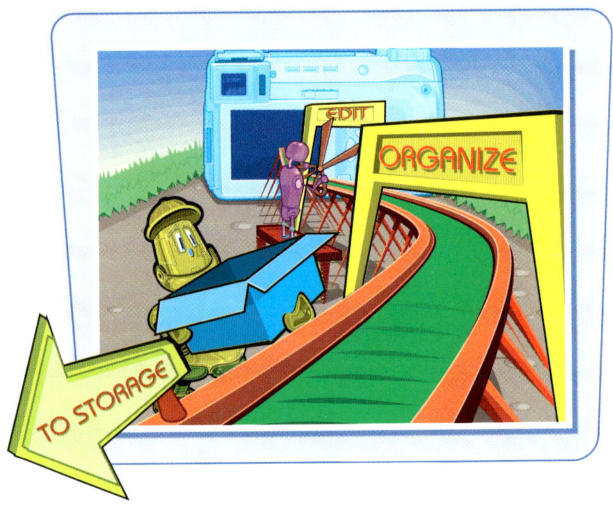

Capture Images

The digital workflow begins by choosing camera settings that will produce the best photo. You can choose a preset scene mode (portrait, landscape, sunset, for example), use a fully automatic setting, or set the camera to operate in manual shooting mode. To learn more about exposure, see Chapter 3.

Confirm that the camera's white balance matches the light in the scene or is set to auto. For more information on white balance, see Chapter 8.

Then compose the image in the frame, adjust the zoom, ensure the autofocus has the subject in focus, and take the picture.

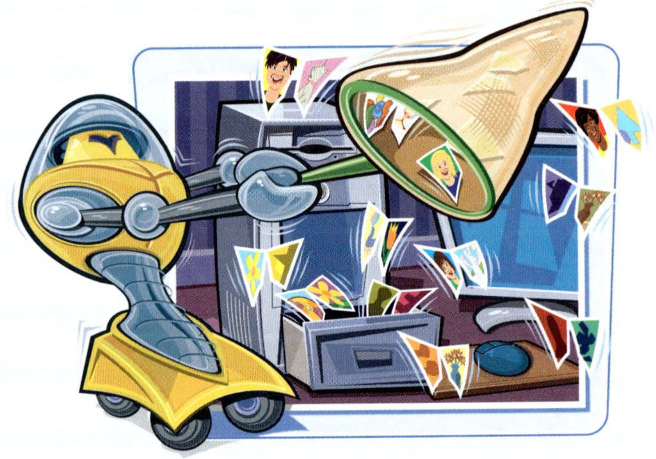

Verify Exposure and Composition

Next, review the picture on the camera's LCD screen to ensure that the exposure and composition are acceptable. As you review the image in your LCD, look for distracting background elements, closed eyes, and other elements that you can improve. If the picture is too light (overexposed), or too dark (underexposed), most cameras set to automatic allow you to easily correct that by adjusting the exposure using exposure compensation. When in doubt, retake the picture and try new things — as many times as you want.

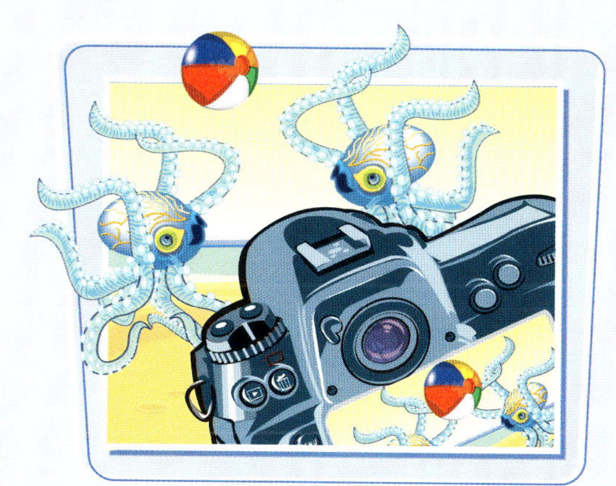

Use the LCD

The LCD screens on today's cameras are getting ever bigger, brighter, and clearer, but it still may be difficult to determine how good the photo is. Learn how to zoom the LCD display to get a closer look at the details of your photo. Unless the picture is hopelessly flawed, do not delete it. Instead wait and evaluate it on your computer — you may be able to save the picture or use the information in the photo to help you learn.

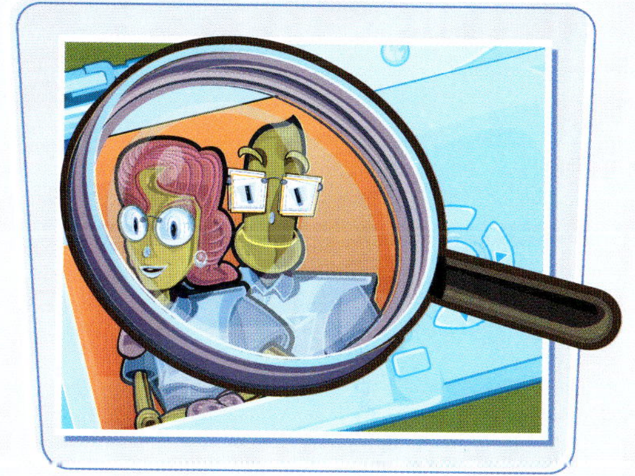

Transfer Pictures to a Computer

You can transfer pictures from your camera to your computer with a USB cable, a card reader, or a docking station. The fastest way to transfer pictures is by using a card reader. Card readers come in many forms, they are inexpensive, and they do not drain your camera battery — which happens when you hook your camera to the computer.

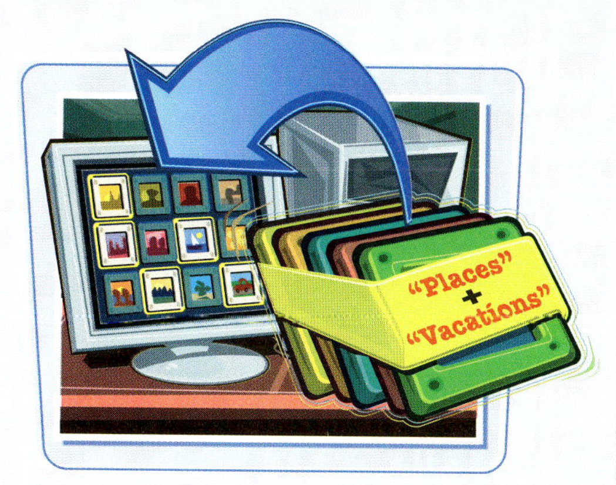

Edit Pictures

You can use image-editing software that comes with your camera or computer, or software that you purchase to edit pictures. Image-editing programs enable you to rotate, adjust color and saturation, correct red eye, remove unwanted elements (even people), crop, resize, sharpen, combine, and add text to digital pictures. There is no end to the things you can do to your digital photos. See Chapter 12 to learn more about working with image-editing software.

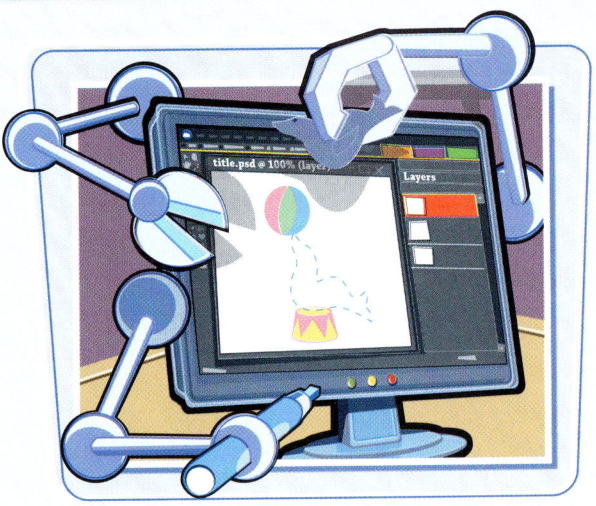

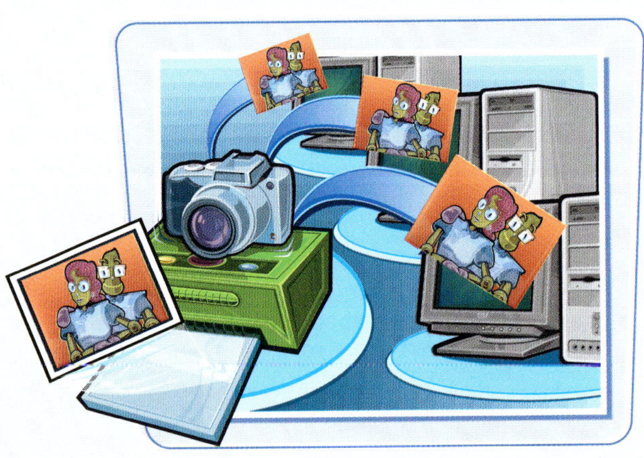

Print and Share Pictures

After you edit, crop, and sharpen your pictures, you can print them on a home photo-quality printer, or at a commercial printing service — either online or at your local photo lab and even grocery stores. In many ways it is just like dropping film off to be processed, but now you only have to print the photos you know that you like. You can also share them in e-mail messages, on social networking Web sites, or on a photo-sharing Web site.

Organize and Store Digital Negatives

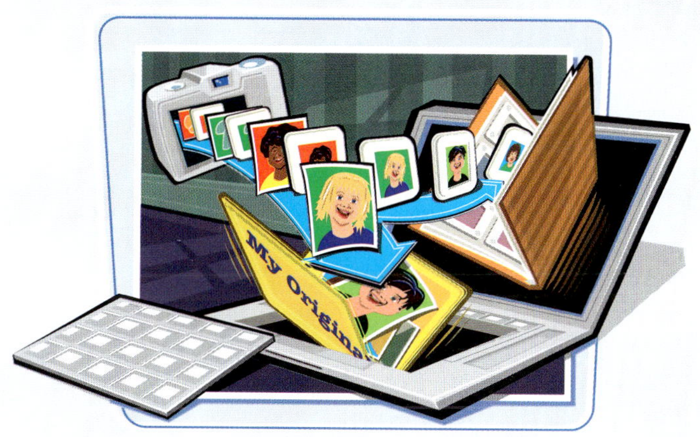

You should not alter the original image, which is the equivalent of a film negative. If you need to make changes to an image, get in the habit of making changes to a copy and keeping the original file untouched. This is not as hard as it sounds. Some image editors automatically apply your changes to a copy rather than to the original.

It does not take long until your picture collection will become large, so take advantage of the photo organizer programs that are available. Even with a photo organizer program, take some time to come up with a smart way to label and organize the folders of photos — either by date or event, or whatever makes sense to you and you can stick with. You can always find a particular photo quickly without spending hours searching for it if you consistently assign keywords and descriptions to your photos using programs such as iPhoto, Windows Live Photo Gallery, Photo Organizer, or Photoshop Elements.

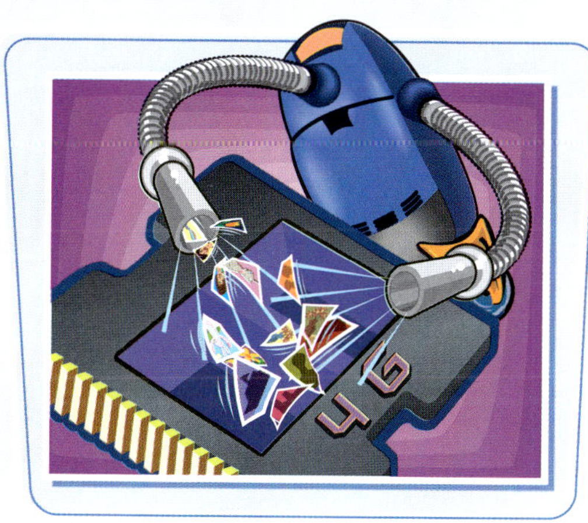

Clear the Memory Card

After your pictures are on your computer, you can safely delete pictures from your memory card. Many image editors offer to delete pictures after they have been transferred, but you should be sure that the images have been successfully placed on your hard drive because when the images are deleted from the card, you cannot get them back. The optimum choice is to delete all the photos in the camera by formatting the card using your camera after you have downloaded the photos. The card format option is typically found as a menu option accessed from the menu on the LCD screen of your camera. Using this method also helps to maintain the internal file structure of the memory card, which should keep it working smoothly.

Chapter 2

What You Need to Get Started

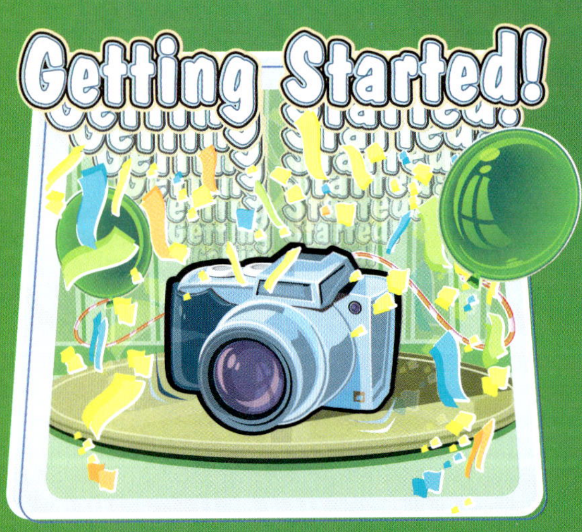

Knowing the basics about digital cameras, resolution, lenses, batteries, and accessories helps you choose the right camera for you. Having the right equipment for your digital darkroom enables you to edit and print your images faster and easier.

Quick Steps

Choose a Digital Camera 14
Consider Digital Camera Accessories 16
Build a Digital Darkroom 20
Choose a Photo Printer 22

Choose a Digital Camera

When choosing a digital camera, consider the size of camera, the resolution, how much control you want to have over the camera settings, the quality and focal range of the lens, the shooting modes you use most often, the life of the battery, and the type of storage media available.

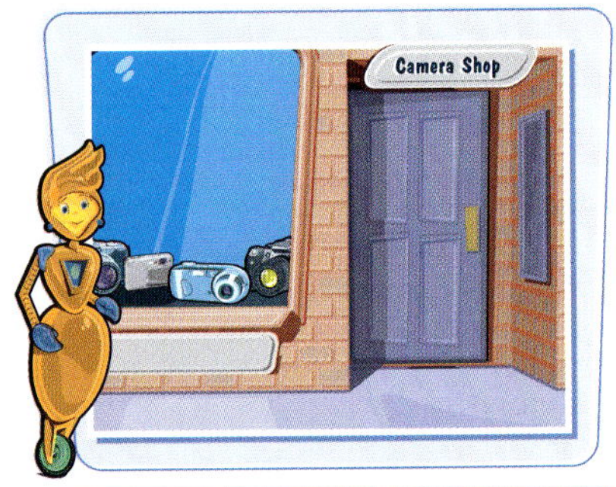

Compact

Compact, or point-and-shoot, digital cameras typically capture photos with image resolutions ranging from 10 to 14 megapixels. They include a built-in flash and zoom. Although compact cameras offer limited manual controls, they often provide a number of handy shooting presets that allow you to optimize the settings for better pictures more easily.

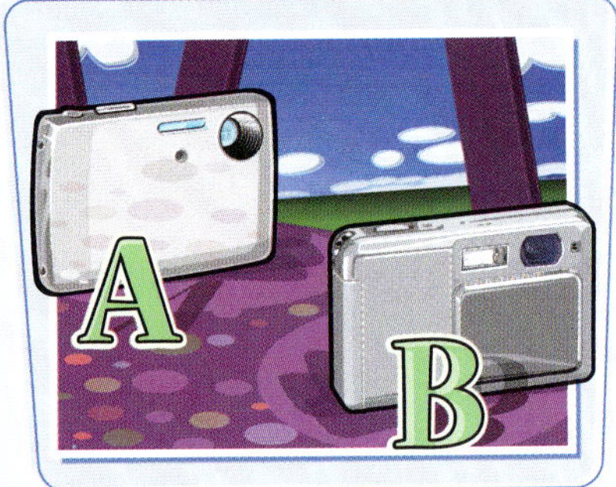

Advanced Non-SLR Cameras

Advanced non-SLR (single lens reflex) digital camera resolution ranges from 8 to 15 megapixels. Also called *prosumer* (professional/consumer) cameras, they feature more exposure control and greater zoom ranges than compact cameras but are also larger, heavier, and more expensive. These cameras often have exotic features like extreme telephoto and wide-angle lenses, high-speed shutter, and high-definition video all built into one.

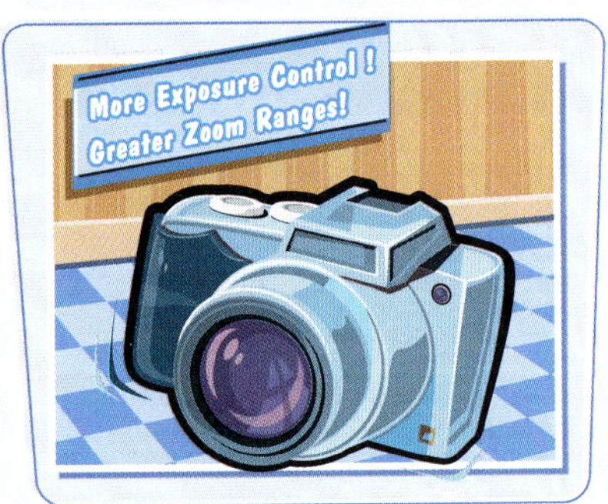

Digital SLR

Resolutions for digital SLR (dSLR) cameras range from 10 to 25 megapixels. These cameras offer all the features and controls found on film SLR cameras. The choice of professional photographers and serious hobbyists, dSLR cameras offer a wide variety of high-quality interchangeable lenses and flashes and nearly limitless control. Image quality on these cameras is noticeably better because of their larger sensor size.

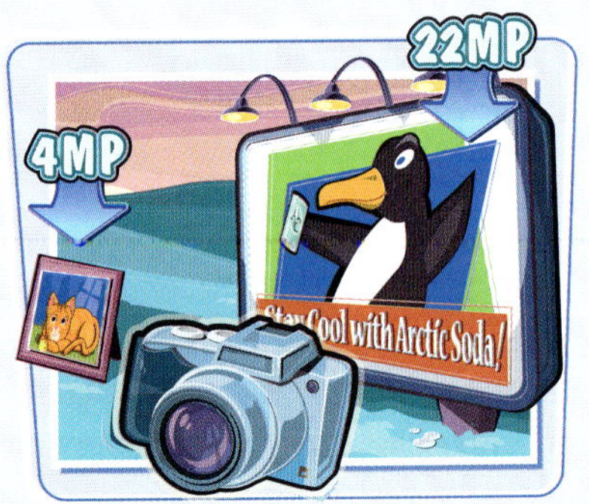

Lens Considerations

Most compact cameras come with a 4× zoom lens with a 35 to 135mm range. Getting the largest *optical* (not digital) zoom factor allows you a lot of flexibility. The optical zoom factor is the amount of magnification produced by the internal lenses in the camera. The digital zoom is created by enlarging the pixels that make up the image, producing an image that appears slightly out of focus and grainy. Lenses that go wider are great for landscapes and groups; lenses that are more telephoto are used for sports and wildlife. The drawback of a large optical zoom is that it makes the camera physically larger. You can learn more about lenses in Chapter 3.

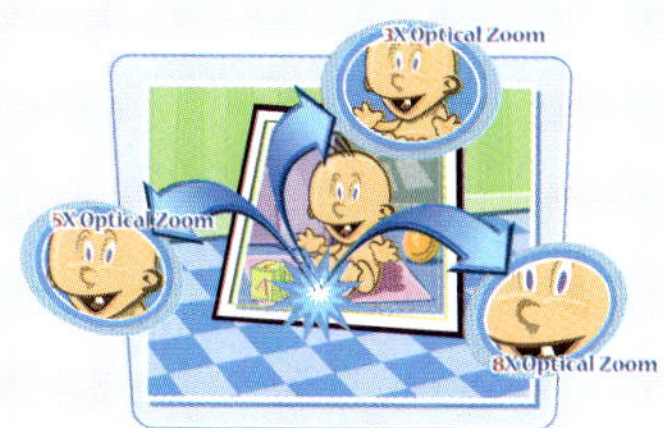

Evaluate Exposure and Scene Modes

A camera that has both automatic and semiautomatic exposure modes allows you more flexibility and creativity. Most compact cameras include scene modes that automatically set the camera's aperture, shutter speed, and flash based on the scene mode that you choose. The scene modes help take the guesswork out of setting your exposure, especially at the extremes — photos of the beach at noon are very different than a sunset party.

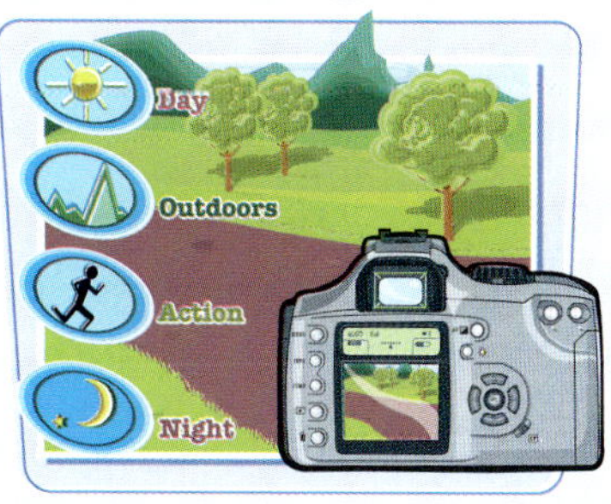

Batteries

At this point, most digital cameras use product-specific rechargeable batteries. These cameras' rechargeable batteries are very reliable and long-lasting. A few cameras still use disposable and rechargeable batteries interchangeably. This is convenient because you can use disposable batteries when you cannot recharge your batteries and use rechargeable batteries all other times. It is very important to buy the right type of battery, and get at least one extra set of batteries to ensure uninterrupted shooting.

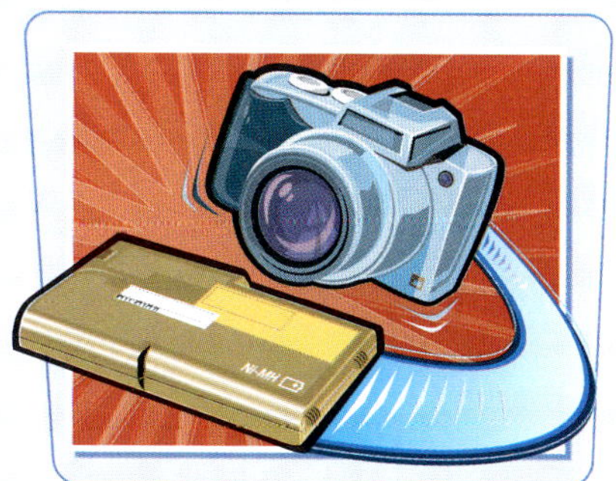

Storage Media

Digital cameras store pictures on removable memory media called memory cards, of which the most used are SD (Secure Digital), SDHC (Secure Digital High Capacity), CF (CompactFlash), Memory Stick, and XD. These cards come in a variety of capacities and can be used in your camera as well as MP3 players, cell phones, and PDAs (Personal Data Assistants). If you currently have one of these, it is possible to share the cards between the devices and your camera. The size you need depends on how many images you want to get on a card and the resolution of your camera, and the type you need depends on the camera you buy. The cards are physically small, but can store a lot. It is preferable to have a larger-capacity card than trying to manage several smaller cards.

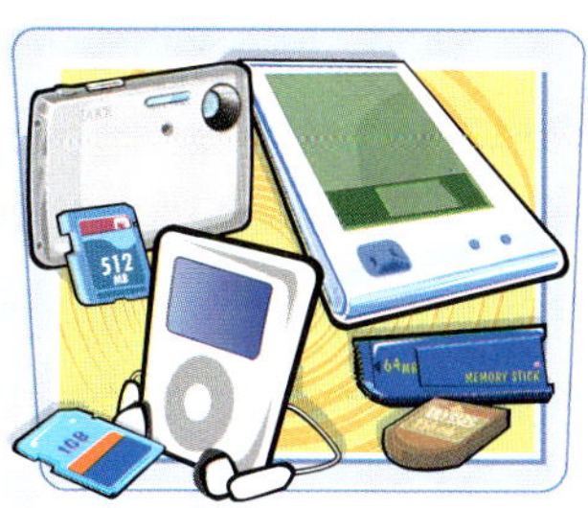

Consider Digital Camera Accessories

Although most digital cameras come with everything you need to take your first pictures, you can add helpful accessories. Accessories include higher-capacity memory cards, a card reader, extra or better batteries, an accessory flash, accessory lenses, and a tripod.

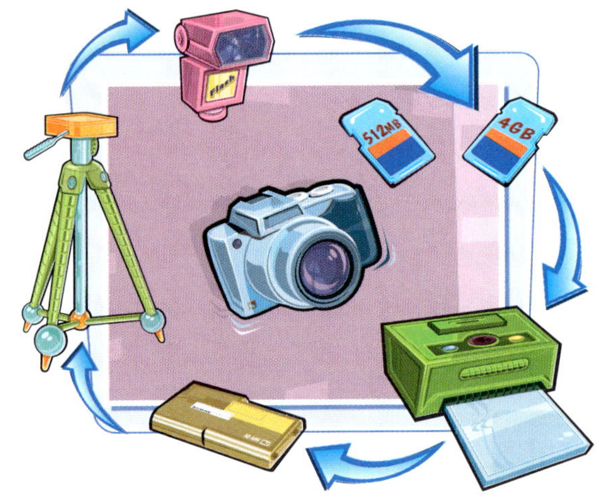

Photo Storage Devices

Laptop computers are great photo storage devices, and with all of the WiFi hot spots at schools, libraries, coffee shops, and public common areas, not only can you easily get your photos onto your computer, you can also quickly get them to your e-mail or Web site. If you are taking your camera with you but do not want to deal with a laptop, you may want to consider a photo storage device. These devices come in a variety of shapes and prices. Some are designed specifically to store and preview photos; others are MP3 players or even video players that provide the option of storing photos. These have large built-in hard drives but limited computing functions.

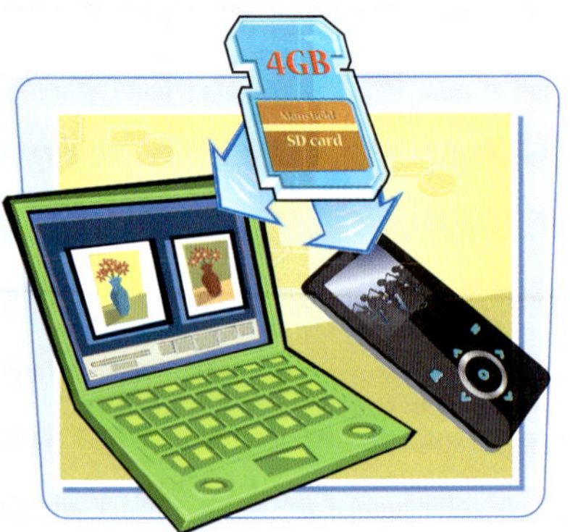

Memory Card Capacity

The number of images a memory card can hold depends on the resolution of the camera, and the file format and compression you set using the image-quality menu on the camera. Memory cards are relatively inexpensive. 1GB and 2GB cards are plentiful, and a 4GB card can hold nearly 600 highest-resolution JPEG photos from a 12-megapixel camera. To see how much it will hold on your camera, plug it in and format the card. Your camera's instruction manual should also have a listing of how many images you can get on a card at different resolutions.

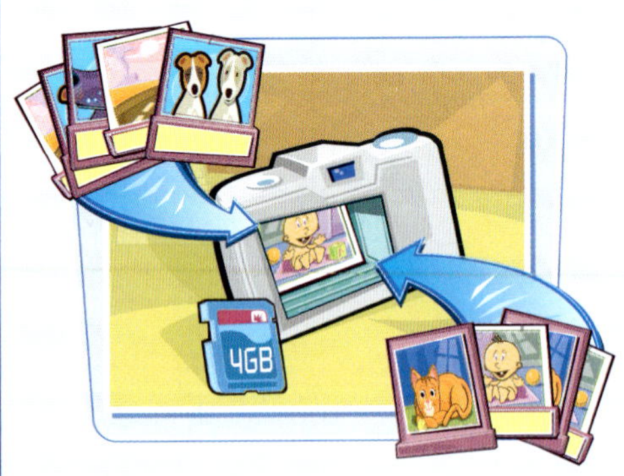

Card Readers

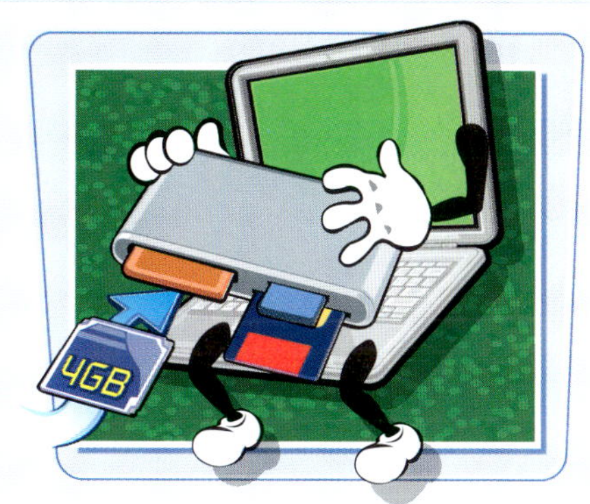

You can easily transfer pictures from your camera to your computer using a USB cable or camera dock. However, a memory card reader provides a faster and inexpensive way to transfer images. Most card readers connect to the computer using a USB cable, and some card readers accept multiple types of memory cards. Virtually all new card readers use a USB 2.0 connection, which is currently very common and very fast. Many cameras are now able to use the high-capacity SDHC cards. If those are the cards you are using, make certain that your card reader has that capability. For owners of a notebook computer, memory media–specific PCMCIA (PC Card) readers are available.

Accessory Lenses

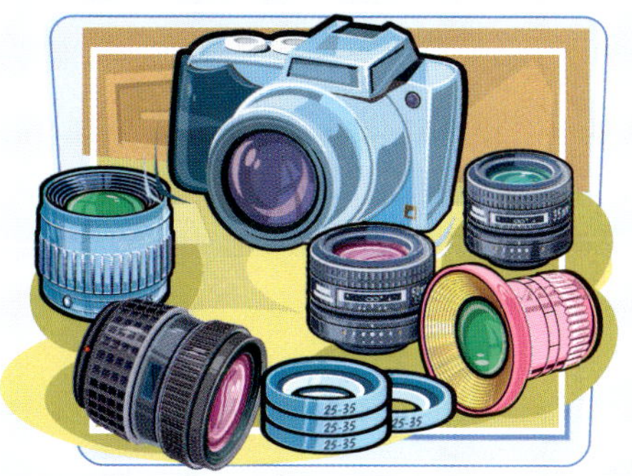

If your camera accepts accessory lenses, the lenses offer you additional photographic flexibility and are typically wide-angle or telephoto lenses. Look for accessory lenses from the manufacturer of your camera and from aftermarket suppliers. For compact digital cameras, accessory lenses may require step-up or step-down rings. The ring attaches to the camera's lens, and then the accessory lens attaches to the other side of the ring. For dSLR cameras, make sure that the lenses you buy will work with your camera; after that the sky is the limit! Each brand of camera has many different lenses designed to work optimally with your camera. Aftermarket lenses also do a good job and may save you a little money.

Accessory Flash Unit

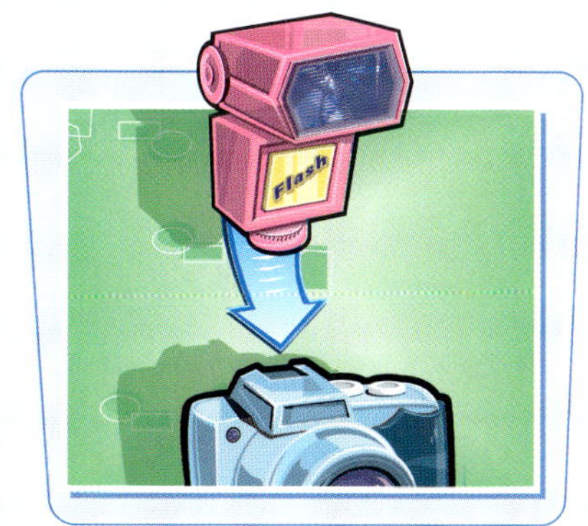

If your camera has a flash mount, or *hot shoe,* you can add an external flash unit. The advantage of an external flash is that it has more power, offering greater distances for flash shots. Because it is higher above the camera, it dramatically reduces red eye in the photos you take. Using your camera-branded flash will maximize all the automatic flash technology in today's digital cameras. For some cameras this even allows multiple flashes to communicate wirelessly for creative lighting in your photographs. To learn more about lighting and flash photography, see Chapter 4.

Consider Digital Camera Accessories *(continued)*

Travel Accessories

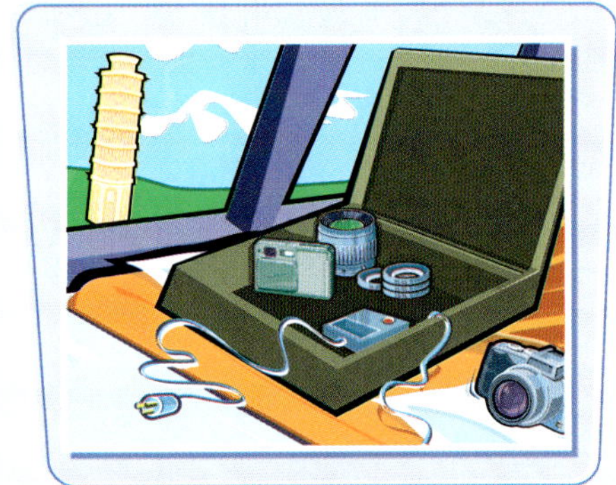

If you are traveling to another country, check what power and power connectors are used in that country. If you are sure your battery charger works with that power, check for the proper adapter. Voltage is rarely a problem but frequency is. A charger that works only on 60 Hz will burn out in a few minutes if plugged into a 50 Hz power outlet. So it is best to have one that works on 50/60 Hz plus have the proper power connection for the country you are visiting.

Tripods

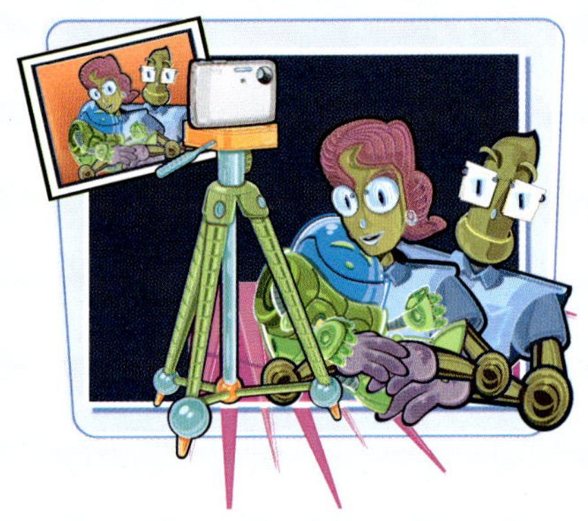

You can take sharp pictures in lower-light conditions if your camera is absolutely stable, and if the subject does not move. You can stabilize your camera by using a tripod. Tripods range from small tabletop versions, which are suitable for small digital cameras, to full-size tripods suitable for large digital cameras. It is great to use a small tripod for your compact digital camera for parties and family get-togethers, so you can be in the photos by using the timer or a remote control.

Camera and Accessory Bag

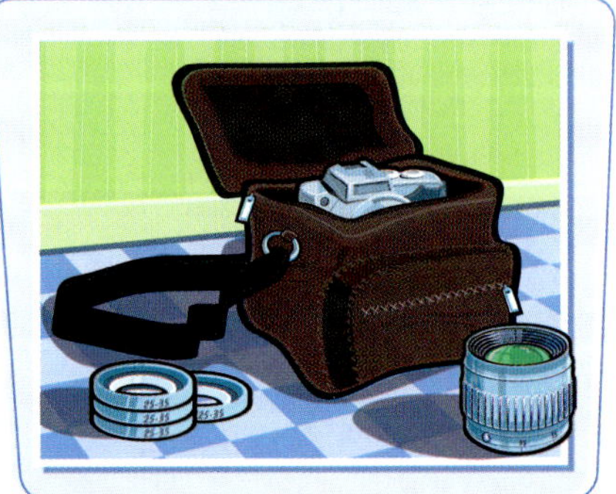

There are many brands and styles of camera bags, which range from backpacks to sling bags and even ones that look like purses. Bags range in size from small pouches to full-size bags with compartments for flash units, lenses, and spare batteries. Remember that a camera bag is there to: keep your stuff together, keep it organized, and keep it protected.

Some photographers like water-resistant camera bags, and some like to keep their camera and accessories in everyday bags, like book bags, messenger bags, and even diaper bags — all of which have plenty of room and pockets and do not get a second look from thieves. Just make sure your camera is in a well-padded place in the bag and that things do not rub against each other.

To protect easy-to-lose memory cards, you can buy hard- or soft-sided memory card cases that hold multiple memory cards.

Filters

Filters, including a *UV filter or Skylight*, can protect the lens of some digital cameras and help in cutting down on haze. You can also use a *polarizing* filter on some digital cameras (if the camera lens had threads to accept a filter) to reduce reflections and to make colors more vibrant. If you are buying a polarizing filter, make sure it says "circular polarizer" on the filter case. Linear (noncircular) polarizer filters confuse autofocus systems. Although digital cameras do not require color-correction filters, you can use some color filters.

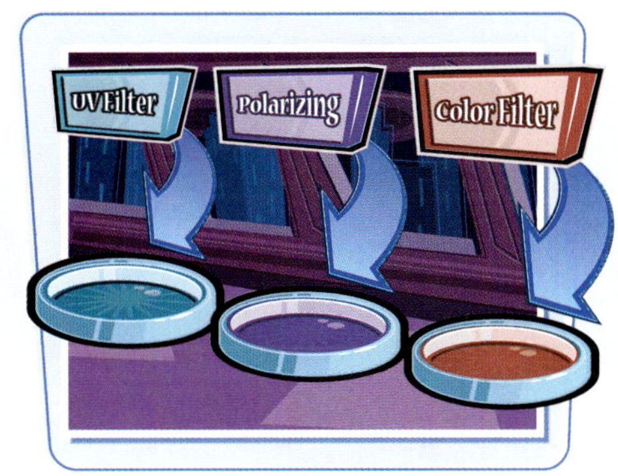

Creative Filters

You can use filters to add all sorts of effects to your photographs. There are filters that add starbursts and halo effects to lights. A *diffuser* filter creates a light fog effect by using a soft focus. Color filters alter or enhance the colors of your picture. *Graduated* filters or *grads* affect only part of the image and are great for affecting the sky in a photo. You can also reproduce the effects of some creative filters in most image-editing software.

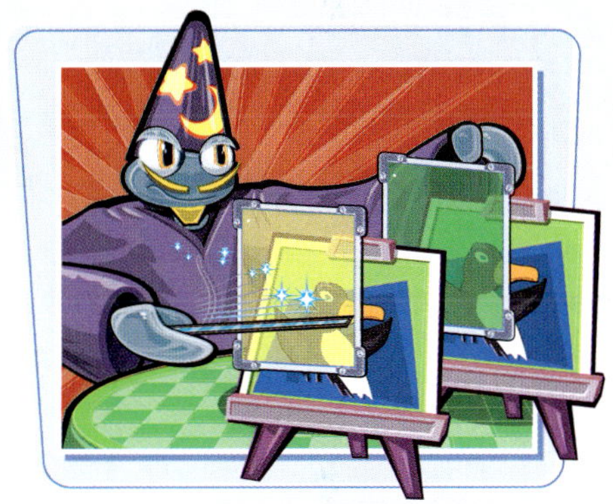

Cleaning Supplies

To clean your lens, you can use microfiber lens-cleaning cloths and a blower brush. You can also use a lens pen. A *lens pen* has a brush on one end to sweep away particles, and a circular pad with lens-cleaning fluid to wipe away smudges on the other end. You can clean the exterior of your camera with a clean, soft cloth like you would any other electronic equipment.

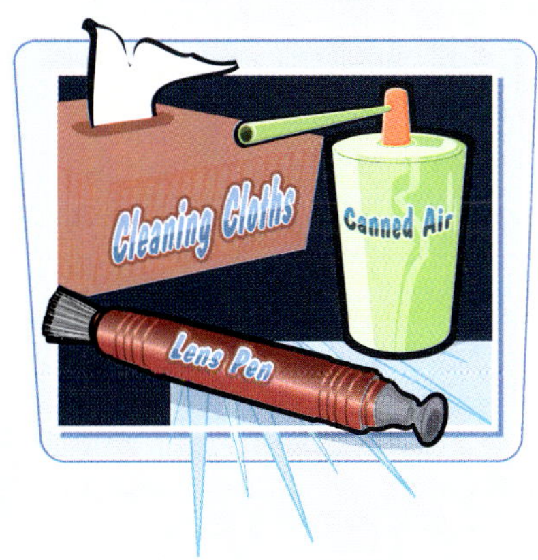

Build a Digital Darkroom

Unlike film photography, digital cameras do not require chemicals and a room without light to develop photos. Your digital equivalent of a darkroom is your computer in combination with your image-editing software and maybe even your photo printer. Armed with this equipment you can ensure that your pictures have great color and contrast, and that they are precisely cropped. To create this virtual digital darkroom, you need a computer, monitor, and software for editing images.

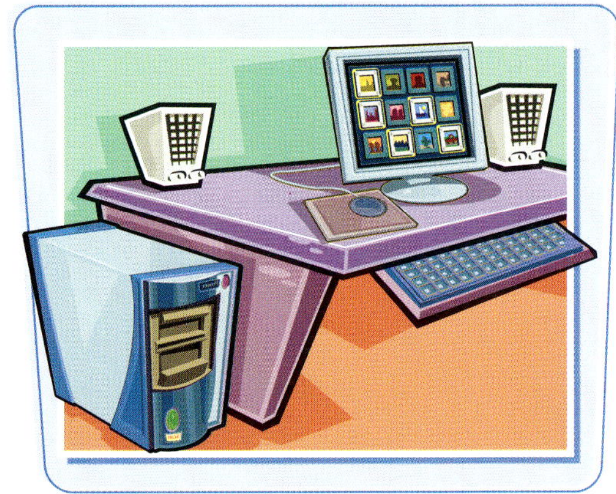

Computer

Digital photo files and photo-editing tasks require more hard drive space and RAM than text files and processing requires. To speed up digital photography work, it is helpful to have a computer with sufficient RAM (at least 1GB), a hard drive with free space to store photos, and a reasonably large monitor that you can calibrate for accurate color.

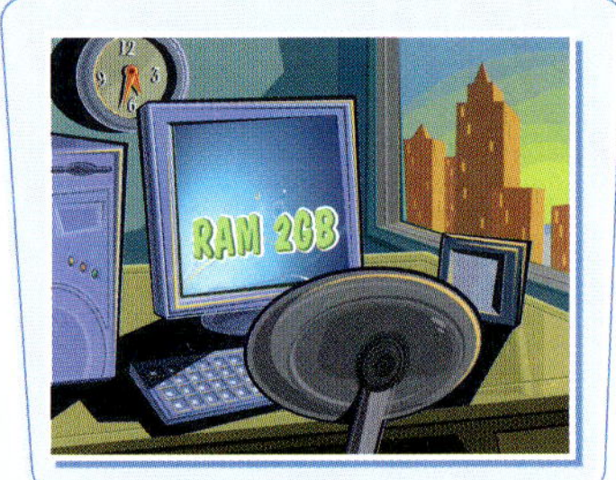

Minimum System Requirements

A good way to determine if your computer RAM and hard drive space is adequate for image editing is to check the system requirements for both the image-editing program and the operating system. You can find this information on the software product box.

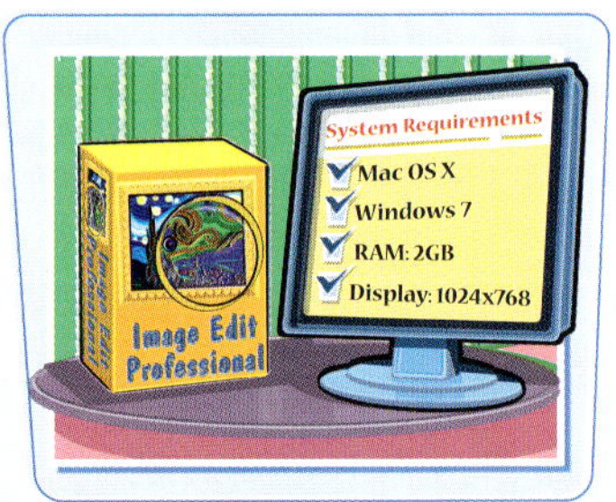

CD or DVD Archiving

As your digital image collection grows, it is good practice to archive images on CDs or DVDs. A recordable CD stores 700MB at a cost of 10 cents or less per CD. A recordable DVD stores 4.7GB of data. DVD prices vary by brand and DVD format, but they cost a little more than CDs. The newest high-capacity storage is Dual Layer (DL) DVD, which offers more than 8GB of storage. Make sure you check your computer to determine which DVD format you need: DVD-R or DVD+R.

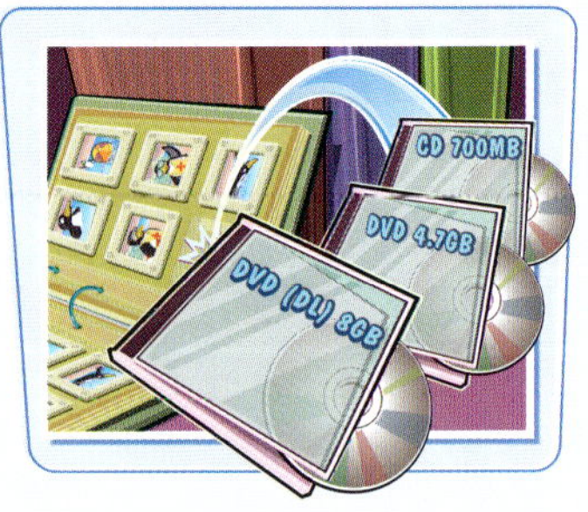

Hard Drive Archiving

The cost of external hard drives continues to go down, making 250GB, 500GB, and even 1TB-plus drives ever more reasonable. External hard drives are connected via USB cords, or FireWire (IEEE 1394), or even via a network, making it much easier to access your archived info on a hard drive than going back to find a single disc with your photos. Some of these drives are very compact and are powered by the USB cord, making them extremely portable. Setting up a routine backup of your photos to an external hard drive is very simple.

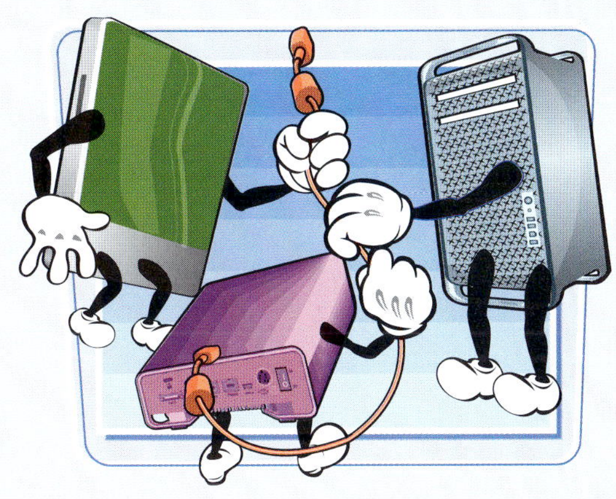

Choose an Image-Editing Program

An image-editing program allows you to adjust the contrast and color, and to rotate, crop, and add text and special effects to your pictures. In addition to basic image editing, most software helps you organize your images, e-mail them to friends, print them, and even helps you assemble impressive slide shows — which can be used for digital scrapbooking.

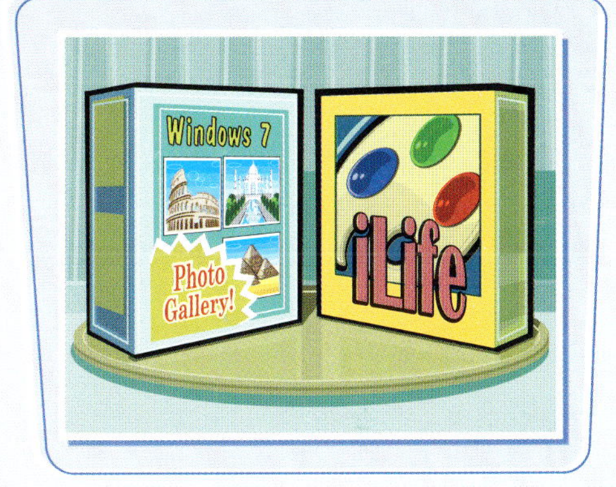

Monitor Types, Sizes, and Settings

Both CRTs and LCD flat-panels display digital images accurately. Nearly all displays sold today are flat-panel displays. 20-inch monitors are practically standard issue on new computers today. Screen resolution should be at least 1024×768 pixels. Digital photo editing requires that the color depth be set to 24- or 32-bit depending on your graphics adapter. If you purchased your computer in the last few years, it is already set up at an adequate resolution and color-depth setting. Larger monitors help by displaying more of the image at a larger magnification, and multiple monitors allow you to have your photo on one monitor and your toolbars and panels on the other monitor.

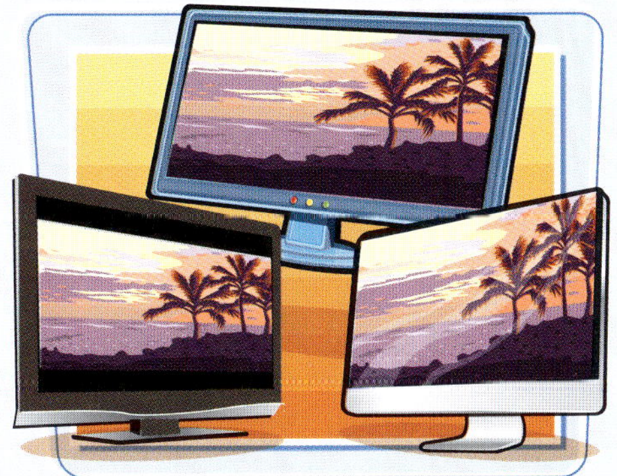

Choose a Photo Printer

High-quality, affordable photo printers, along with premium photo paper, enable you to easily print your own photos that are indistinguishable from your photo developer's. You can choose from a wide variety of dedicated photo printers that produce fade-resistant prints in a large variety of sizes. Most printers also sell a diverse selection of media ranging from preprinted cards to museum-quality paper, for those special photos.

Inkjet Printers

Inkjet printers, the most common printer type, use four or more ink colors — as many as twelve ink colors for the very best photo printers. They spray tiny droplets of colored ink (usually organic dyes) onto the paper to print the photo. Depending on the quality of the ink and paper, inkjet prints can last many years without fading. There are also larger desktop inkjet printers that make great enlargements.

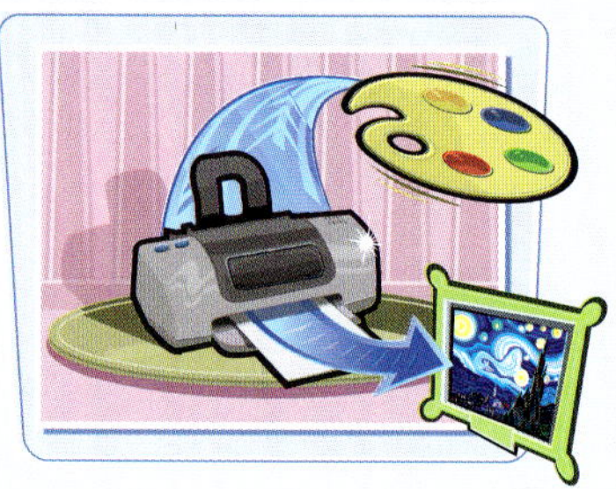

Dye-Sublimation Printers

Dye-sublimation, or *dye-sub,* printers apply heat to a printer ribbon, producing a colored gas that bonds with the paper to create the photo. Dye-sub printers produce continuous-tone prints that most closely resemble traditional film prints, and the print life is comparable to high-quality inkjet prints. The disadvantage of dye-sub printers is that they can be expensive to buy and to operate. The most common types of dye-sub printers are for small (4×6-inch) prints and passport-type photos.

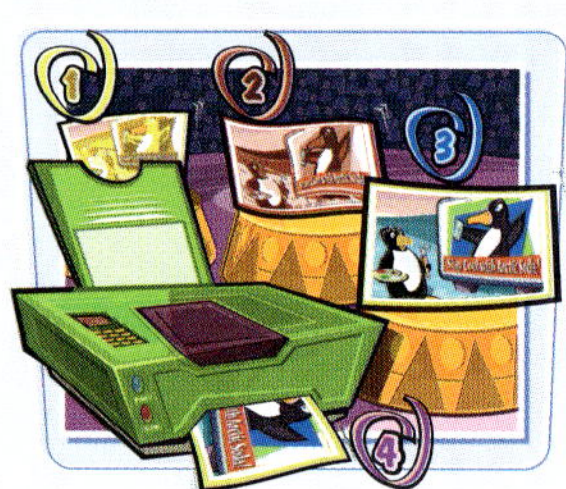

Print Directly from Memory Media

Direct printing lets you print pictures without transferring pictures to your computer first. On some printers, you can insert the memory card into a slot, and then print all or some of the images. On direct-print printers, you can attach your digital camera to the printer using a USB cable, and then print all or part of the images.

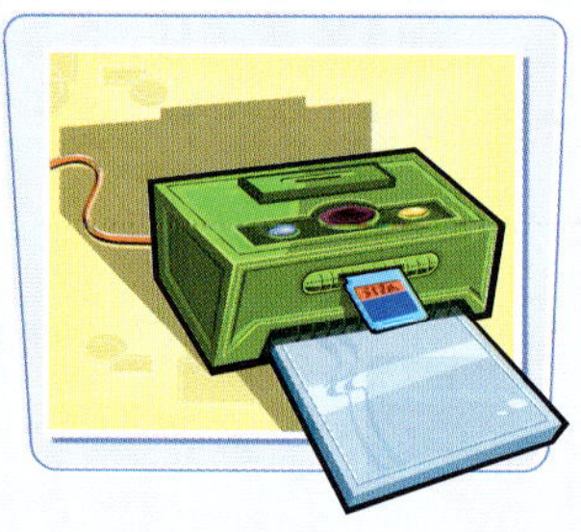

Print Speed

Usually the print speed published by the manufacturer is for draft-quality printing, and not for the best photo-quality printing. Print speed is measured in pages per minute (ppm). Printers set at the highest quality settings take much longer to print the same size print. Printers are constantly getting faster and quieter.

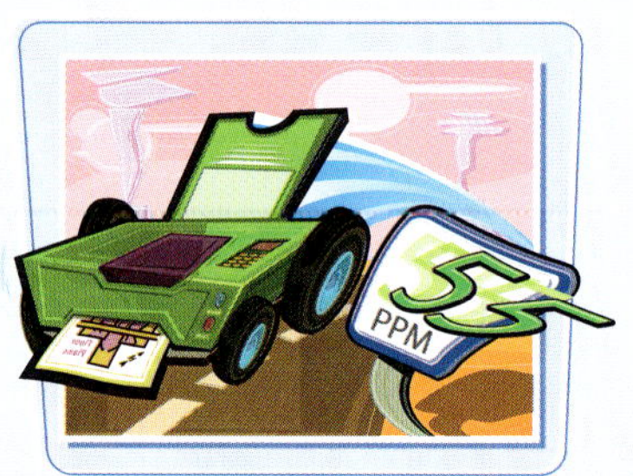

Paper Size

Printers commonly use 8.5×11-inch paper to print an 8×10-inch image. Many printers allow for the use of roll paper, as narrow as 4 inches, letting you make your own 4×6's — other printers use 44-inch-wide roll paper for huge prints. There are many sizes in between. Paper sizes now reflect proportion of the sensor — 11×17 and 13×19 paper are now common sizes for enlargements.

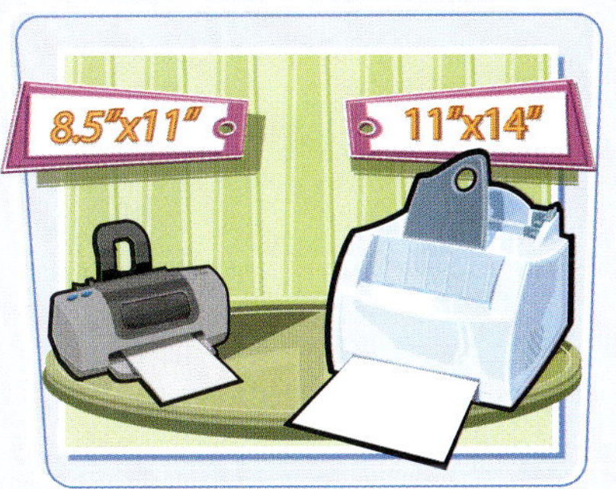

Connection

Most printers connect to the computer using a USB cable. Some professional printers use either a USB or a FireWire (IEEE 1394) cable interface. Some printers even have network inputs, like a Cat 5 cable, allowing multiple computers access to the printer via a network.

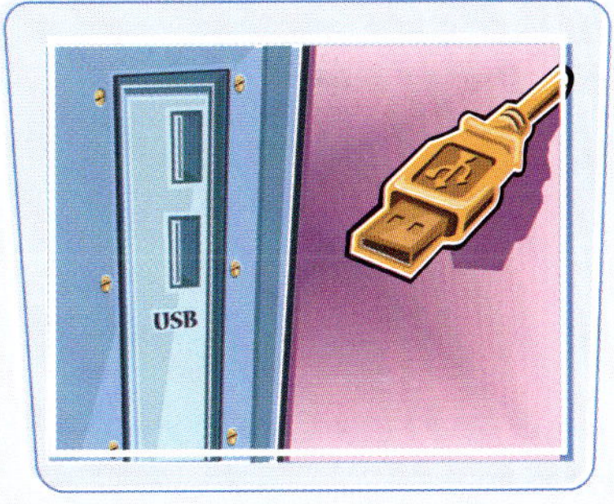

Cost

The manufacturer cost-per-print estimates are usually not figured at the best setting of the printer, which uses more ink. Color print costs range from approximately 18 cents to $2 or more per 8×10-inch print. Some printers' software is actually able to tell you how much paper and ink you have used to determine your cost. Using the highest-quality settings means using the most ink, which is also more costly.

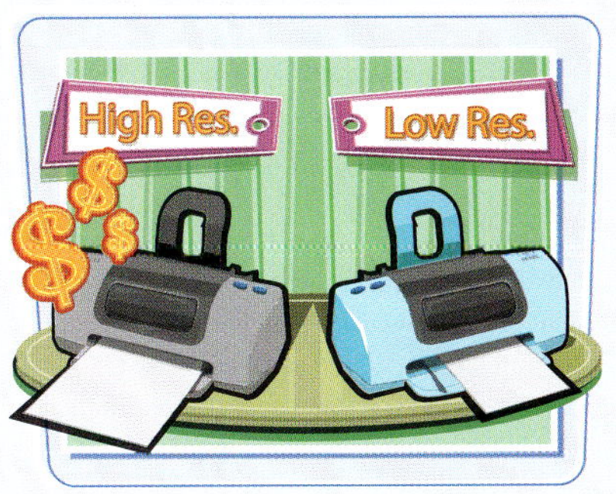

Print Quality

New inkjet printers usually offer a maximum color resolution of 4800×1200 dots per inch (dpi). When you evaluate printed samples from different printers, look for smooth, continuous tones, fine gradations of color, and color accuracy and fidelity.

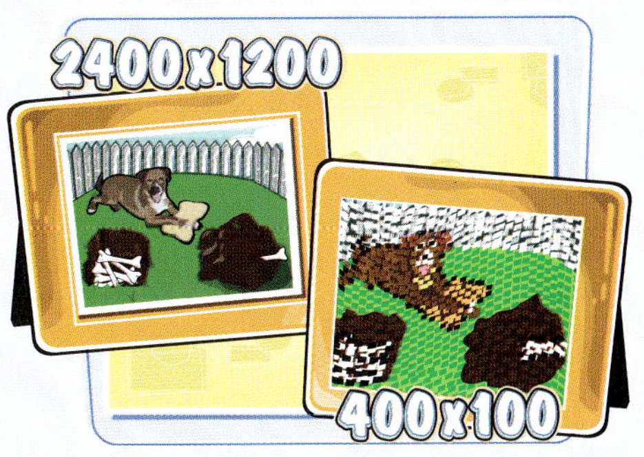

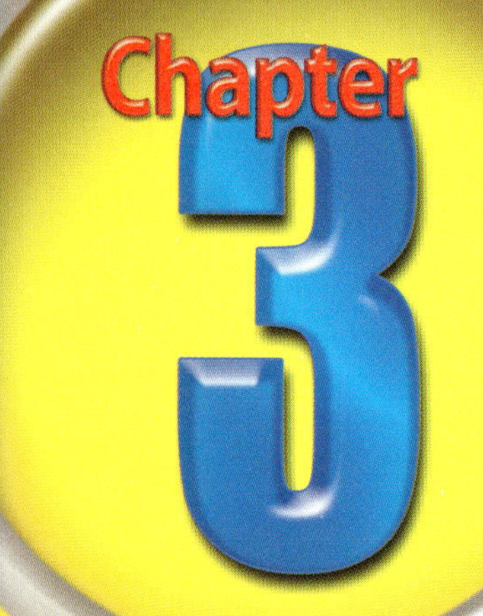

Controlling Exposure and Focal Length

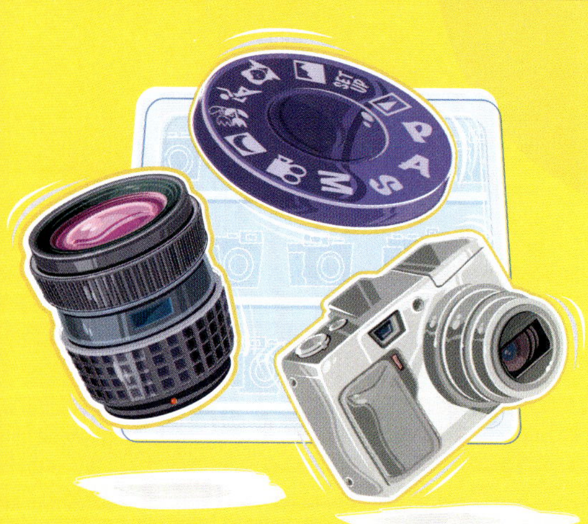

There are many settings that affect your digital camera photographs. The camera automatically controls most of these settings in response to the amount of light illuminating your subject and the distance of the subject from you. From aperture to shutter speed to focal length, you can mix and match different camera settings to gain creative control over your pictures. Any change in the light requires a change in the exposure. To learn how to best capture the correct exposure, all you need is an understanding of the basic elements of photography.

Quick Steps

Learn About ISO 26
Learn About Aperture 27
Control Depth of Field 28
Understanding Shutter Speed 29
Discover Exposure Modes 30
Learn About Focal Length 32
Use a Wide-Angle Lens 33
Use a Telephoto Lens 34
Use a Zoom Lens 35
Learn About Digital Camera Lenses 36

Learn About ISO

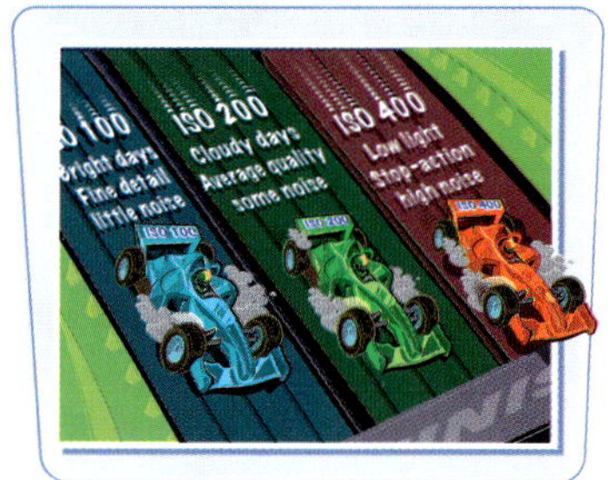

The sensitivity of film to light is described as the *speed* of the film. Film that is very sensitive is called *fast* film and can result in better photos taken in lower lighting conditions than can be achieved with slower speed film. Similar to film speeds, the ISO settings on digital cameras indicate the digital image sensor's speed, or sensitivity to light. The numbers on the camera's ISO approximate the sensitivity of the same ISO number on film.

ISO stands for International Organization for Standardization, which created a standard measurement for the film speed of color negative and positive (slide) film. The name ISO replaced ASA (American Standard Association) in 1974, but the measurement system was the same.

What Is Your ISO?

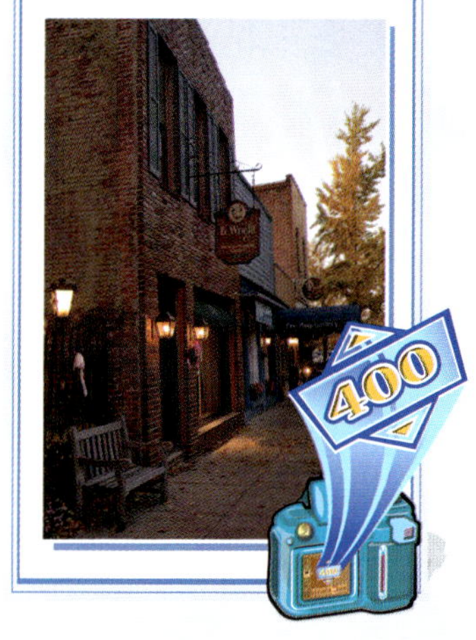

ISO is the first of three parts of the exposure calculation, and just as with film is designated with numbers such as 100, 200, 400, 800, 1600, with each one being twice as light sensitive as the previous. The lower your camera's ISO number, usually 80, 100, or 200, the better the image quality. Even with the advances in digital cameras' high ISO capabilities, it is important to use the lowest ISO possible to maximize your image quality. The drawback to using high ISO settings is that it can result in increased *noise,* small multicolor flecks, in the picture. In many cases though, getting the shot, even if it means more noise, is more important than optimal image quality.

On a sunny day, using 100 or 200 is great, but once you get in the shade or it gets cloudy, or the sun starts to go down, you will need a higher ISO to maintain a good exposure. To get an exposure bright enough might mean using ISO 200 or 400. Indoors the light level is even less. Your eyes automatically correct for the light level, but unless you are going to use a flash, using ISO 400 to 800 makes a lot of sense. At night and indoors, using the flash at these higher ISOs allows the flash to recycle quicker and allows the light level inside to more closely match the flash — so you can see everything in the photo.

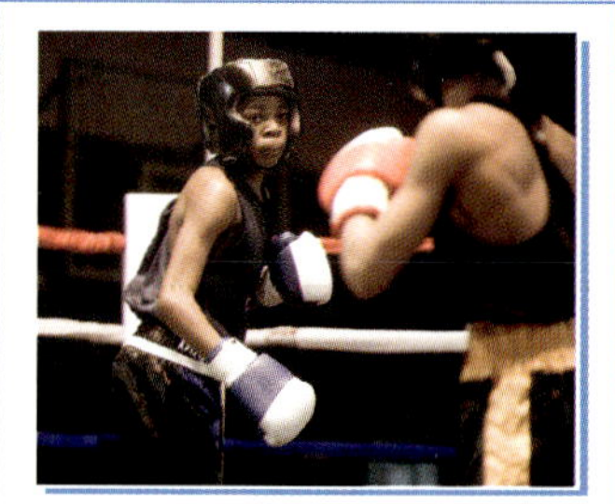

ISO Settings

Each step up or down of the ISO is considered a "stop," so changing the ISO from 200 to 400 without changing any other settings creates a photo twice as bright. Although many digital cameras can control the ISO setting automatically, on most digital cameras you can set the ISO either from a dial or from the camera menu. Some digital cameras allow you to increase the ISO to very high numbers — ISO 3200 and higher for some dSLRs. Choosing a faster or higher ISO allows you to take properly exposed pictures even in scenes with very low light.

Learn About Aperture

The camera ***aperture***, controlled by a diaphragm mechanism, determines how much or how little the lens opens to let in the light that strikes the image sensor. The size of the aperture also affects how much of the image is in focus.

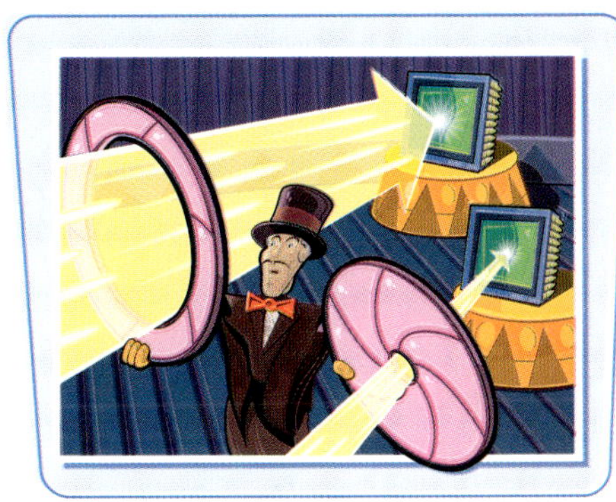

What Is the F-Stop?

Aperture is shown as f-stop numbers, such as f/2.8, f/4, f/5.6, and f/8. These numbers refer to whether the diaphragm mechanism opens a little or a lot. A wide f-stop, such as f/2.8, allows more light to strike the image sensor. A narrow f-stop, such as f/16, lets in less light. Lenses that offer larger apertures are referred to as fast. They tend to be physically larger and more expensive than the same focal length, offering a smaller aperture due to the larger and better glass it takes to make the lens.

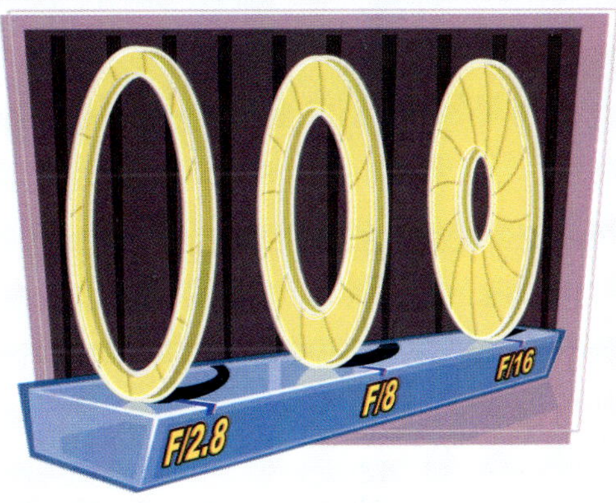

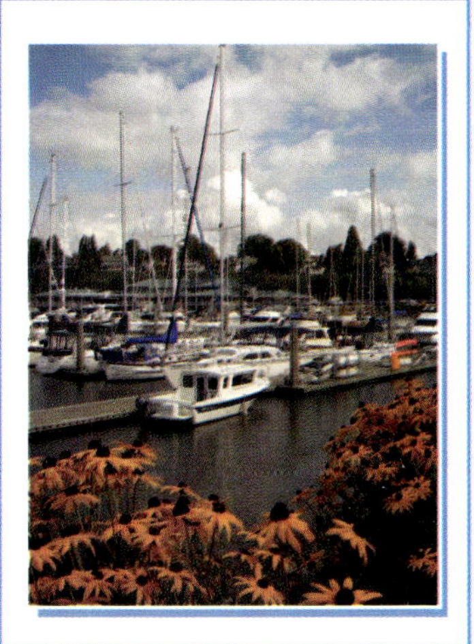

Set the Aperture

An easy semiautomatic exposure mode is aperture-priority, which is usually designated with an A and can be selected through one of the camera's menus or dials. When the camera is set to aperture priority mode, then you can control the aperture by choosing the f-stop, and the camera automatically sets the correct shutter speed. This allows you to easily select how much depth of field is in your photograph.

Control Depth of Field

When the automatic focus mechanism of your digital camera focuses on a subject, you can only be sure that the subject is in focus. Objects closer and farther from the camera may not be in focus. How much of the image is in focus is controlled by the ***depth of field***, which refers to the area in front of and behind a subject that is in acceptably sharp focus. In general, the zone of sharpness extends one-third in front of and two-thirds behind the point of focus.

Pictures with a soft background show little depth of field, achieved by setting a wide aperture such as f/4, moving closer to the subject, or selecting portrait mode, if your camera offers it. Pictures with the foreground and much of the background in focus show extensive depth of field, achieved by setting a narrow aperture, such as f/11, moving farther from the subject, or selecting a landscape mode, if the subject is far enough away.

Adjust the Aperture

To increase the depth of field in a photo where you want as much of the scene in sharp focus as possible, choose a narrow aperture such as f/8 or f/11. To decrease the depth of field in a photo where you want the background to be out of focus, choose a portrait mode or select a wider aperture such as f/2.8, f/4, or f/5.6. A good way to remember this is the larger the f/stop number, the more the depth of field.

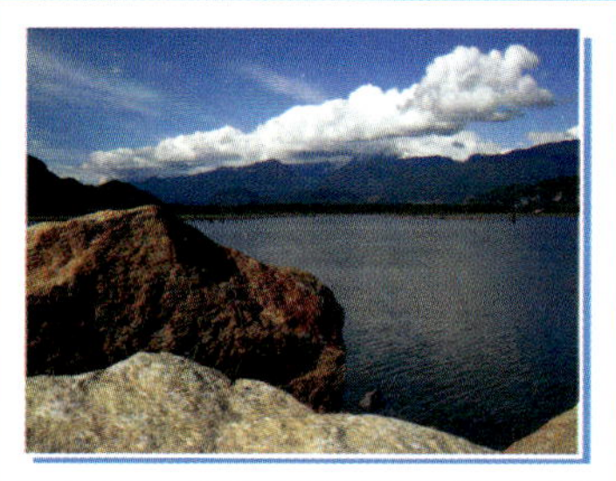

Change the Camera-to-Subject Distance

Regardless of the f-stop you choose, the farther away you are from a subject, the greater the depth of field. The closer that you focus on a subject, the zone of acceptable focus, or depth of field, gets smaller. So naturally a tight portrait will have more depth of field than a wide landscape shot.

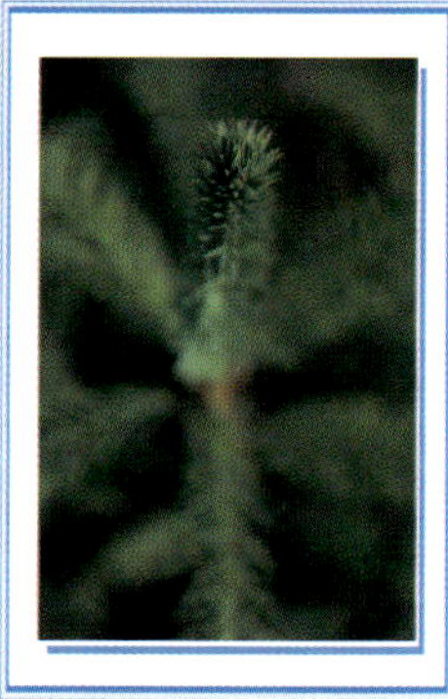

Change Lens Focal Length

Focal length determines how much of a scene the lens *sees*. A wide-angle lens or zoom-out setting sees more of the scene than a telephoto lens or zoom-in setting. A wide-angle setting provides greater depth of field than a telephoto setting. Depth of field becomes greater, every time you zoom wider, and becomes lesser every time you zoom the telephoto longer.

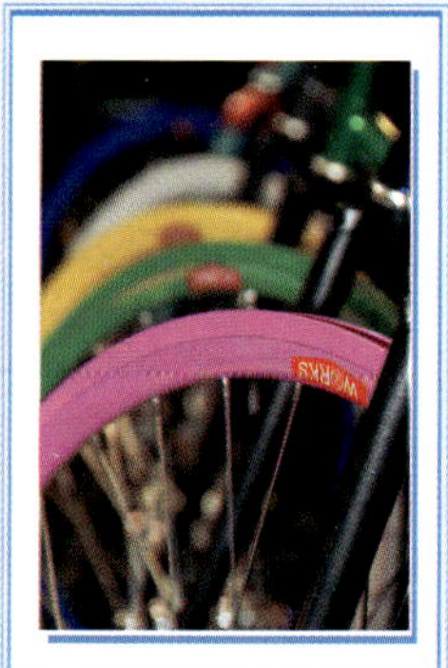

Understanding Shutter Speed

The shutter speed controls how long the *shutter*, a curtain-like mechanism that covers the sensor, stays open to let light from the lens strike the image sensor. The longer the shutter stays open, the more light hits the sensor, and the less time it stays open, the less light hits the sensor.

Shutter speeds are described by how long they allow light into cameras in fractions of a second. They range from slow (1, 1/2, 1/4, 1/8, 1/15 second); moderate (1/30, 1/60, 1/125 second); to fast (1/500, 1/1000, 1/2000 second). Increasing or decreasing the shutter speed by one setting halves or doubles the exposure respectively.

Set the Shutter Speed

Because changing your shutter affects how long the shutter is open, the shutter determines how much stop action or blur is in a scene. With an action scene mode, the camera selects a fast shutter speed to freeze subject motion. In semiautomatic modes, you can set the shutter speed using one of the camera's menus. To make sure you do not have blur from your hands moving the camera, your shutter speed should be faster than 1/60 second. With shutter speeds slower than 1/60 second you should consider a tripod to stabilize the camera.

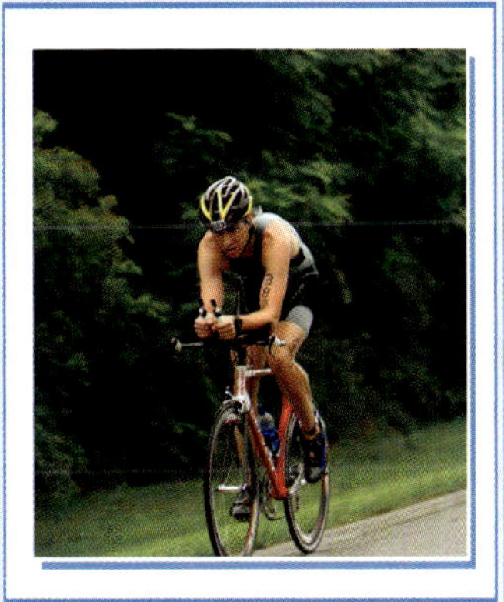

Freeze or Blur Subject Motion

To freeze motion in normal scenes, set the shutter speed to 1/250 second or faster. To capture motion as a blur, use 1/30 second or slower and mount the camera on a tripod. Using very slow shutter speeds (1/2 second, 1 second, and longer) you can really show the passage of time, such as with water moving.

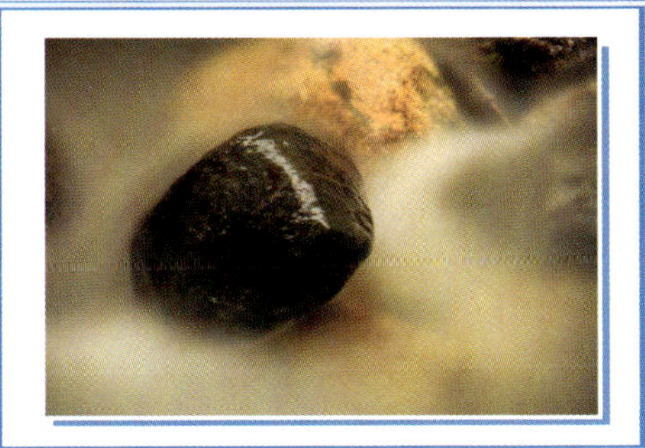

Pan-Blur

At a slower shutter speed, such as 1/15 second, you can follow subject movement with the camera and blur the background, as shown here. This technique is called a *pan-blur*.

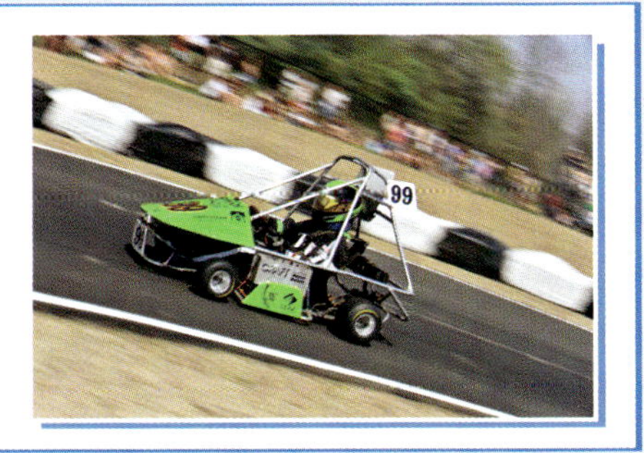

Discover Exposure Modes

Digital cameras offer several ways to control the exposure settings. Ranging from fully automatic (often called P for program or point-and-shoot, as well as the preset scene modes) to specific exposure modes, each method of control offers advantages and disadvantages. Although serious photo buffs eschew the automatic settings, on average, these settings offer the greatest insurance for getting a good photo. Selecting a preset scene mode lets you get a pretty good result — easily, whereas one of the priority auto exposure modes gives you some creative control over depth of field and whether you freeze or blur motion with the aid of all the camera's technology.

Auto Mode

Auto mode, which is often called program mode, works well when you want to just point and shoot. In this mode, the camera selects the aperture, or f-stop, and shutter speed for the correct exposure. Although auto mode may not be the most creative way to use your camera, it works well when your goal is to quickly capture a picture.

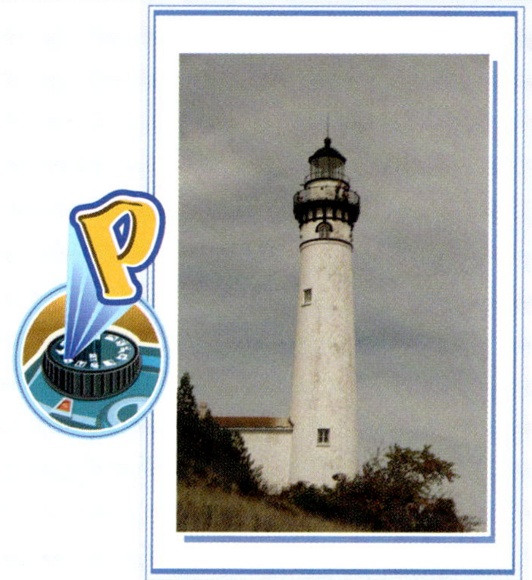

Aperture Priority Mode

You can use aperture priority mode when you want to choose the aperture, or f-stop, and have the camera automatically set the shutter speed. Aperture priority mode works well when you want creative control over depth of field. If you choose a narrow aperture (large f-stop number) in a low-light scene, you may need to steady the camera on a tripod due to the slow shutter speed.

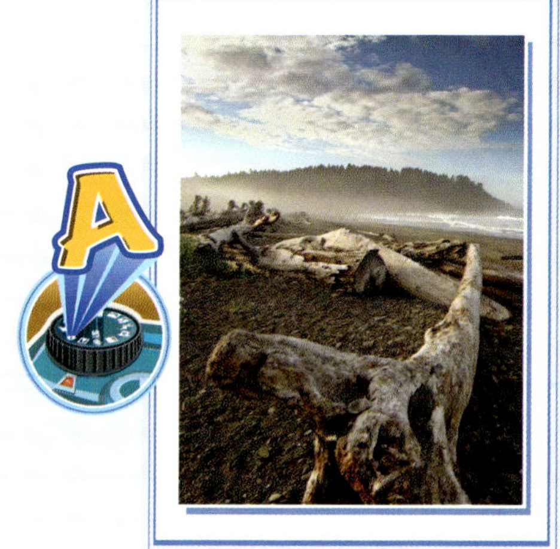

Shutter Priority Mode

You can use shutter priority mode when you want to choose the shutter speed and have the camera automatically set the appropriate aperture, or f-stop. Shutter priority mode works well when you want to control how action appears. A fast shutter speed freezes action. A slow shutter speed shows motion as a blur, as shown.

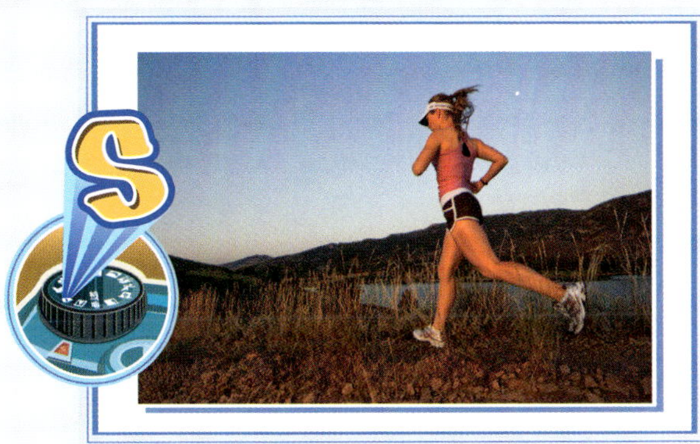

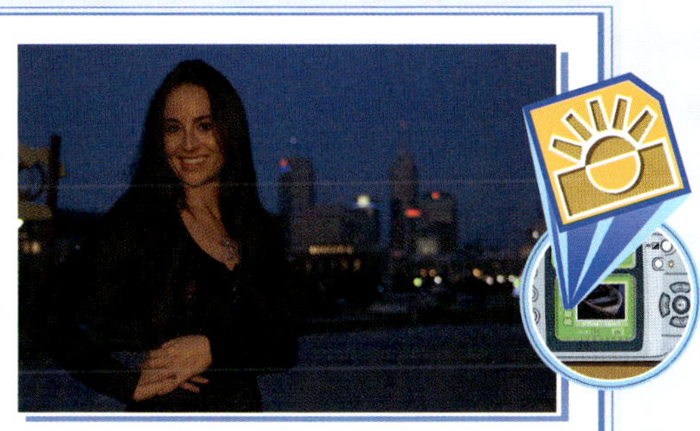

Subject Modes

You can use a subject or scene mode when you want the camera to automatically set the exposure based on a specific scene. Common scene modes include sports, landscape, portrait, and close-up. Newer cameras offer special modes such as sunsets, fireworks, snow, beach, sunrise, and night portrait. Scene modes work well when you want to point and shoot and have the camera's computer take care of the settings when getting the best results might be a little tricky.

Manual Mode

You can use manual mode when you want to choose the shutter speed and the aperture. This gives you the maximum amount of creativity. In most cases the camera's meter tells you what it thinks is the best setting, but then you can adjust the aperture, shutter, and ISO until you get exactly what you are looking for. Manual exposure is typically used when the lighting is relatively tricky and when you want the exposure to be the same no matter how the scene is lit.

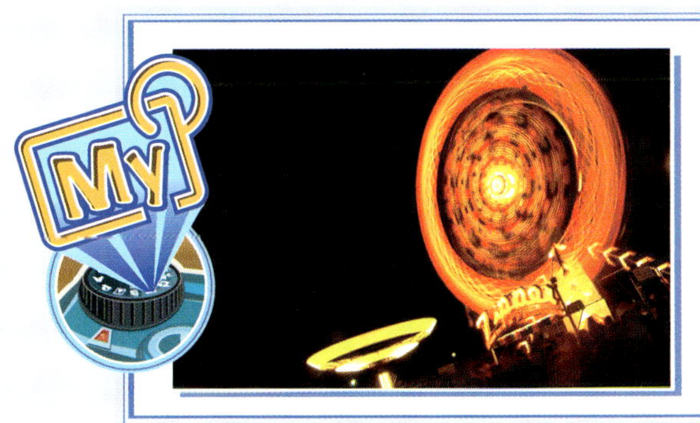

Learn About Focal Length

Focal length determines the angle of view, or how much of a scene the camera's lens sees. In addition, focal length plays a role in determining the sharpness or softness of the background and foreground objects in a scene, or the depth of field.

To learn more about depth of field, see the section "Control Depth of Field," earlier in this chapter.

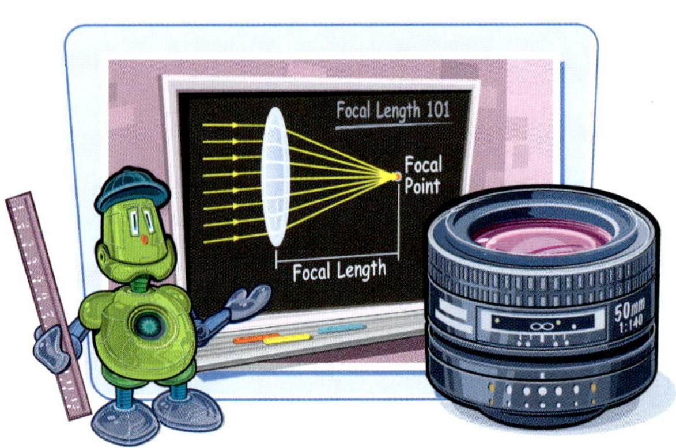

Focal Length Defined

Focal length describes the angle of view of the lens, or how much of the scene the lens sees. For example, on a 35mm camera, a normal lens, like a 50mm, is able to see about 40 degrees of the scene, but it has about the same real view as what we see. A superwide lens like an 18mm lens has an angle of view of 90 degrees, encompassing a broad sweep of the scene, whereas a telephoto lens of 200 has a much narrower view, only about 10 degrees.

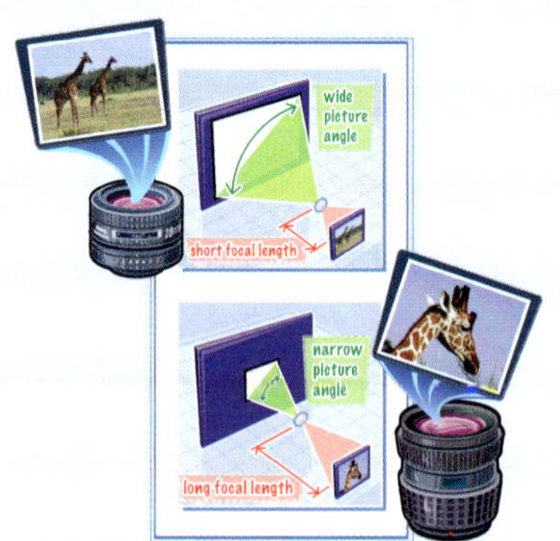

Use a Normal Lens

On a 35mm camera, a 50mm lens is considered a normal lens because it sees approximately the same angle of view as the human eye. In reality our eyes see near 180 degrees of a scene. On most digital cameras, a 35mm lens is closer to normal because the image sensor is smaller than the traditional 35mm film frame, which magnifies the view approximately 1.5 times depending on the camera sensor. This is why all digital camera makers list the focal length as being "equivalent" to a specific 35mm focal length. This is helpful for traditional film photographers because focal length is a term they understand.

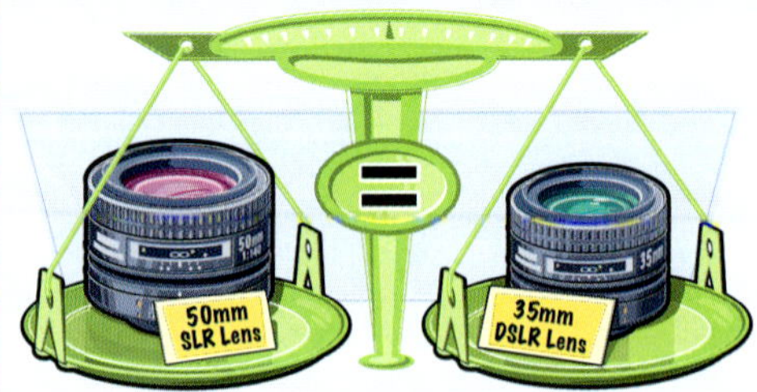

Use a Wide-Angle Lens

A wide-angle, or wider than 50mm lens provides a broad angle of view and extensive depth of field — especially at small apertures. Use a wide-angle lens or zoom setting to photograph landscapes, panoramas, large groups, and small areas where you want to capture the entire scene.

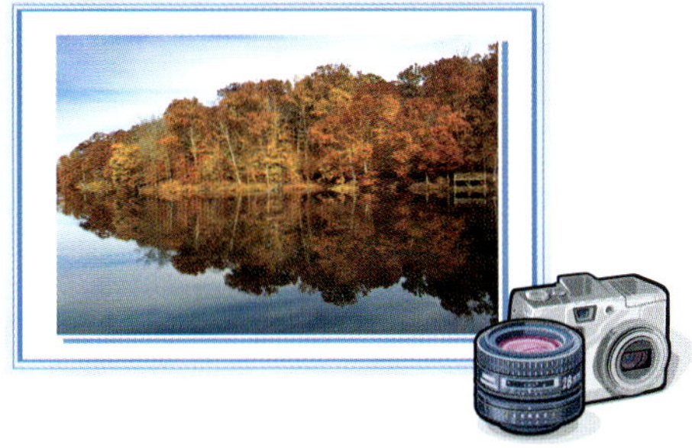

Wide-Angle Distortion

Wide-angle lenses distort the relative size and spacing of objects in a scene. For example, objects close to the lens seem larger than they are, whereas distant objects seem farther away, and farther apart than you remember seeing them. A wide-angle lens, or a zoom lens at its widest setting, can also create a distortion called *barrel distortion*, which is evident in buildings or other tall elements where the edges bend inward, giving straight lines a kind of "inflated" look.

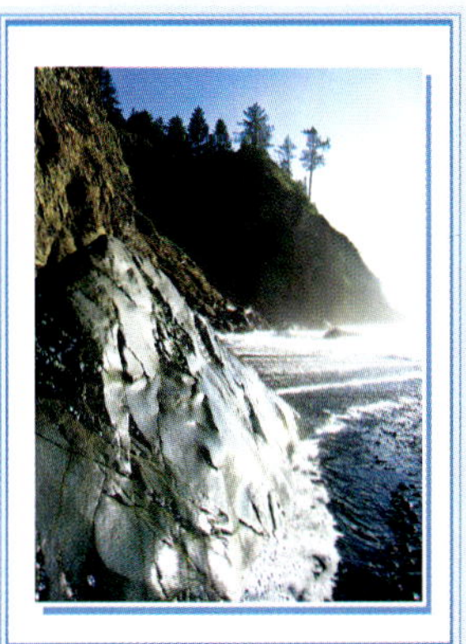

Maximize the Wide

Because wide-angle lens seem to push far-off subjects even farther away, it often helps to place something into the foreground of the scene to give your photos a visual anchor. With the additional depth of field, and a moderate aperture setting, you should be able to get plenty of sharpness throughout the scene.

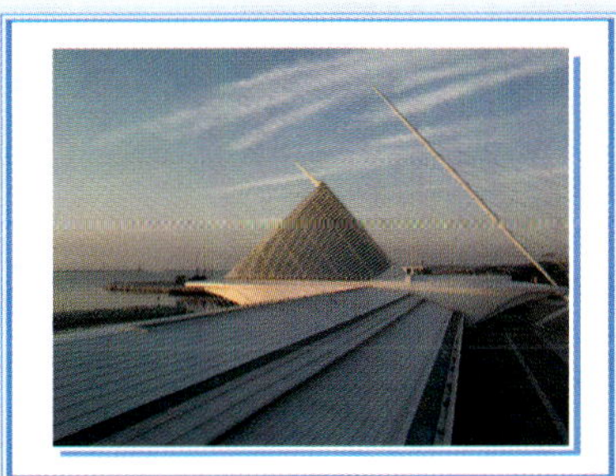

Aspherical Lens

An aspherical lens has a nonspherical surface. These lenses help to produce better edge sharpness and straighter lines by making sure that all the wavelengths of light focus to the same point. These lenses are also lighter in weight than standard lenses because they do not need additional lens elements, or additional glass, to correct for edge sharpness.

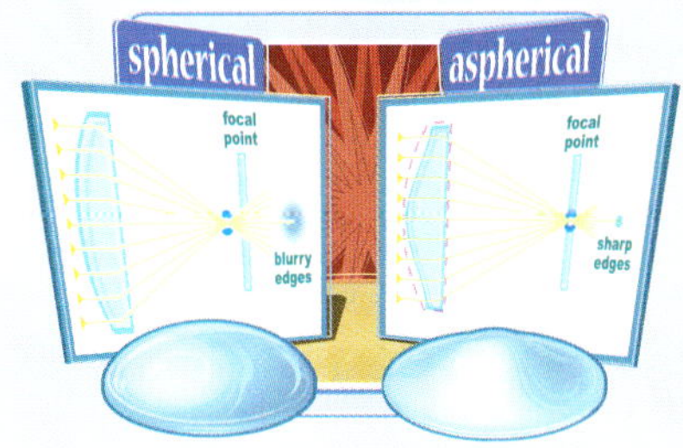

Use a Telephoto Lens

A telephoto lens, or one longer than 50mm in 35mm film terms, provides a narrow angle of view and limited depth of field. You can use a telephoto lens or zoom setting to isolate a subject from the background, bring distant objects closer, and compress objects with the background.

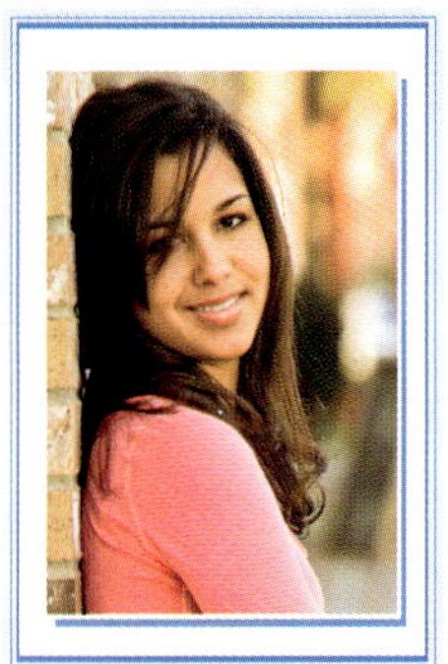

Telephoto lenses and zooms with low-dispersion glass provide increased sharpness, especially at the frame edges, and they provide better color. When you shop for a compact camera or a telephoto lens, look for lenses identified as ED, extra-low dispersion; LD, low dispersion; SLD, super-low dispersion; L, luxury; or APO, apochromatic.

Telephoto Compression

Because telephoto lenses compress perspective, elements in a scene appear closer together than you remember seeing them. You can use this compression to create a layering effect in photos.

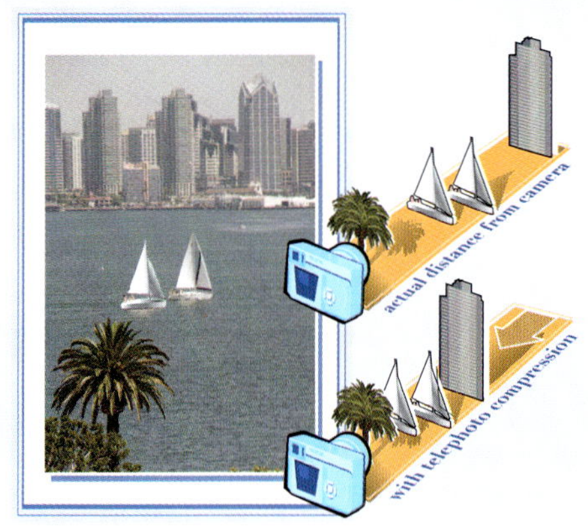

Bringing It Closer

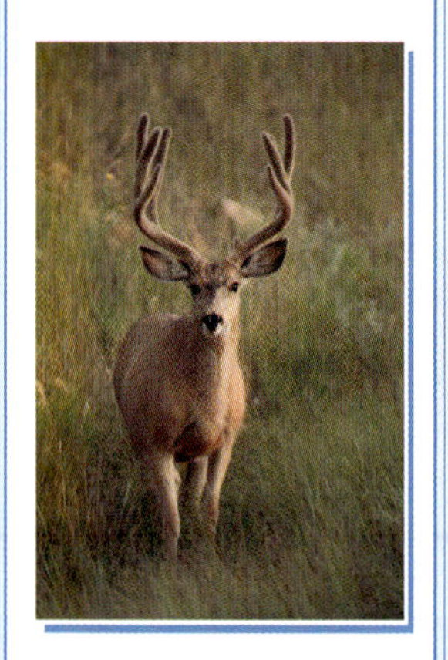

Telephoto lenses are mostly used to isolate and bring subjects that we otherwise cannot see very well closer to us. These lenses are great for sports, wildlife, and portraiture. Telephoto lenses magnify these subjects in relation to the 50mm normal lens — for example, a 200mm lens brings subjects 4× closer, a 300mm lens is 6×, and a 600mm lens makes things appear 12× bigger.

Use a Zoom Lens

Most digital cameras that are not SLR cameras have a built-in zoom lens. Most dSLR cameras come with a zoom lens included in the kit. A zoom lens enables you to change the focal length of the camera at the touch of a button or twist of a ring. A zoom lens combines a range of focal lengths within a single lens. There are zoom lengths of every sort — wide zooms, telephoto zooms, normal zooms, and all-in-one zooms that go from very wide to very long.

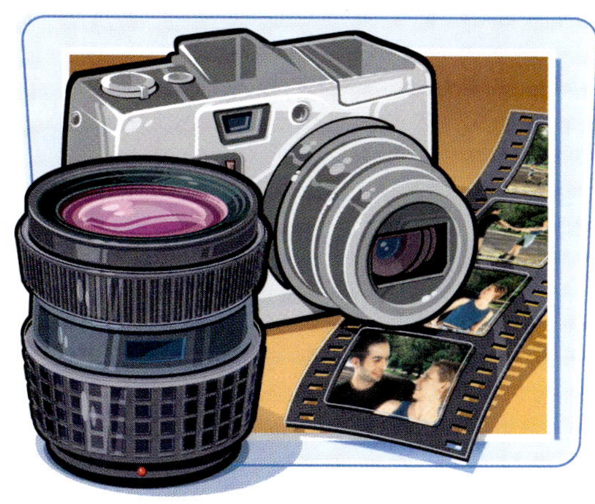

Choose a Zoom Lens

A large zoom range is very helpful because of its versatility. The trade-off of having a large zoom factor is that the camera is typically larger and a little bulky. The ability to zoom in, enabling you to capture details at a distance, is a great advantage. Having a zoom with a wide setting is equally helpful for shooting in small spaces and capturing wide expanses.

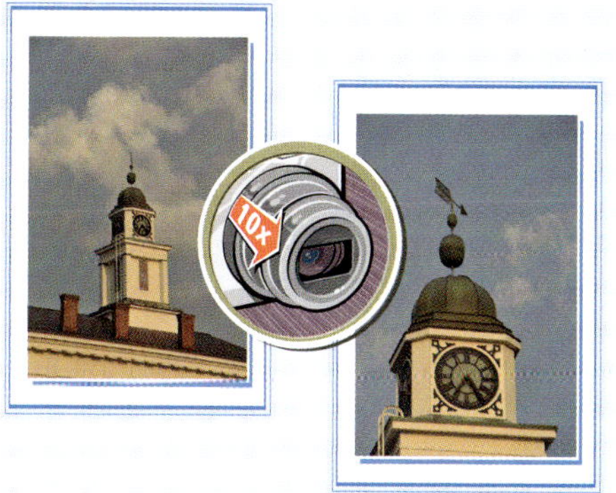

Prevent Blurry Pictures

Zooming in on your subject exaggerates even the slightest camera movement, which can result in blurred images, especially with photos at slower shutter speeds. When shooting at slower shutter speeds, you can stabilize your camera by mounting it on a tripod. Many new cameras now offer a built-in vibration reduction that reduces the effects of camera shake. This feature has many names, such as Image Stabilization, Vibration Reduction, and Super Steady Shot. This often allows you to hold your camera 2 to 3 shutter speeds slower.

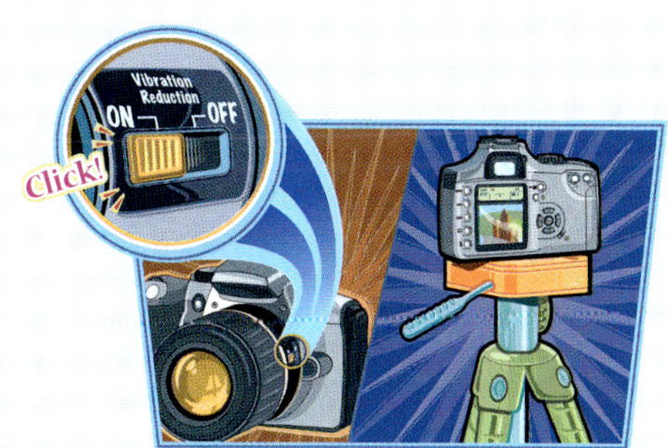

Learn About Digital Camera Lenses

Understanding a Multiplication Factor

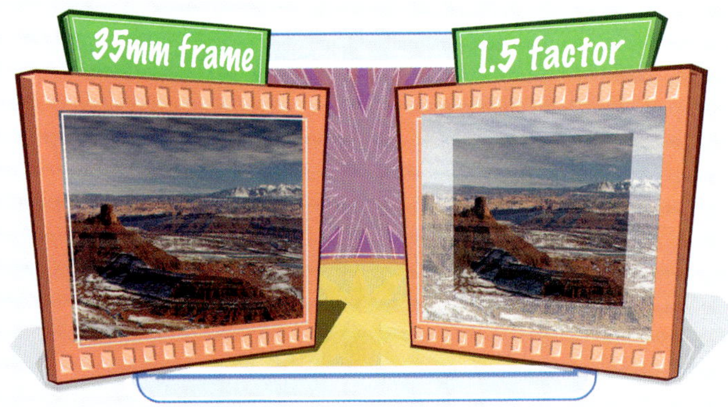

Digital cameras with image sensors smaller than a 35mm film frame reduce the angle of view and produce an apparent lens magnification. Magnification varies by factors ranging from 1.3 to 1.5 times. At a 1.5 factor, a 100mm to 300mm lens provides a 150mm to 450mm equivalent angle of view. This gives greater magnification when you photograph distant subjects, but gives a narrower view of the scene at wide-angle settings.

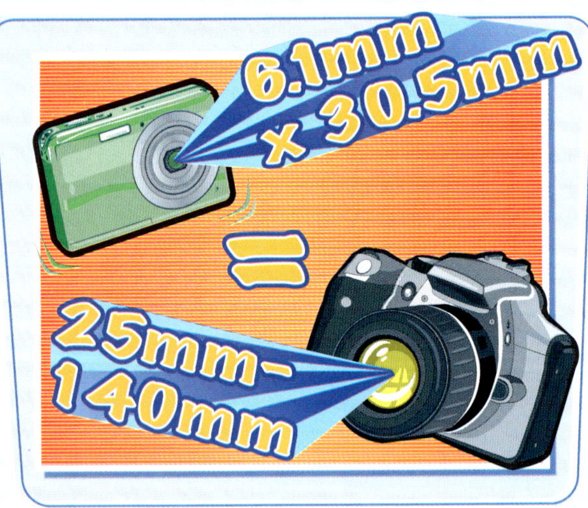

Lenses with Compact Digital Cameras

Compact digitals have even smaller sensors yet. These sensors are roughly 7.2mm×5.3mm — as compared to a 35mm film which is 36mm×24mm. Lenses for cameras might seem impossibly wide, but on a compact digital camera the equivalent to a normal 50mm lens is a 7.4mm lens. Thus a compact digital camera with a very good zoom range might be something like a 6.1mm×30.5mm lens, which would be equivalent to a 28–140 in 35mm terms.

Optical Versus Digital Zoom

Many digital cameras offer optical and digital zoom. Optical zoom magnifies the scene by changing the focal length. Digital zoom crops the scene, which magnifies the center of the frame to make the subject appear larger. Some cameras add extra pixels to round out the image size or resolution. This cropping effect often degrades image quality. Always avoid using digital zoom.

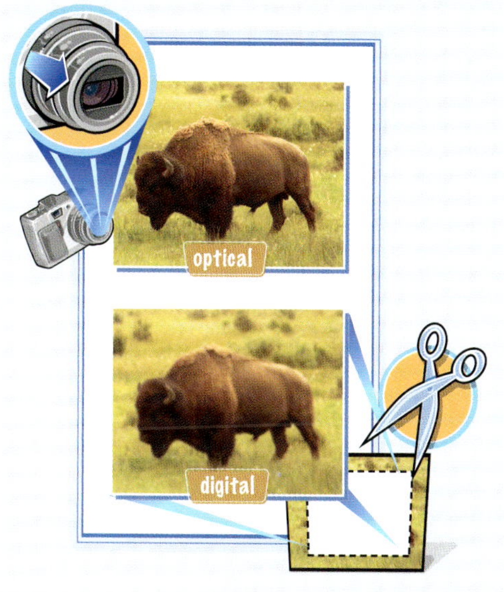

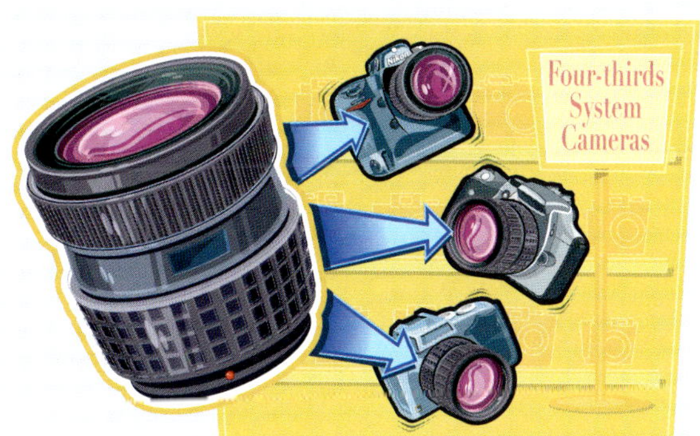

Digital-Specific Lenses

Several companies, including Olympus, Panasonic, Leica, Kodak, and Fujifilm promote the *four-thirds system* that establishes a new common standard for the interchange of lenses developed for digital SLR cameras. The four-thirds system allows the development of dedicated digital camera lens systems with a sensor measuring only half the size of a 35mm film frame. The four-thirds system produces a 2× multiplier for the new digital lenses.

Nikon, Canon, and Sony all have created a significant variety of different lenses for their smaller, APS-C (1.5×)-sized sensor. These lenses are more compact to correspond with the smaller cameras that are made around the smaller sensors, and sometimes have even better zoom range than their 35mm counterparts.

continued

Full Frame Sensors

The size of the sensor in most digital cameras is physically smaller than a 35mm negative, whereas some professional digital SLR cameras have larger, more expensive sensors that are the same size as a 35mm negative, and which are called full frame sensors. The two major advantages of a full frame sensor are the resolution, which results from getting more pixels on the larger sensor, and the larger possible pixel size, resulting from the larger sensor and lessening the amount of noise present in high ISO photos. These cameras and their lenses are also physically larger and heavier. Some full frame sensors are able to create usable photos at well above ISO 6400.

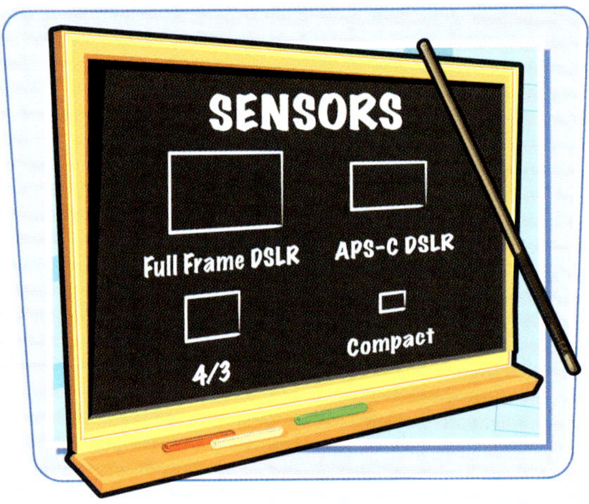

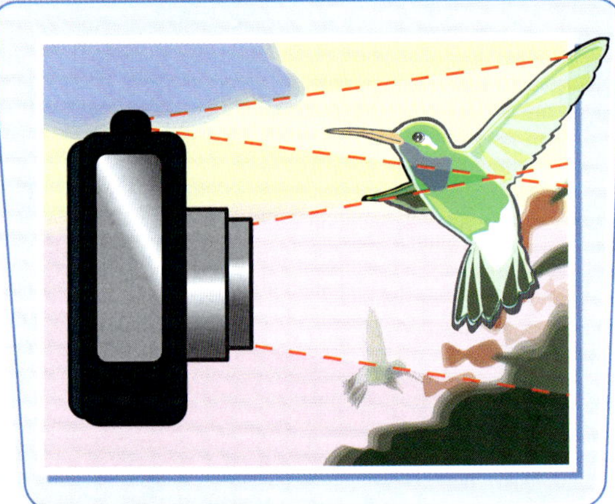

What You See versus What the Lens Sees

Many compact digital cameras feature optical viewfinders, but the viewfinders are separate from the lens. As a result, you do not see in the viewfinder exactly what the lens sees. The closer you move to the subject, the greater the difference, or *parallax,* becomes. To get an accurate view of what the lens *sees,* you should use the LCD. Viewing the image on the LCD can be tricky on a bright sunny day, but accessories are available that put a hood over the LCD to allow you to see the LCD on the brightest of days.

Macro Lenses

Macro lenses allow you to focus very close and are specifically designed for the best results when taking photos of very small items such as jewelry, flowers, or stamps. Macro lenses are generally telephoto lenses so that you can focus close to a small subject without being too physically near to that subject. Many telephoto zooms have a macro setting, which also lets you focus close, but not as close as a true macro lens.

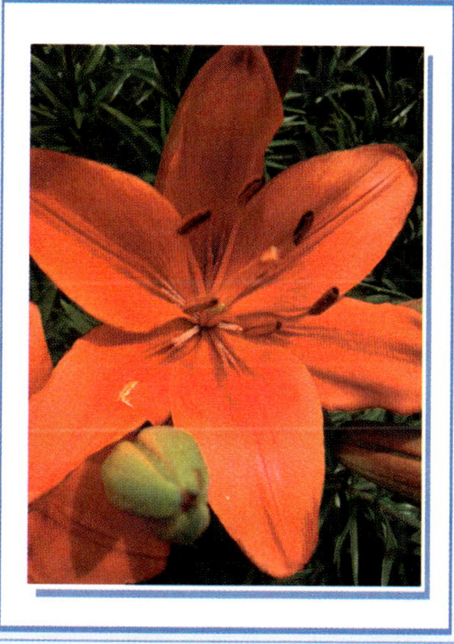

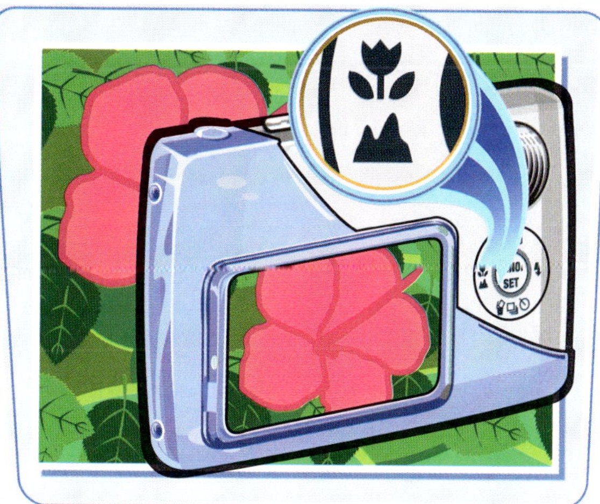

Macro Setting on Compact Cameras

Compact digital cameras have a close-up or macro setting, which is generally designated with a flower icon. This macro setting actually adjusts the camera or lens, allowing the lens to focus closer and limits the lens from taking a photo at far distances. On most digital compacts, that setting is maximized at the wide setting.

Chapter 4

Understanding Light

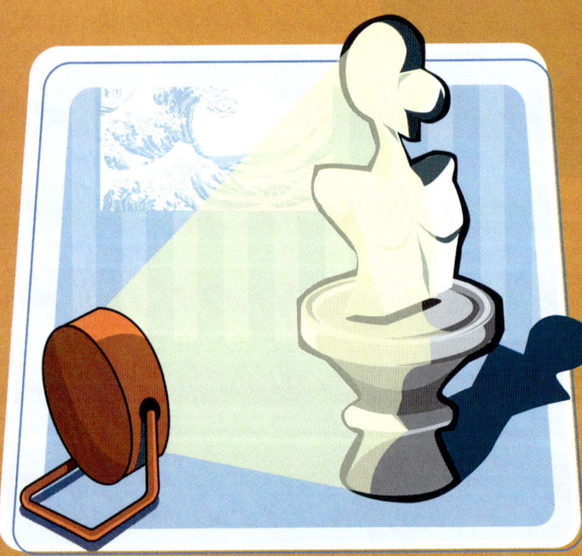

Learn how to use light to create a mood or atmosphere, define a shape or a form, and bring out details in your photographs.

Quick Steps

Learn About the Color of Light 42
Measure and Correct Light for Color 44
Learn About Light Quality 46
Use a Flash 50

Learn About the Color of Light

You can use the qualities of light to set the mood and to influence a viewer's emotional response to the picture. You can also use light to reveal or partially hide the subject's shape, form, texture, and detail, or use light to show colors in the scene as vibrant or subdued.

Our eyes automatically adjust for the difference in the color of light sources. You can also use the camera's technology to make sure that your photos look how you see them.

Light and Color

All colors within the color spectrum are contained in visible light. The amount of any particular color within the light is determined by its source, and for outdoor light, the time of day. For example, more reddish orange color is seen at sunset when the sun's low angle causes light to pass through more of the heated earth's atmosphere. Midday light on an overcast day produces a bluish color, whereas indoor light, such as candlelight and tungsten light bulbs, creates an amber tone. Knowing how these different light sources affect your photographs helps you make better choices.

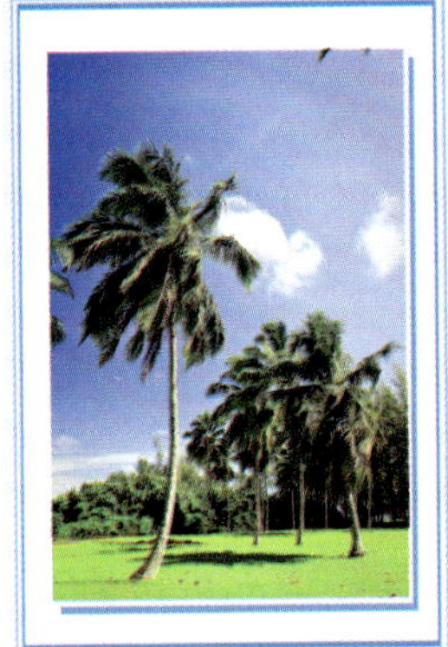

Sunrise

Cobalt and purple hues of the night sky predominate during early sunrise. Within minutes, the landscape begins to reflect the warm gold and red hues of the sunrise. Early morning light is produced by sunlight passing through the atmosphere at a low angle, which means that the light is going through much more of the earth's atmosphere than it would if the sun were directly overhead. (This same increase in atmospheric layers has a magnifying effect, which explains why the sun and the moon appear so much larger when they are close to the horizon.) Later in the morning as the sun gets higher in the sky, the light shifts to a rich blue. Most photographers agree the best shooting light for clear skies is an hour after sunrise until around midmorning, and then again when the sun is within a few hours of setting.

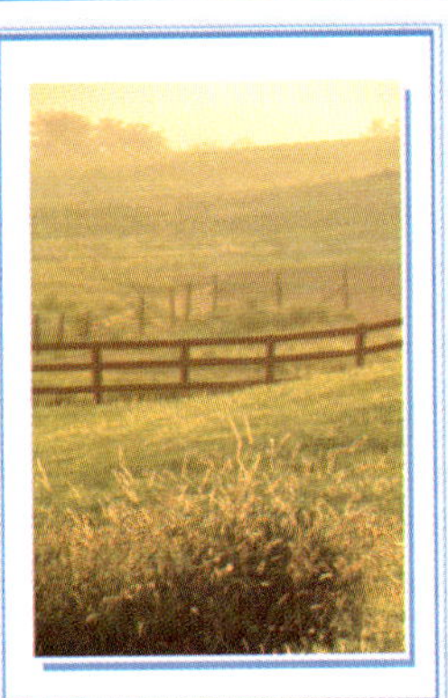

Midday

During midday, bright overhead light produces harsh shadows and a bluish colorcast. For some types of photography, particularly portraiture, this is not the time to take the most beautiful photos. Midday light can work well for photographing shadow patterns, flower petals, and plant leaves made translucent against the sun, and for natural and man-made structures such as rock formations and buildings.

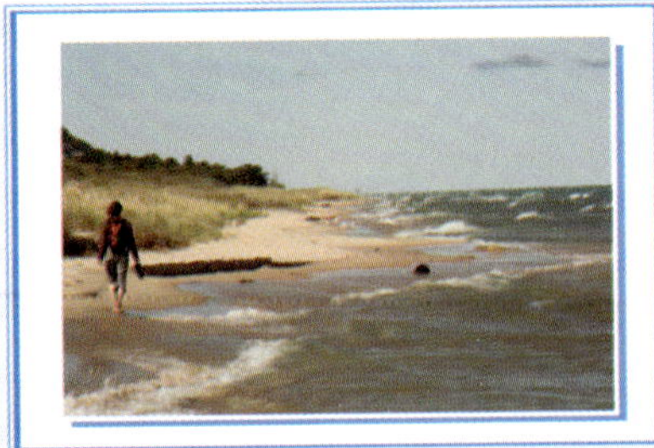

Sunset

During the time just before, during, and just following sunset, the warmest and most intense color of natural light occurs. The predominantly red, yellow, and gold light creates vibrant colors, whereas the low angle of the sun creates soft contrasts that define and enhance textures and shapes. Sunset colors create rich landscape, cityscape, and wildlife photographs.

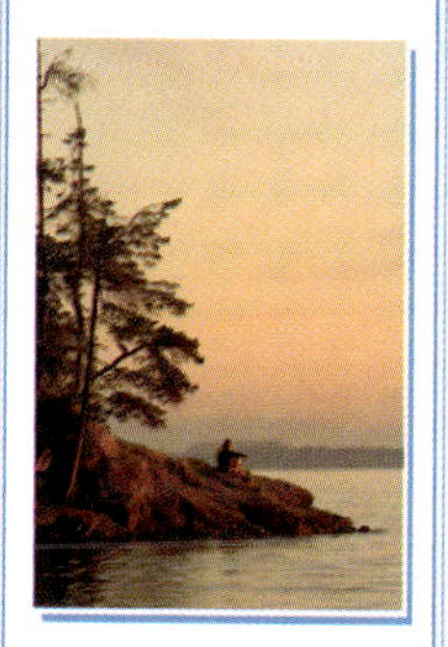

Electronic Flash

Most on-camera electronic flashes are balanced for the neutral (white) color of midday light, although sometimes these strobes tend to make their subjects slightly bluish. Electronic flash light is neutral, and in the correct intensities, reproduces colors accurately. On the negative side, using a flash can bring out unwanted details, such as wrinkles, and produce hard shadows; in very dark situations, the flash creates a bright subject and makes everything else too dark.

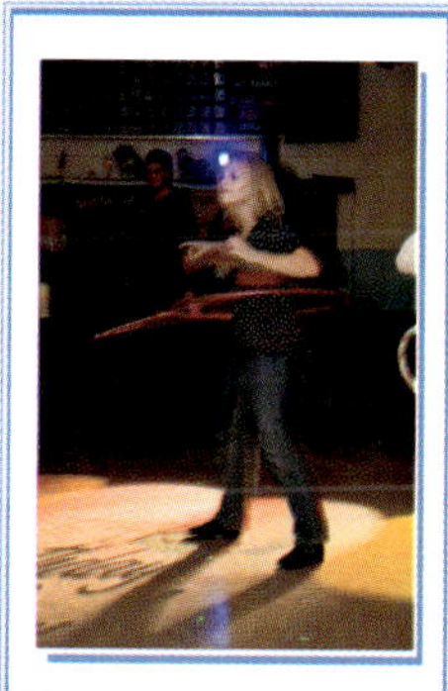

Household or Candlelight

Tungsten is household light. Tungsten light, like firelight and candlelight, appears warmer than daylight and produces a yellow/orange cast in photos taken using a digital or a film camera. Although this colorcast can be easily corrected, in many cases it is desirable because of its warm, inviting feel.

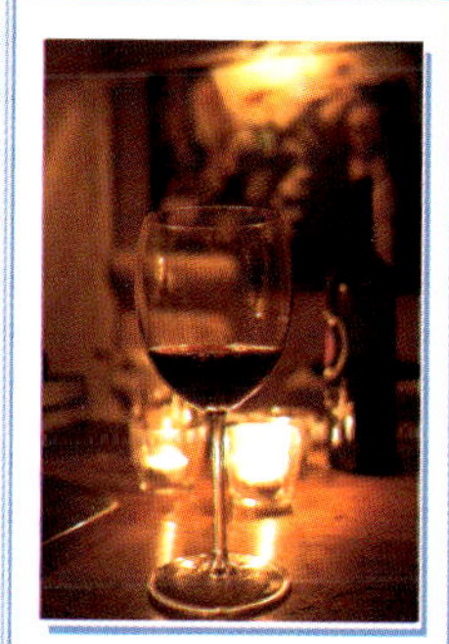

Fluorescent Light

Commonly found in offices and public places, fluorescent light typically produces a green cast in photos taken using a digital camera that has the white balance set to daylight or auto. Typically this colorcast is seldom seen in the photo because when the subject is lit by fluorescents, the light is low enough to cause the camera's automatic flash to fire. The flash produces sufficient light to overcome any colorcast produced by the fluorescent lighting. Fluorescents, compact fluorescents, mercury vapor, and sodium vapor lights are all common types of lights in buildings and cities at night, and each of these creates its own type of colorcast. The white balance on today's cameras seems to get ever better at figuring out the different color automatically to make for normal-looking photos, but keep your eye out when a lot of different lights are around.

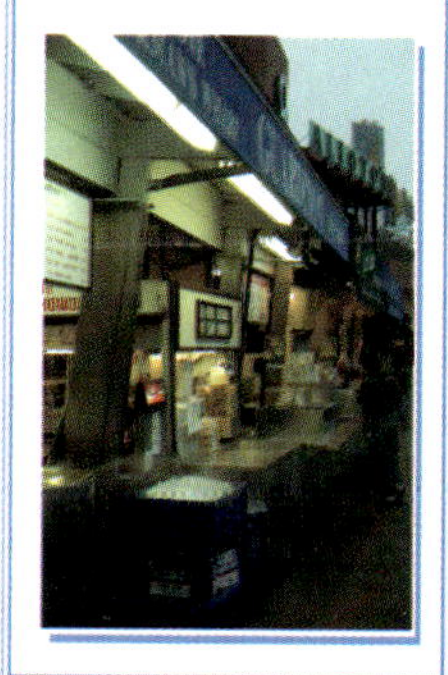

Measure and Correct Light for Color

In film photography, the color composition of the light is controlled by attaching color filters in front of the lens to compensate for or enhance various ranges of color. This is because the color balance of the film is determined by its chemical composition and cannot be changed. Digital cameras allow you to control the color balance of the sensor by manually changing the white balance (WB) setting.

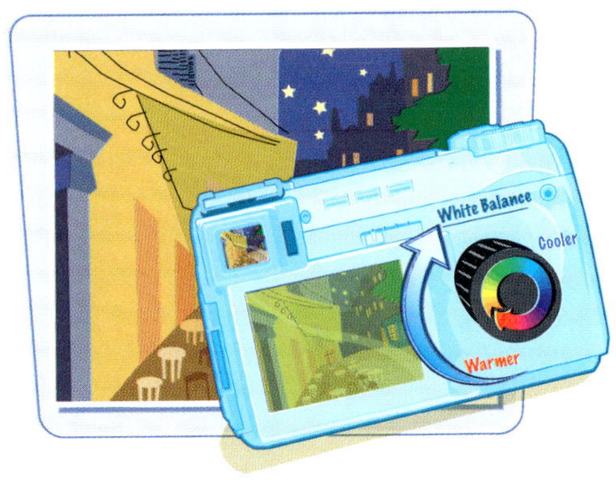

How Light Color Is Measured

In photography, image color is measured as a temperature. Each color of light corresponds to a temperature measured on the Kelvin (K) scale in degrees, with white sunlight being about 5000 K. It works the opposite way you would expect it to. The higher the temperature, the cooler (or more blue) the light, so a heavily overcast day would be about 9000 K. The lower the temperature, the warmer (or more yellow/red) the light — candlelight being about 1000 K. In short, subjects lit by cool, higher-temperature light appear bluer; when lit by warmer light, subjects appear amber.

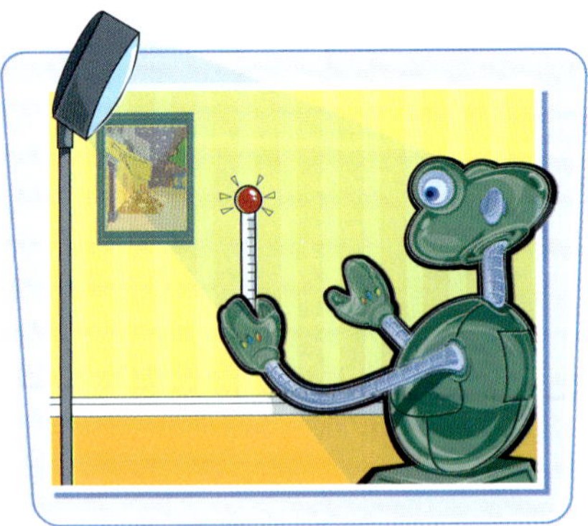

Light Meters

Camera light meters assume that everything you focus on is neutral gray, which reflects 18 percent of the light and absorbs the rest. Today, the 18 percent gray card is used for metering and for calibrating the white balance setting of a digital camera. When the light meter in a modern digital camera evaluates a scene, it reads hundreds of areas of light and dark in the image frame and adjusts the camera to capture the greatest amount of detail without over- or underexposing the image. In today's cameras the light meter works with the onboard computers to figure the best exposure and white balance automatically even in some very tricky situations.

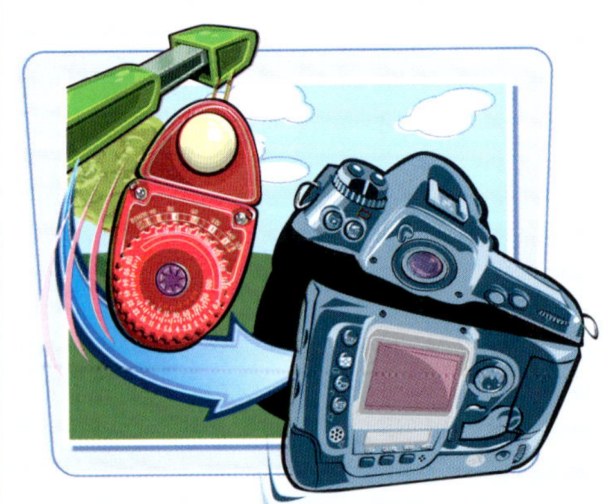

Why Correct for Light?

The human eye automatically adjusts to changing light color and sees white as being white in different types of light. Digital sensors simply read the light as it is, so as the color temperature of the light illuminating the subject changes, so does the colorcast on the finished photo. To achieve the desired color in a photo, either the white balance of the camera must be adjusted or the color of the photo must be corrected using the computer.

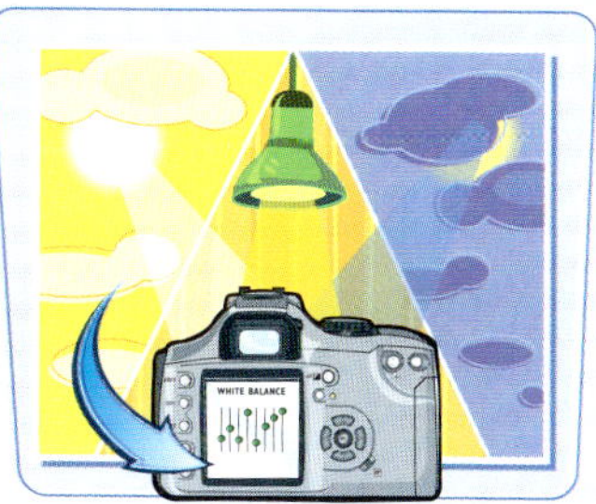

Automatic White Balance

There are several ways to achieve desired color rendition using a digital camera. You can manually set the white balance or let the camera set it for you automatically. Automatic white balance is getting better with every new generation of digital cameras, and in many cases it is the best solution, especially when there are multiple light sources. The camera reevaluates the WB with each shot, so inconsistencies have the opportunity to occur.

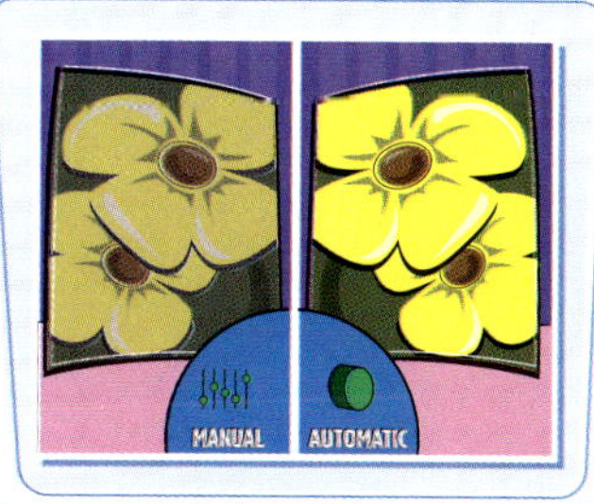

Set White Balance

On digital cameras, you adjust the white balance to tell the camera the temperature or type of light in the scene. White balance options, such as Bright Sun, Tungsten, Shady, and Fluorescent, are set using one of the camera menus. Choose the setting that matches the predominant light in the scene. Some cameras allow you to adjust settings with a + or − to get more precise color. Newer cameras offer multiple scene selections, such as sunset, fireworks, and outdoor action. These scene mode settings not only control the exposure but the white balance settings as well.

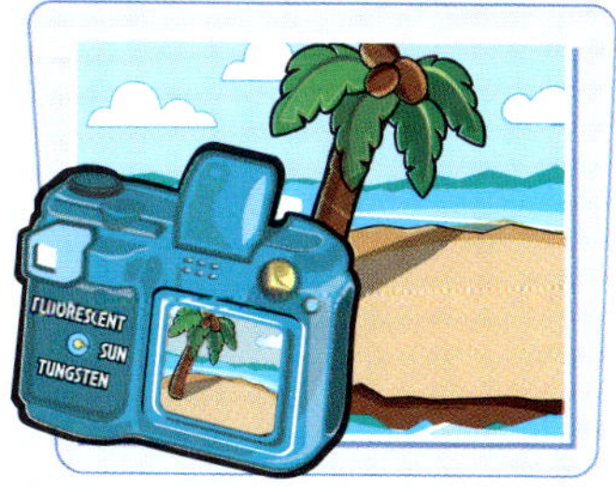

Manual White Balance

If the auto settings are so good, why would you use the manual settings? Manually setting your white balance is the most accurate way to get your color correct. It is also the most consistent because the auto WB is looking for an average colorcast, but even a slight change in the scene can offset the color in auto WB. Also, you may want to change the WB to a different setting for your own creative purposes.

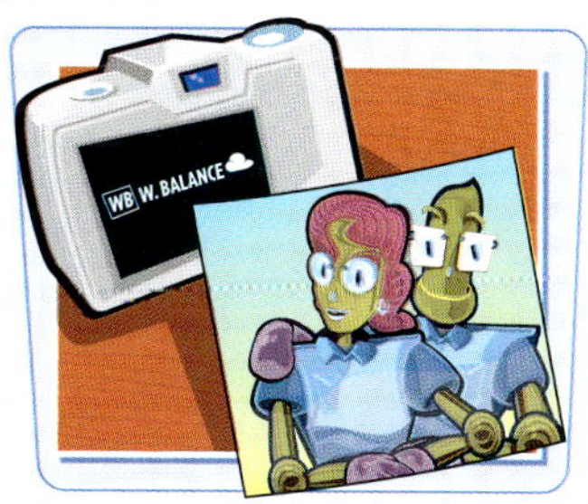

Learn About Light Quality

Photographers describe light by many names. These names often describe the effect that the light has on the resulting photo. Hard light creates shadows with well-defined edges. Soft light (also called diffused light) creates shadows with soft edges. Understanding the effect that each type of light produces helps you use both types of light, and variations in between, effectively. In addition to types of lighting, the direction that the light is coming from also affects how accurately the automatic light meter can read the scene and produce optimum exposure settings.

Light Quality

Light quality is somewhat hard to quantify because it changes from photo to photo. Light quality helps to build a mood or tone in your photos. An overcast day might be dark and moody or it might help create a soft and gentle-looking portrait. Learning to evaluate the light helps you to better create your own best photos.

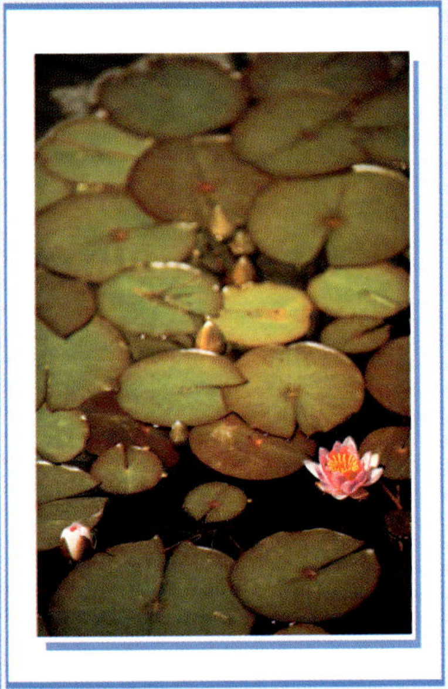

Hard Light

Hard, bright light creates a concentrated spotlight effect. Hard light from the bright sun, a flash, or a bare light bulb creates shadows with sharp edges, and obliterates highlight and shadow details. Hard light can be good for landscape and for fall color photography. Hard light can lead to challenging photos of people. To prevent shadows on faces caused by hard light, use a fill flash, or if possible, move the subject to a shady area.

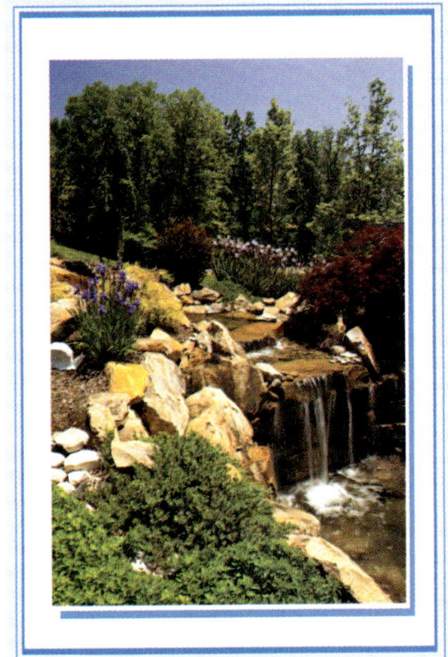

Soft Light

Soft light is diffused light spread over a larger area. Atmospheric conditions, such as clouds, diffuse natural light, creating shadow edges that transition gradually. Open shade is also considered soft light. Soft light works well for easy portraits and close-up photography. Even though an overcast day produces a bluish colorcast, the diffused light it offers allows you to get photos of subjects without harsh shadows.

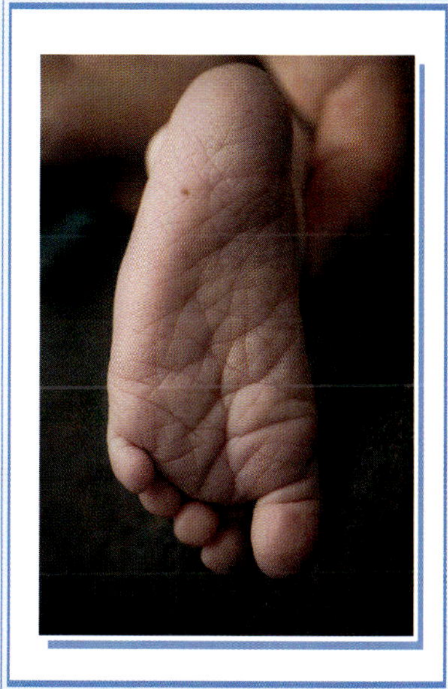

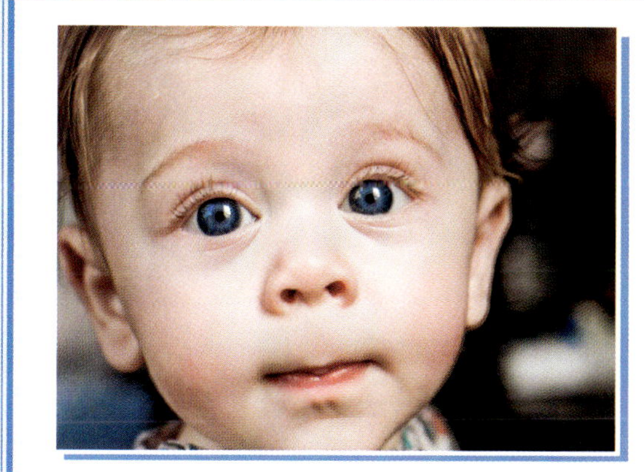

Front Lighting

The simplest type of light comes from the front of the scene. Front light allows for bright scenes and easy exposures. If you are taking photos outside, try to keep the sun at your back for nicely front-lit photos. Strong front light can sometimes be too bright though, and all the light from the scene can come straight back into the camera. Front-lit portraits might be better if the light is slightly softer.

continued

Side Lighting

Side lighting happens when light comes across the scene, and can be called *cross light*. This type of light is usually seen out of doors in the early morning or late afternoon and helps to create great texture and depth within the photograph. Many portraits are done with some side lighting, but once again, are probably most flattering when the light is slightly softer.

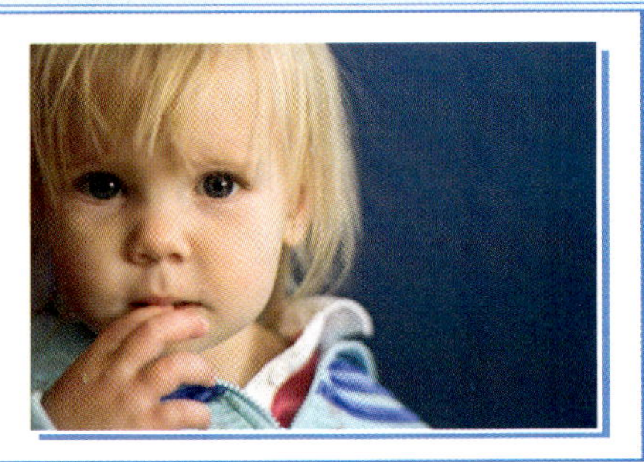

Top Lighting

Top lighting illuminates the subject from overhead, such as what happens in the middle of a sunny day. This hard lighting produces strong, deep shadows, especially under the eyes, nose, and chin when shooting people. But if the day is overcast, shooting a portrait in this light is great, with a huge soft-light source from above. Many photographers also adjust their flashes indoors so that the light hits the ceiling and bounces down in a top-lighting situation. Doing this creates more natural-looking flash shots.

Backlighting

Light positioned behind the subject creates a condition called *backlighting*. Depending on the angle, backlight can create a great thin halo of light that outlines the rim of the shape of the subject. Backlight is a tricky lighting situation, but it can be beautiful and dramatic. You may need to overexpose the scene (using exposure compensation) to make sure enough light falls on your subject. Backlight is also used for silhouettes and other dramatic types of photos.

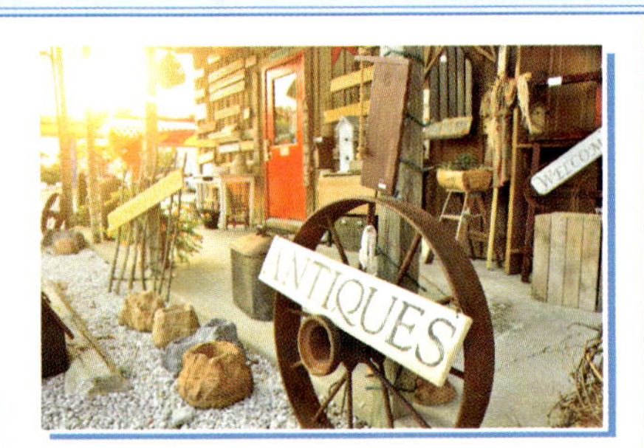

Learn About Fill Light

Sunlight is a very bright light source, and thus the shadows it casts are very dark. The contrast between the light and dark is simply too much for your sensor. To help close the gap between the brights and darks when you have shadows that hide some element in your photographs, you use some other light source like a strobe or some sort of reflector to "fill in" the shadows with light. Many times this is just a tiny bit of light to get some sparkle into the subjects' eyes.

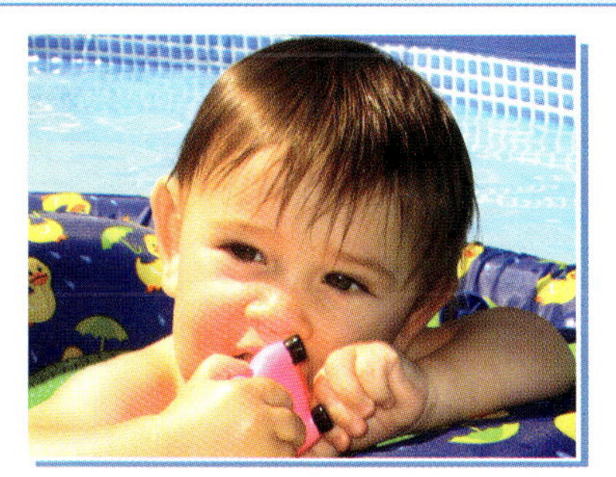

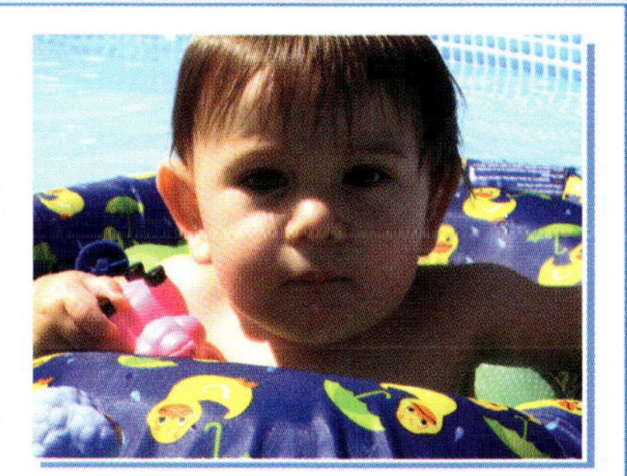

Use a Reflector

A reflector can be just about anything that can reflect some sunlight back into the subject and fill in the shadows. You can get all manner of reflectors at your camera shop, but you can use paper, cardboard, tin foil wrapped on cardboard, a building, mirrors, or even have someone with a white shirt move close to your subject to reflect some light.

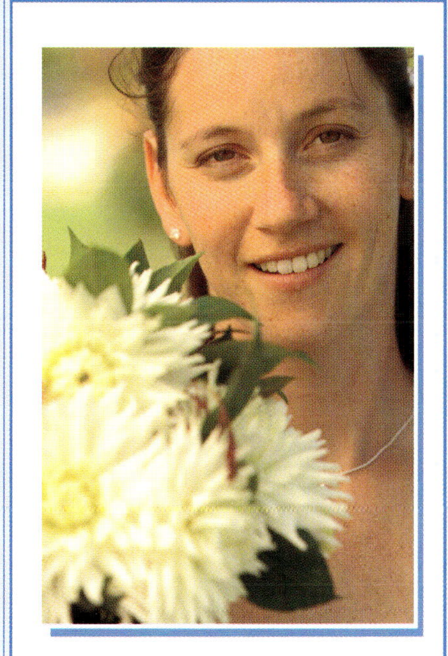

Use a Flash

Your electronic flash is a powerful tool. When you need to add light in a low-light scene, the camera automatically fires the flash to provide enough light for a good exposure. When a light source is producing shadows on a subject's face, use the camera's built-in flash unit or an external unit to fill in those shadows to create a well-illuminated photograph.

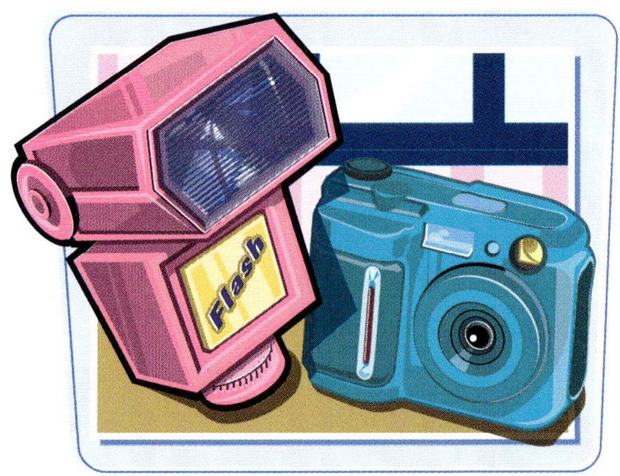

Flash Distance

To get the best flash pictures, indoors or outdoors, it is important to know the distance that the flash travels, and then to stay within that distance when taking pictures. On most compact cameras, the flash range is 10 to 15 feet. Be sure to check your camera's manual to find the exact range of your flash.

With one of the large hot shoe–mounted strobes, you may be able to angle or twist the flash head so that you can direct and bounce the light. In that case, make sure the flash will make it all the way to the bouncing surface (ceiling or wall) to get enough light on your subject.

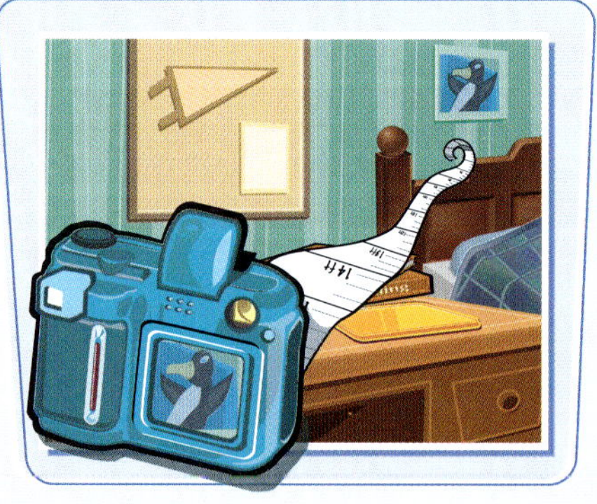

Flash Compensation

Today's digital cameras automatically sense when the flash has produced the optimum exposure and adjust the amount of flash for your exposure. Some digital cameras and accessory flash units allow you to control the flash intensity. Use your LCD to determine just how much flash power is being used automatically, and if it is still too dark or too light, use flash compensation. You can set the flash to different levels of power, measured in exposure values (EV). To decrease the flash output and create a softer light, you can set it to a negative EV value, and if you need to increase it, you set it to a positive value. This is particularly helpful when using the flash for daylight fill flash.

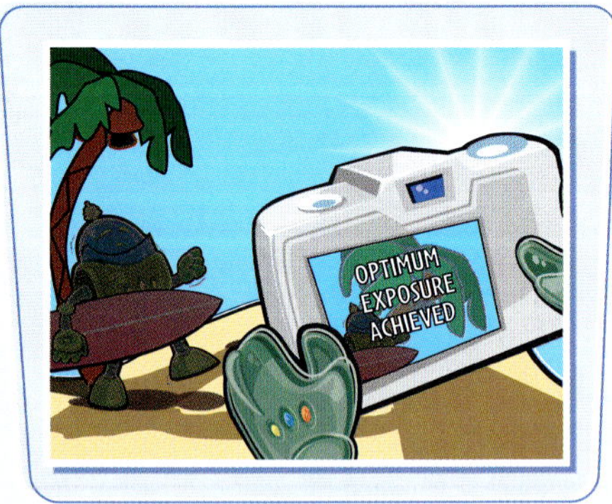

Use Flash Outdoors

With your compact digital camera, it might actually help if the default flash setting was to flash in bright sunlight. Shadows on faces and even small still-life subjects can be brought to life with even just a little strobe power. Look for shadows in eye sockets or underneath hats, and use your flash to brighten up the scene. Flash outdoors is even helpful in overcast situations to add some contrast or in a backlit scene like a sunset to help balance the light coming back to the camera.

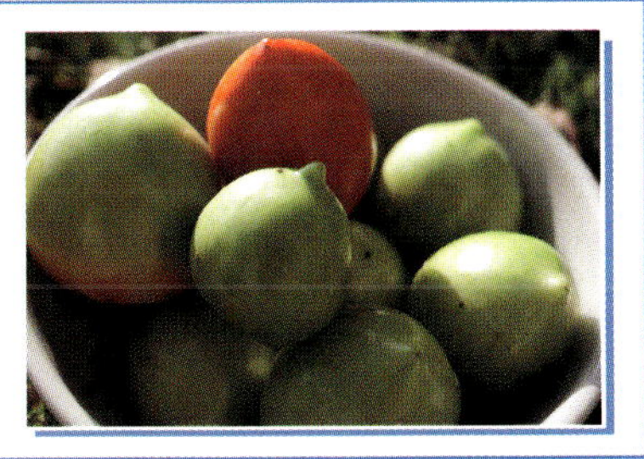

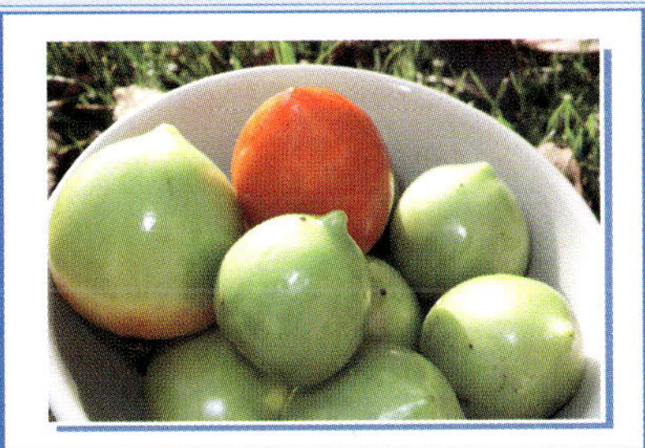

Without Fill Flash

Harsh overhead (top) lighting and backlighting create problems, such as unattractive shadows in portraits and silhouettes. In this picture, without a fill flash, deep shadows appear under the nose and chin of the subject.

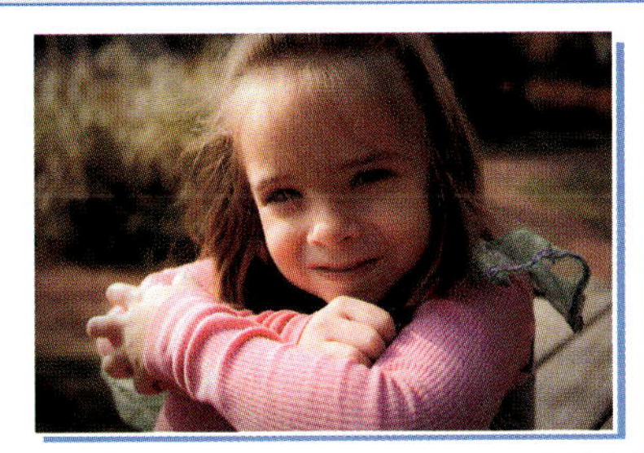

With Fill Flash

In most cameras today, just opening the flash or changing the flash mode to manual produces the necessary flash exposure to work as an effective fill flash. Even though the flash mode may be called manual, the automatic sensor still regulates the amount of power in the flash. In this picture, fill flash lightens the deep shadow areas by adding light to the front of the subject.

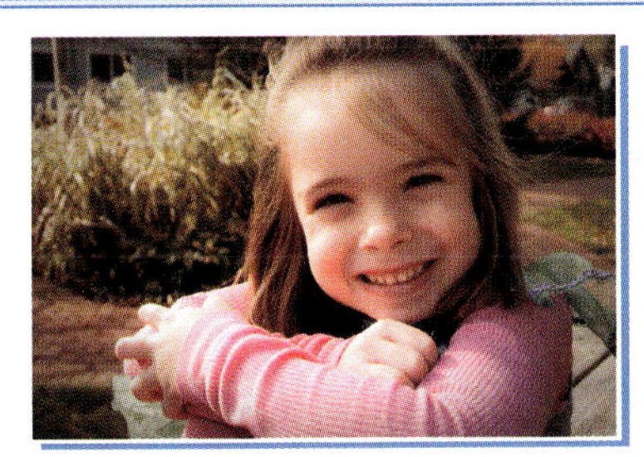

Chapter 5

Learning About Focus

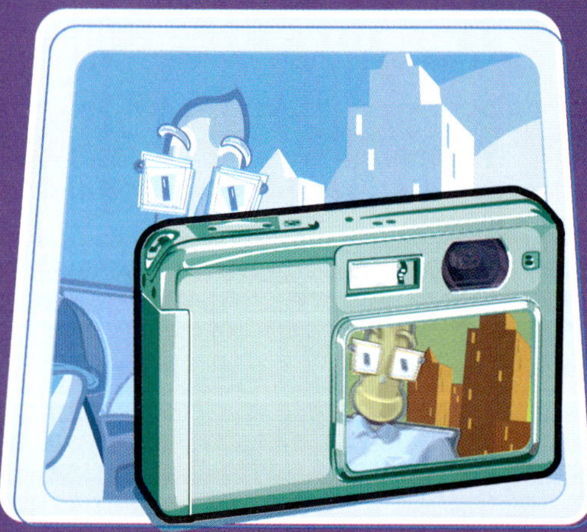

Focus is essential to taking good photographs. A blurry or out-of-focus subject makes the picture unusable. Even though all digital cameras have an autofocusing system, focus problems are the leading cause of ruined photos in digital photography. In this chapter, you learn how to focus precisely, and what to focus on in a scene.

Quick Steps

Understanding Focus Systems.......... 54
Focus on an Off-Center Subject.......... 56
Use Focus Modes.......... 58
Discover Focus Techniques.......... 59

Understanding Focus Systems

All digital cameras have autofocus built-in. These systems vary from camera to camera and their abilities range from a simple type of autofocus that focuses the camera on the subject in the center of frame, to more sophisticated systems that can follow and focus on objects moving across the lens; and even more advanced focus systems automatically focus on a face and take the photo only when people smile.

With a little understanding about how the autofocus system on your camera works, you can ensure that your photos are consistently in focus.

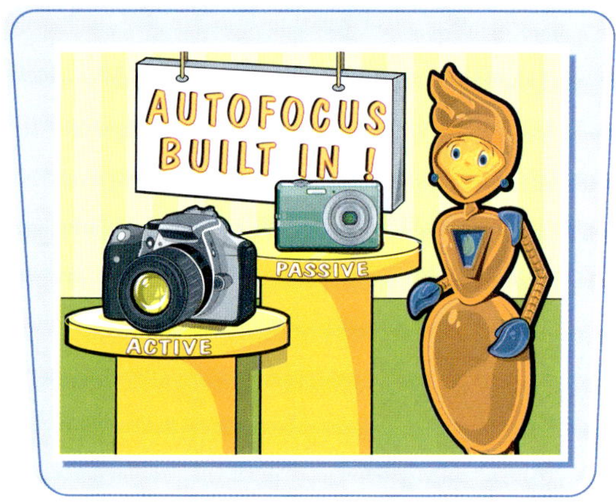

Fixed Focus Systems

Fixed focus systems do not adjust the lens to focus, but rely only on having such a great depth of field that everything more than a few feet in front of the camera is in focus. Although the method is simple, fixed focus systems often display only reasonably sharp pictures. Single-use film cameras often use a fixed focus system, as do budget digital cameras such as the ones found at drugstores and discount marts. This is also how focusing works on most cellular phones that have cameras.

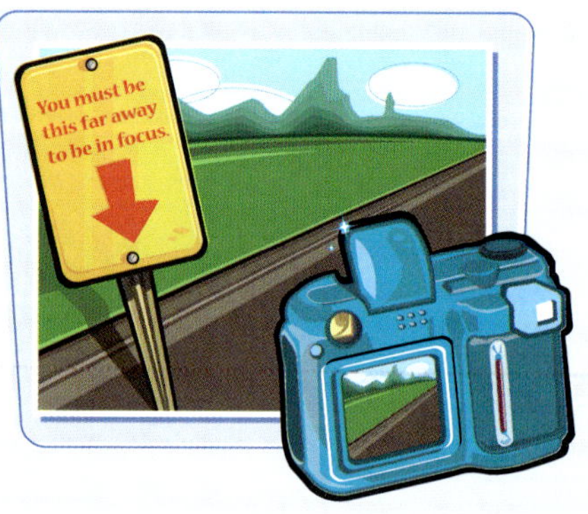

Active Autofocus Systems

Many cameras use an active system that uses a short burst of light or infrared to determine distance. These systems measure the amount of time it takes an object to reflect the light back to the camera, and use this distance to set the focus. Active systems can be fast and precise, but often have problems with shooting through windows and other glass surfaces. Most compact digital cameras use active autofocus systems.

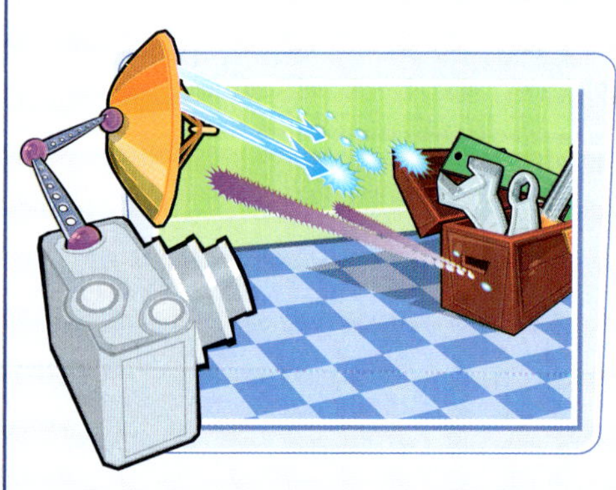

Passive Autofocus Systems

Some cameras use passive autofocus systems, which perform analysis of the image as it comes into the camera. This is done through either *phase detection* or *contrast measurement* as the light comes through the lens. To determine camera-to-subject distance, the camera detects differences in dark and light elements, or *contrast*, in the scene, or differences in colors and textures. Passive autofocus works well in most scenarios, but does not focus as well in low-light situations and with scenes possessed of little contrast difference such as a plain wall or clear blue sky. Some dSLRs have an autofocus assist light to help with this.

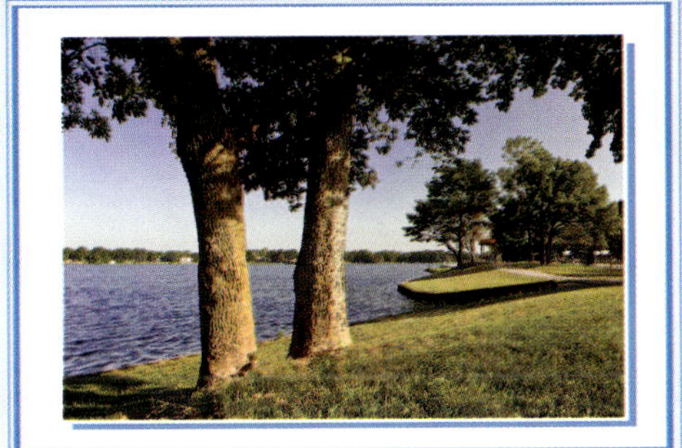

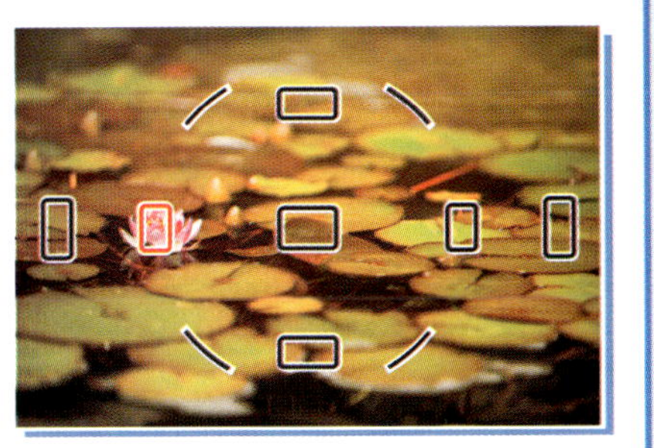

Multipoint Autofocus Systems

Multipoint autofocus systems let you easily compose with and focus on an off-center subject. To focus, you select one of the autofocus sensors, place the subject within the selected sensor, and then focus by pressing the shutter release button halfway down. Some multipoint systems offer focus tracking to maintain continuous focus on a moving subject, whereas others focus on the closest subject regardless of where it is in the frame. Most modern digital cameras have multipoint AF systems.

When Autofocus Fails

Autofocus does not always focus correctly. The most common failure is the camera focusing on the wrong subject. The next most common cause of failure is when too little light is on the subject, or when the subject is just too close to the camera. Most cameras have an indicator (a small icon or a beep) that lets you know when the camera thinks it is in focus. After you take the photo you can see it in the camera's LCD screen, but be aware that even blurred images can appear sharp when viewed on a tiny LCD screen. For important photos, you should use the LCD's zoom feature and make sure the subject, and not the background, is in focus.

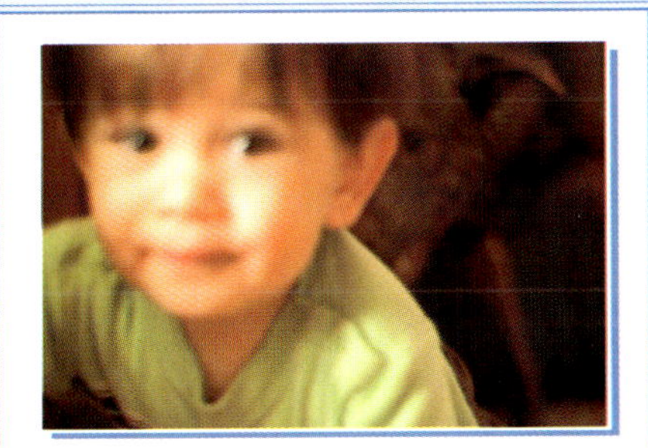

Focus on an Off-Center Subject

When composing an image in the frame, it often looks better to have the subject off-center. But, because the autofocus system of many cameras expects the subject to be in the center, it attempts to focus on whatever is in the center of the frame. This makes focusing difficult with cameras that have a single-center autofocus sensor. To compose an image with the subject off-center, you can use focus lock.

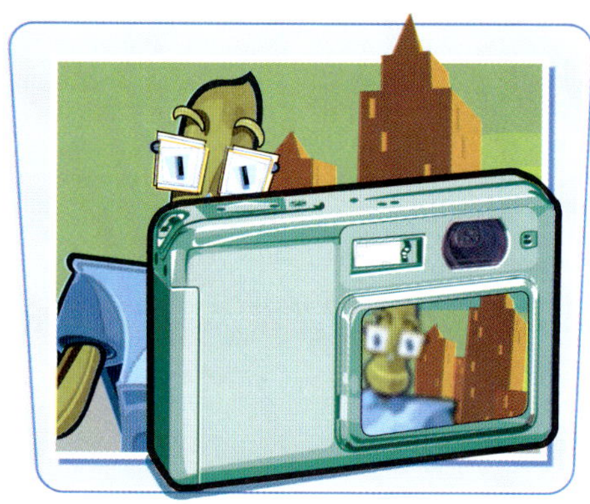

Focus on an Off-Center Subject

1. Frame your subject in the viewfinder or LCD. Make note of where your focus sensor is in your viewfinder or LCD.

   Always set the zoom before focusing.

   For multipoint focusing systems, choose the autofocus sensor you want.

Note: *See Chapter 3 to learn about using a zoom lens.*

2. Place your indicated AF sensor over the subject to be focused on and press the shutter release button halfway down.

   The focus system locks using the center autofocus sensor or the sensor you chose.

3. Check the focus indicator on the camera to ensure the focus is good.

   Many cameras have a green LED that glows in or near the viewfinder when the subject is in focus.

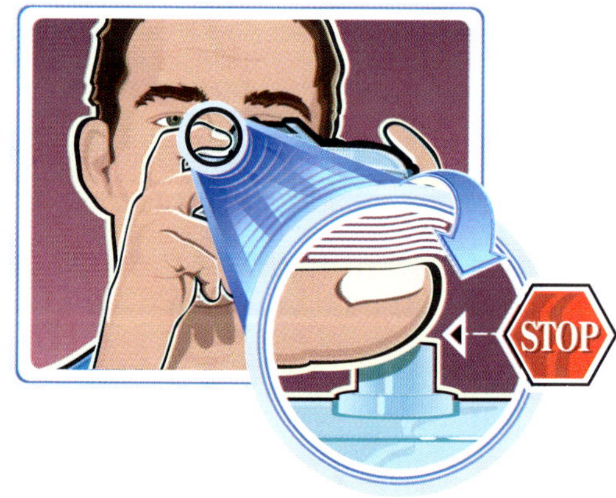

4. If necessary, hold the button halfway down, and then shift the camera to recompose the scene.
5. Fully depress the shutter release button to take the picture.

Note: *If you or the subject changes position, be sure to repeat this process to refocus on the subject.*

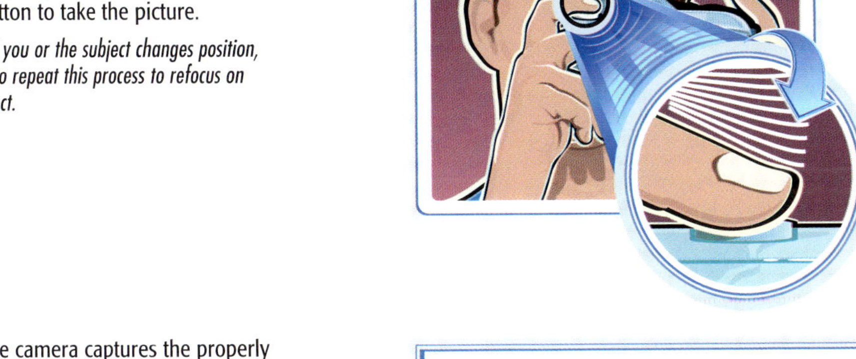

The camera captures the properly focused picture and saves it to memory.

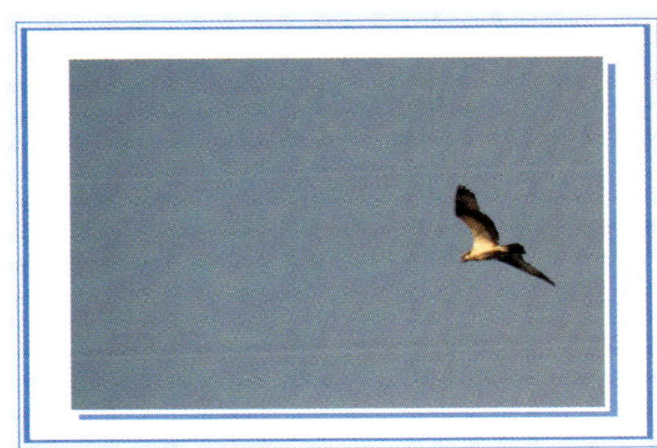

Should I compose my pictures using the viewfinder or the LCD?

The LCD provides an accurate view of the scene that the camera captures, and the viewfinder on some compact cameras may not show the full scene, but if the camera has a viewfinder, it is more stable to bring the camera to your face. If you use the LCD to compose pictures, be sure that the focus indicator shows that the focus is where you want it before you take the picture. When you compose using the LCD in low-lighting conditions, consider supporting the camera on a solid surface such as a tripod or a table, or brace yourself against a solid object to ensure that you get sharp pictures.

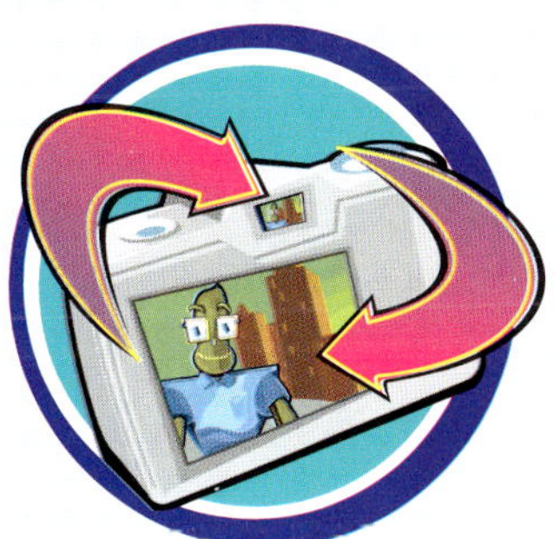

Use Focus Modes

One of the features becoming popular with digital cameras is the ability to select a preset scene mode. Most digital cameras now offer several of these presets. Selecting some of these subject or scene modes affects the focus method used. Make sure to read your camera manual to discover which of the modes affect focus and how they affect it.

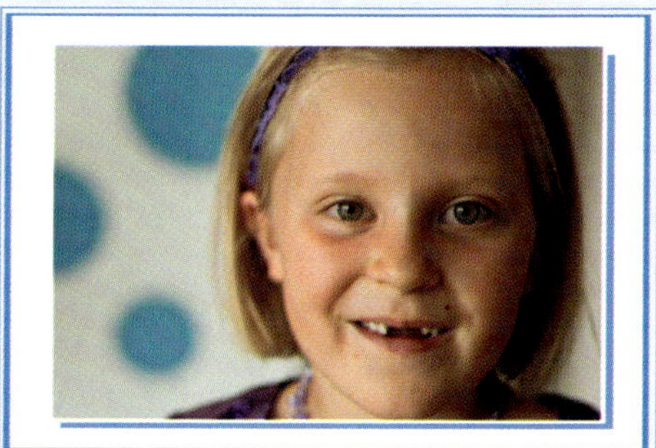

Automatic

Automatic is usually the default setting of the camera. It does not affect the autofocus systems and allows you to take photos at distances from a few feet to infinity. Simply place the focus indicator over the subject to be focused on, press the shutter release part way to focus, and then shoot.

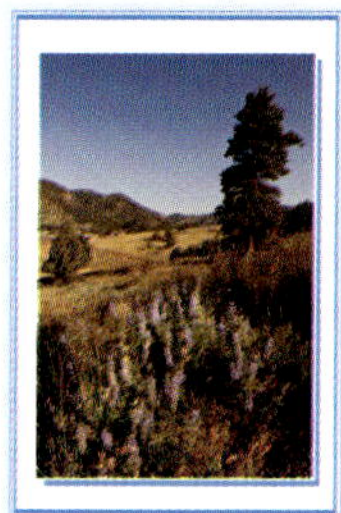

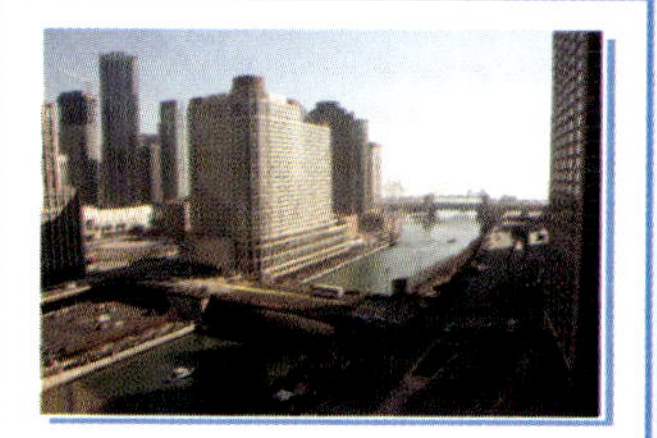

Landscape

If you set your compact digital camera to landscape AF mode, then the camera sets the focus at infinity. This is usually set with an icon that looks like a mountain. The advantage of this mode is that it prevents the camera from continually attempting to focus on a subject that is too far away, which takes time and battery power, and also allows you to focus a compact digital camera through glass. Because the landscape scene mode disables autofocus, the only caution when using this mode is to remember to return the mode to normal auto after you take the photo.

Close-Up or Macro

To change the focus for closer distances, switch to close-up or macro mode, which is usually noted with a flower icon. Depending on your camera, switching to macro mode allows the focusing system to focus on subjects as close as .8 inches from the front of the lens. Check your camera manual to see what the minimum and maximum focus distance is for macro mode. In many cameras, the maximum distance for macro is around 30 feet, which also makes it good for portraits.

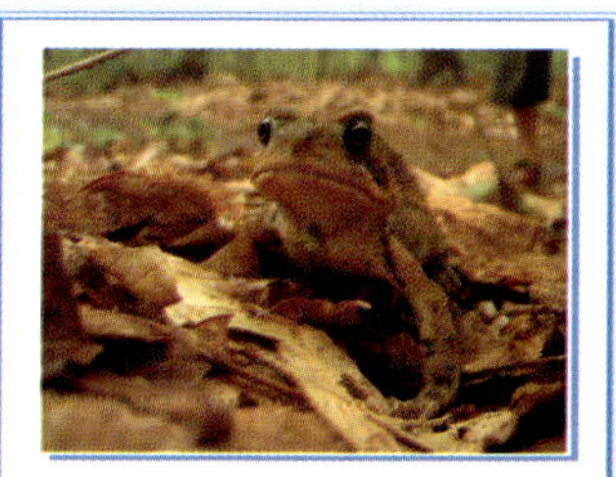

Focus on a Moving Subject

Moving subjects can be a challenge because many camera autofocus systems do not focus quickly enough. One way to ensure that the subject is in the frame when the photo is taken is to establish the focus before you shoot using focus lock. This way the camera is prefocused and does not waste time hunting for the correct focus. dSLR cameras usually have a continuous focus mode that tracks the subject contained within the focus indicator; you then press the button and hold it down. You end up with multiple images to choose from, and the odds are that one of them will be great.

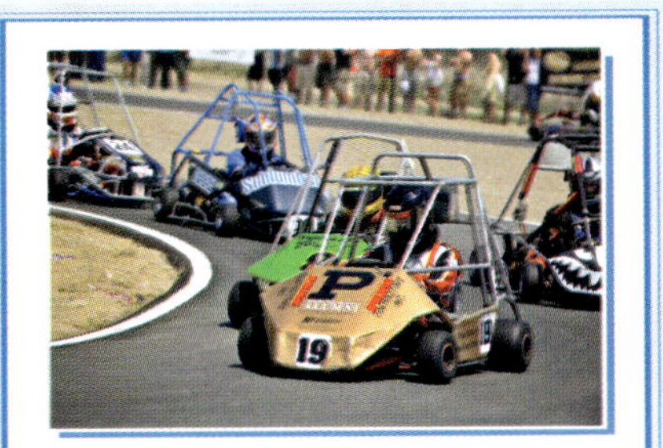

Choose a Point of Focus

When taking a portrait or group picture, focus on the eyes of the person closest to the camera. When photographing a still life, focus on the most important element in the scene. For example, in this picture the focus is on the knife on the cutting board, not the pitcher or the background. For a landscape photo, fix the focus one-third of the way into the scene.

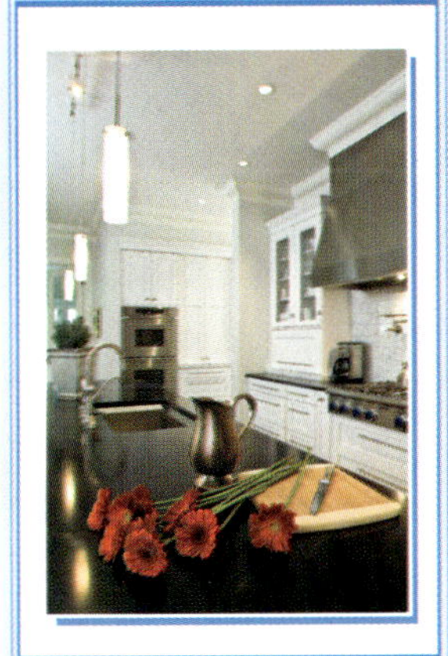

Focus Tips

- Use a tripod if the lighting is low (see Chapter 2).
- Be sure your focus indicator shows that your camera is in focus.
- Use your camera's LCD screen to make sure the photo is in focus.
- For important images, zoom in the LCD preview to make sure the focus is sharp because even blurry images can appear sharp on a small LCD screen.

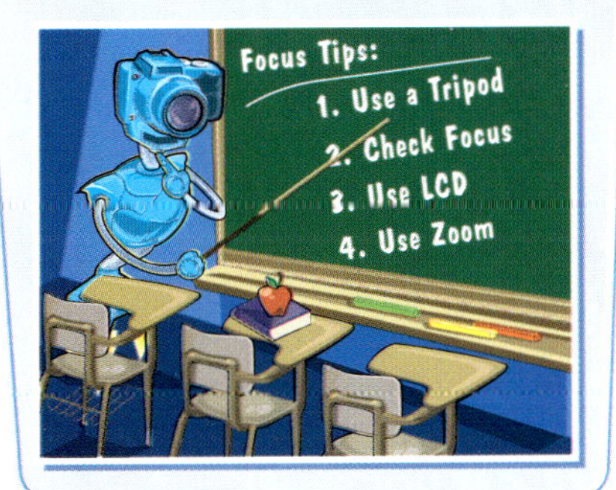

Composing Pictures like a Pro

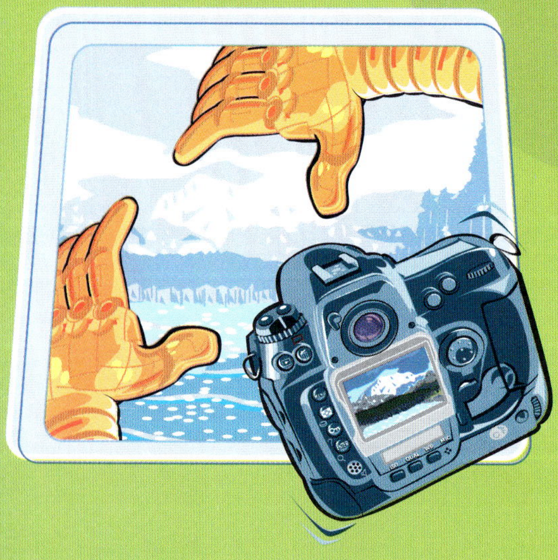

Want to quickly improve your digital pictures? Improving composition is a quick way to get better pictures. This chapter explores some simple techniques professional photographers use that will immediately improve the photos you take. You also learn ways to add interest to all your photos using a variety of composition techniques.

Quick Steps

Visualize Composition 62
Consider Design Principles 64
Discover Rules of Composition 66
Learn to Control Composition 68

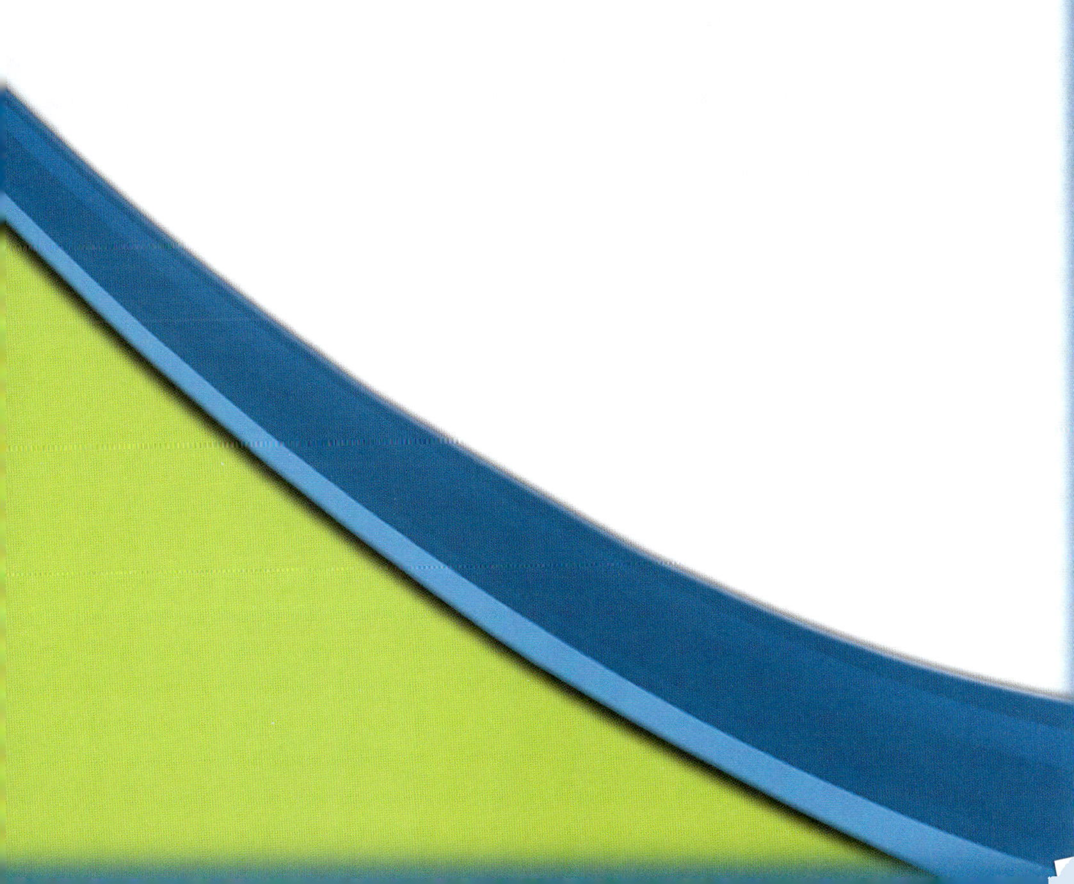

Visualize Composition

The best pictures not only catch your attention, but they also hold your attention. To get these kinds of pictures, compose images carefully and tell a story in each picture. Begin by borrowing established design principles and composition techniques that artists and photographers have been using since the camera was invented. As you progress, add in your own personal style to create signature pictures that viewers will remember.

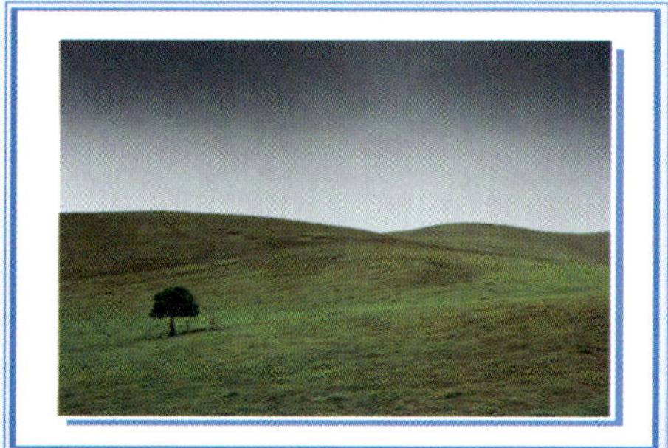

Stand Back and Evaluate

You interpret each scene for your viewers. Your job is to combine your emotional perceptions with the objective viewpoint of the camera. Begin by evaluating all the elements in the scene. Gradually narrow your view to identify individual vignettes. Then look for defining elements, colors, patterns, and textures that can help organize the visual information in the picture.

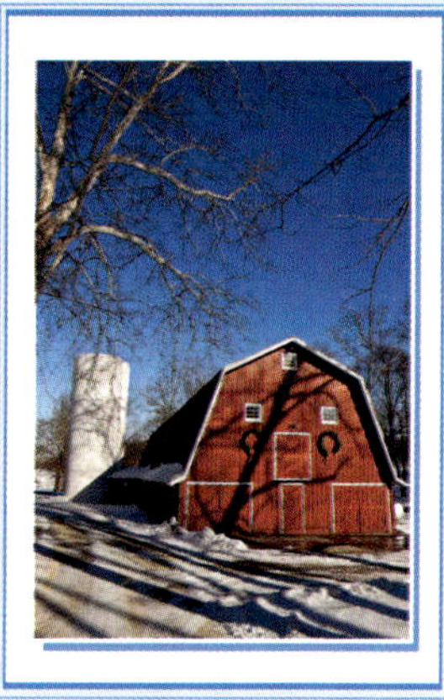

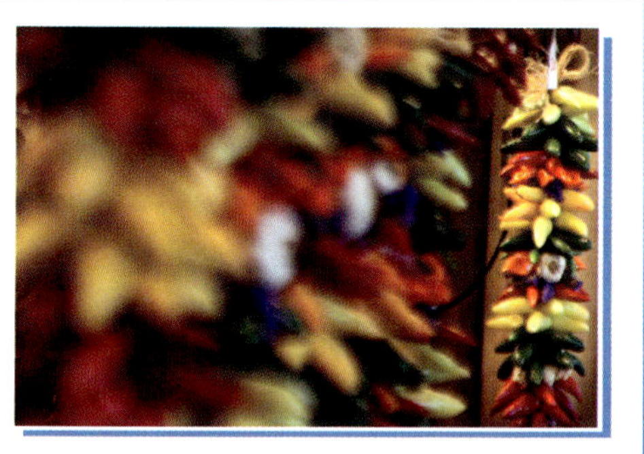

Consider Audience and Occasion

The most important questions to ask during this stage are "Why am I taking this picture?" and "What do I want to tell the viewer?" Answering these questions helps you focus on the important elements in the scene. From there, you can choose to include or exclude visual elements that add to or detract from the message you want to communicate to viewers.

Use Light and Exposure Controls Creatively

When you know the message you want to convey, you can use or modify the light, and choose exposure settings that create the mood, concentrate attention, and provide the perspective of the scene. Once you start visualizing the way the light and shadow works within your photographs, you can begin creating the images that you want instead of just taking pictures. To learn more about exposure, see Chapter 3. To learn more about light, see Chapter 4.

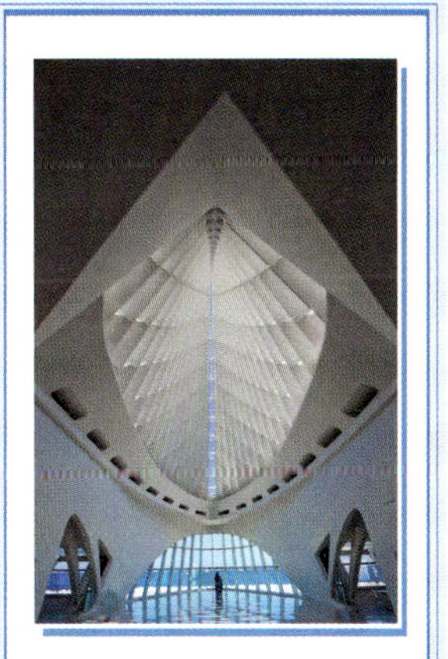

Keep It Simple

Just as with writing or painting, messages are most effectively delivered and retained when they are simple. Strive for a clean shot — an uncluttered visual scene that conveys a single story, or conveys a clear graphic shape, as shown here. To get a clean shot, you can clear away clutter, change your shooting position, or zoom in on the subject.

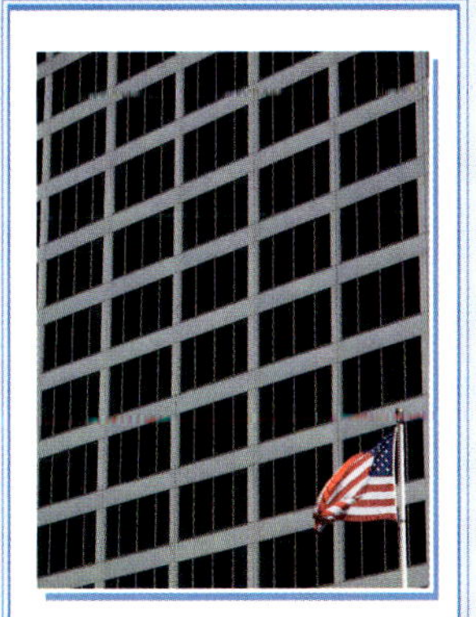

Evaluate the Result

With a digital camera, you can immediately evaluate the success or failure of your images on the LCD. Take advantage of the opportunity to make adjustments, and immediately reshoot the picture. The more pictures that you take, review, and reshoot, the better you become at recognizing composition problems by looking at pictures on the LCD.

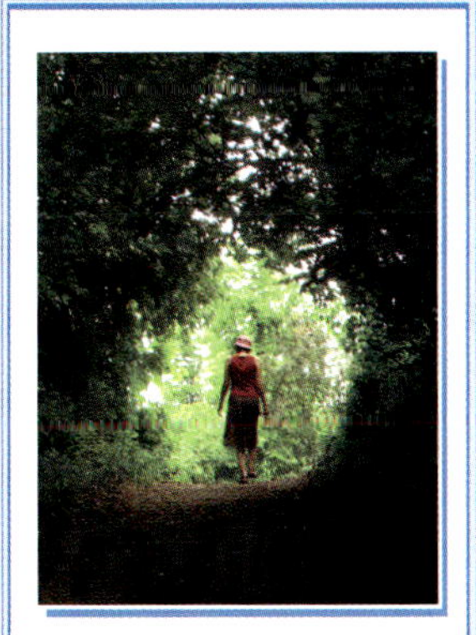

Consider Design Principles

Many principles of photographic composition are derived from the traditional design disciplines of art and graphic design, some of which date back to before the Renaissance. Here are a few of the most widely used principles.

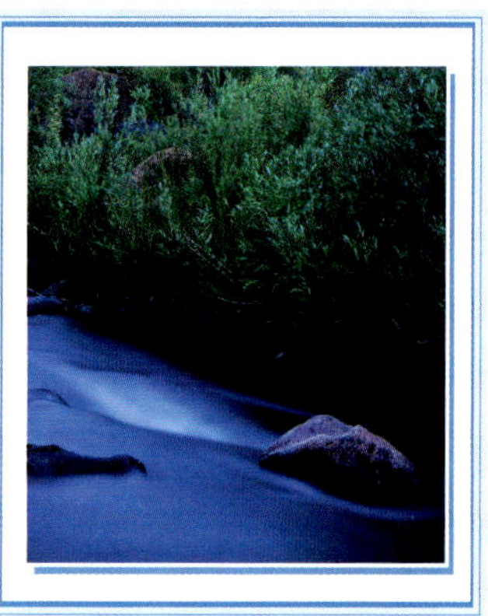

Is Symmetry Good or Bad?

Perfectly symmetrical compositions, images that look the same from side to side or from top to bottom, create balance and stability, but can be viewed as boring compositions. Symmetrical designs, as shown here, sometimes offer less visual impact than photos with some asymmetry and tension. If a composition you are looking at is the same from side to side, look to the top or bottom to add interest.

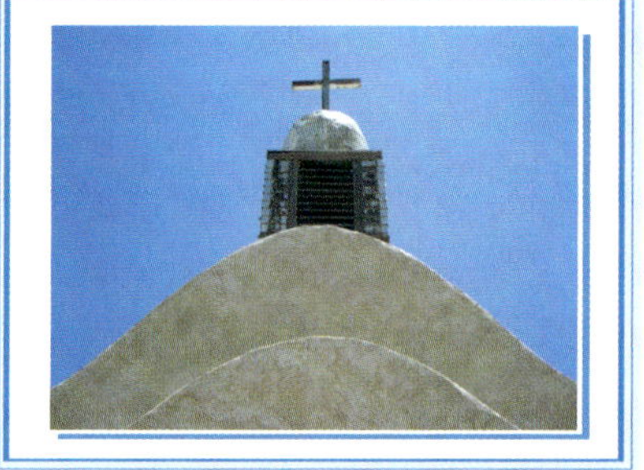

Create a Sense of Balance

Balance is a sense of "rightness" in a photo. A balanced photo does not appear to be too heavy at any point, or too off-center. When composing your pictures, consider the following: the visual weight of colors and tones — dark is heavier than light; objects — large objects appear heavier than light objects; and placement — objects placed toward an edge appear heavier than objects placed at the center of the frame.

What Lines Convey

Lines have symbolic significance that you can use to direct the focus and organize the visual elements in your picture. Horizontal lines imply stability and peacefulness. Diagonal lines imply strength, as shown in this picture, and dynamic tension. Vertical lines imply motion, curved lines symbolize grace, and zigzag lines imply action.

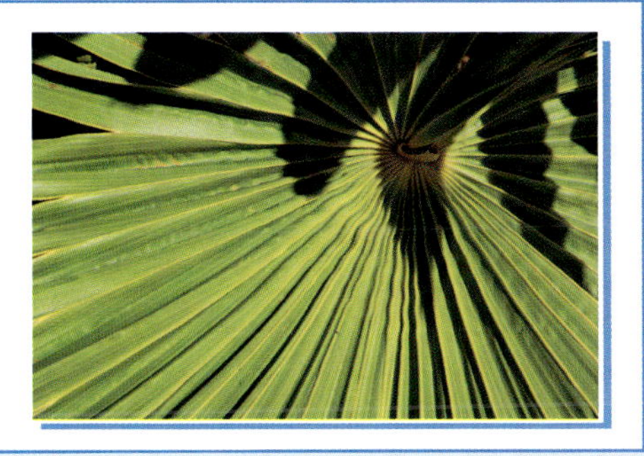

How the Shapes of Objects Affect Photos

The number and kind of shapes in a photo determine where viewers focus their attention. The human shape or form always draws attention in a picture. A single, small shape attracts attention either as the subject or as a secondary element that helps define the subject. Groupings of similar objects invite the viewer to compare size, shape, and spacing between the objects.

Placement of a Subject within a Picture

Just as symmetry can be visually uninteresting, placing a subject or the line of the horizon in the center of the frame is usually equally boring. Subject placement depends on the scene, but placement should identify the subject and create a natural visual path through the photo. Also, motion and implied action should come into the frame rather than travel out of it.

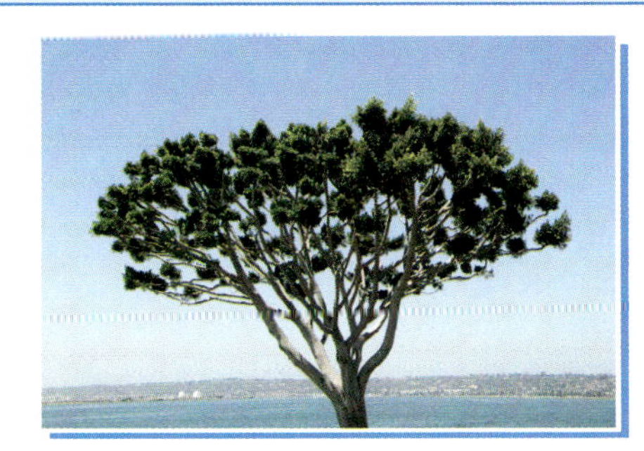

Discover Rules of Composition

There are many established rules and guidelines that you can use to improve your photos. Most of them are simple and easy to remember. There are no binding rules of composition. Some of the greatest artists today broke the rules of composition and technique of their time. The techniques in this section provide a good starting point for designing images. Be sure to experiment and let the subject help define your composition.

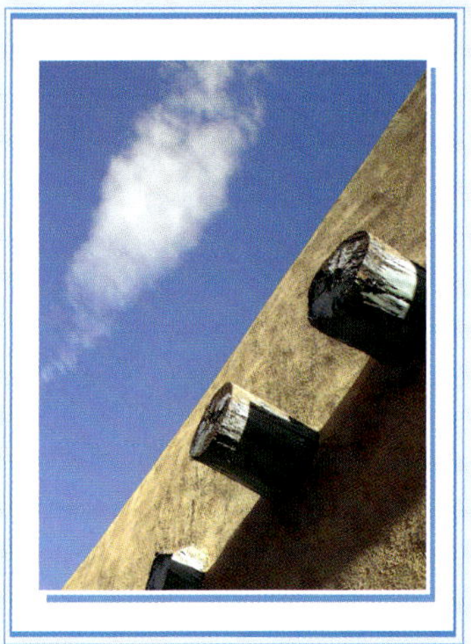

Choose the Orientation

The most basic composition beginsby choosing either a horizontal or a vertical orientation. Some subjects dictate the most appropriate orientation. For example, you can use a horizontal orientation for a sweeping landscape, and a vertical orientation for a portrait, but do not feel obligated to making only horizontal landscapes and vertical portraits. Use your entire frame to build your composition, even if you are using empty space to build balance.

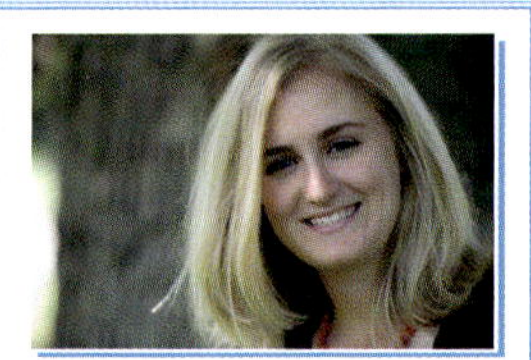

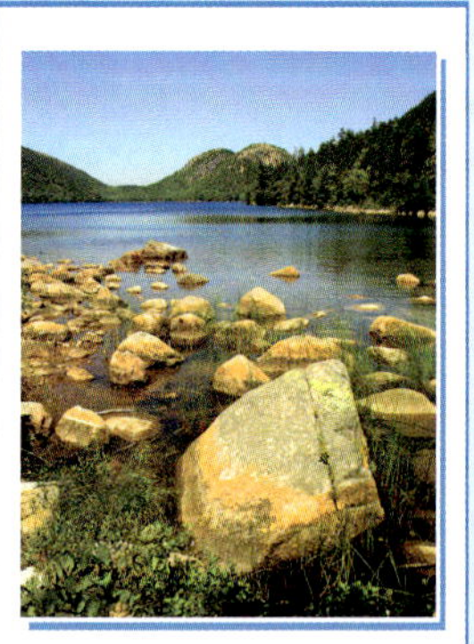

Fill the Frame

Just as an artist fills an entire canvas with a scene, photographers strive to fill the image frame with elements that support the message. Decide exactly what you want in the picture, and then fill the frame with what you choose for the picture. For variation, you can come in very close to the subject to show only part of the subject.

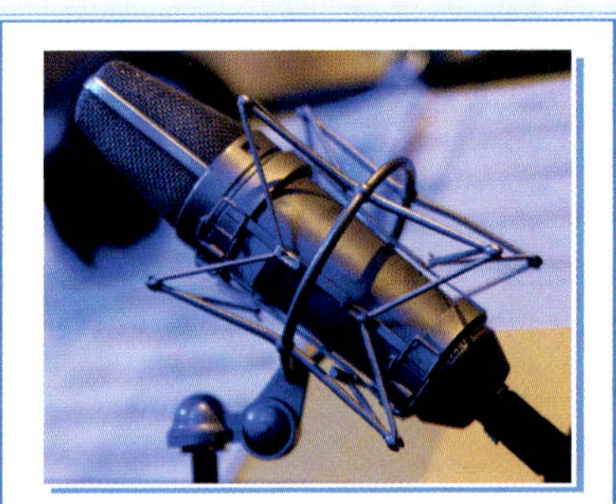

Check the Background and Surroundings

In a picture, the elements behind and around the subject can become as much a part of the photograph as the subject. As you compose the picture, check everything in the viewfinder or LCD for objects that compete with or distract from the subject. Then see if you can move the objects, the subject, or change your position to add interest or to eliminate distractions.

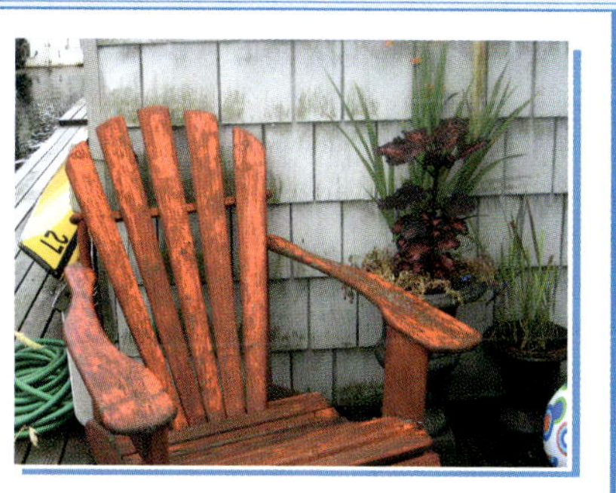

Practice the Rule of Thirds

A popular photography compositional technique draws an imaginary grid over the viewfinder. With the scene divided into thirds both horizontally and vertically, the photographer places the subject on one of the points of intersection or along one of the lines on the grid. In a portrait, you can place the eyes of the subject at the upper left intersection point, which is considered to be the strongest position.

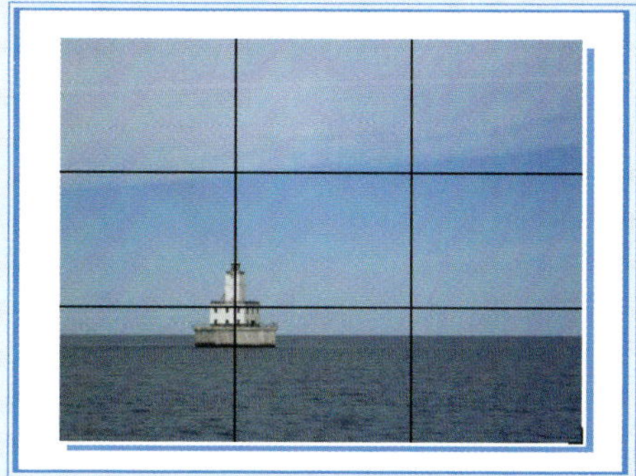

Frame the Subject

Photographers often borrow a technique from painters, putting the subject within a naturally occurring frame, such as a tree framed by a barn door, or a distant subject framed by an archway or foliage. The frame may or may not be in focus, but for best effectiveness, it should add context to the subject.

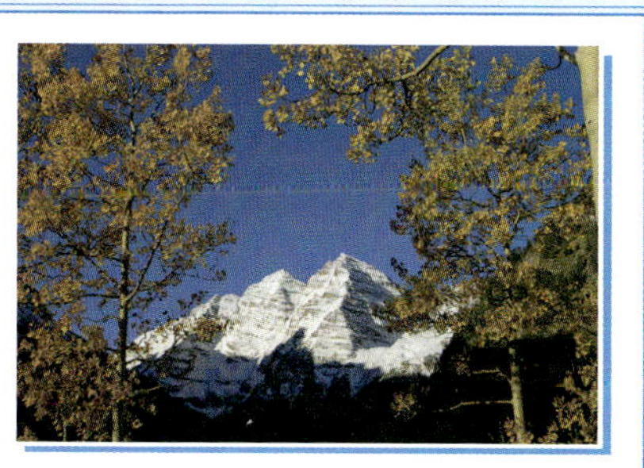

Use Other Composition Aids

Other composition techniques include using strong textures, repeating patterns and geometric shapes, and color repetition or contrast to compose images. These elements can create a picture on their own, or you can use them to create visual motion that directs the eye or supports the subject.

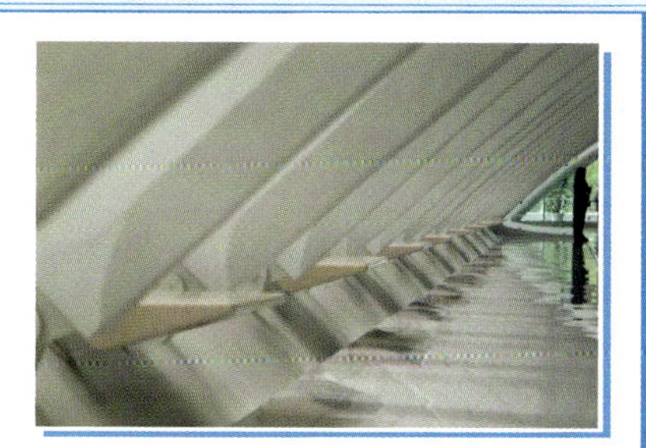

Learn to Control Composition

In a perfect world, you could control all the elements within a photograph. In a studio, everything in the photograph can be controlled by the photographer. In the outside world, you must work with existing conditions, backgrounds, and foregrounds. Here are some ways to get the best composition when you cannot control all the elements in the scene.

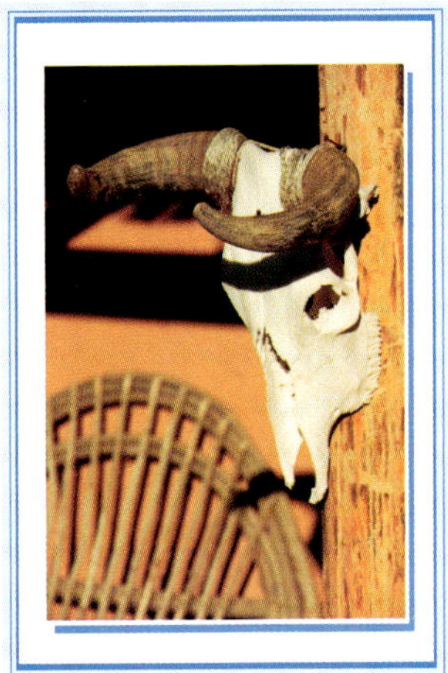

Select Focus and Control Depth of Field

Because the eye is drawn to the sharpest part of the photo, you can use focus to emphasize the relative importance of elements in the picture, or combine selective focus and depth of field to emphasize or subdue elements within the picture. Here, a shallow depth of field blurs a distracting background. For more information on depth of field, see Chapter 3.

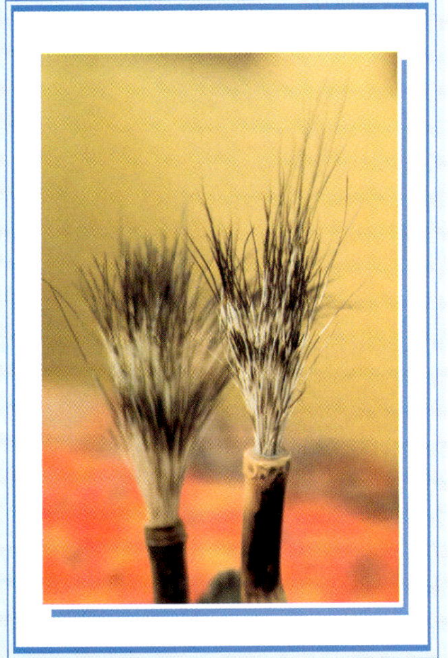

Change the Point of View

Instead of photographing at eye level, try changing your viewpoint. For example, if you photograph a subject from a lower-than-eye-level position, the subject seems powerful, whereas a higher-than-eye-level position creates the opposite effect. Getting on the subjects' level is particularly effective when photographing children and pets.

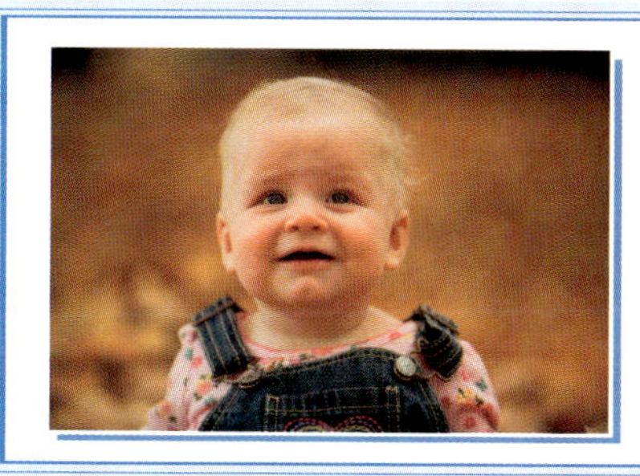

Use Tone and Contrast

You can use *contrast,* or the difference between light and dark tones, to emphasize your subject. Experiment by modifying the amount and angle of light to create more or less contrast, such as waiting for the sun to be in a position to produce long shadows. Or you can change position so the subject is backlit to add dramatic contrast with the lighting of the scene.

Define Space and Perspective

Some techniques to control the perception of space in pictures include changing the distance from the camera to the subject, selecting a telephoto or wide-angle lens or zoom setting, changing the position of the light, and changing the point of view. In this example, a telephoto lens compresses the dry grasses blowing in the wind.

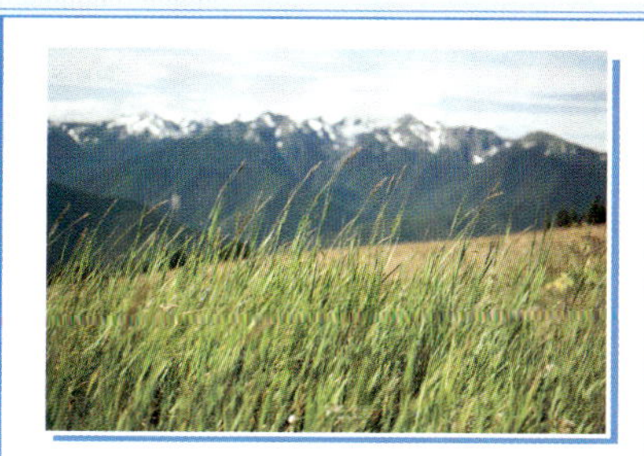

Chapter 7

Putting It All Together

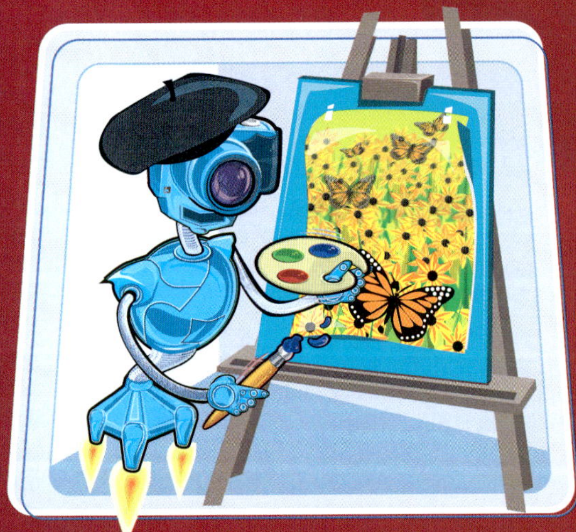

In this chapter, you can practice and see the results of using different exposure factors, lenses or zoom settings, lighting, and scene modes.

Quick Steps

Experiment with Depth of Field 72

Mix and Match Settings 74

Change Shutter Speed for Effect 76

Focus Selectively 77

Compose Creatively 78

Explore Different Lighting Options 80

Try Creative Techniques 82

Experiment with Depth of Field

Learning to control depth of field (DOF) in a picture gives you the ability to choose what part of the scene is in focus and what part is blurred. You can also control the amount of blurring, from mild softness to unrecognizable blurs. You can use depth of field to guide the attention of the viewer and to create artistic effects.

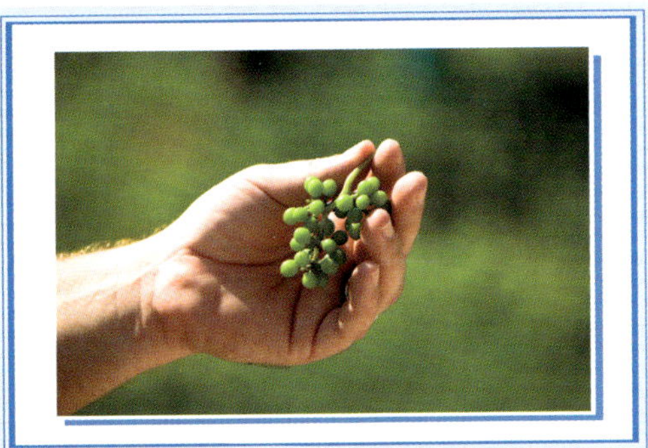

Control Viewer Focus

You can control depth of field in several ways. The easiest way, if your camera has one, is to select its portrait or macro scene mode. The portrait mode preset on your camera should not be confused with the term describing the orientation of the photo as in portrait and landscape. The portrait mode sets the camera to use the widest possible aperture to shorten the depth of field. The macro mode also produces a short depth of field because the subject is so close to the lens. You can also use aperture, focal length, and camera-to-subject distance, individually or in combination, to control depth of field. Other than scene mode, increasing the aperture (using a smaller f-stop) or getting closer to the subject is the next best way to decrease depth of field in a photo. Be aware that you cannot always see the correct depth of field when composing the image, only after you have taken the photo and are reviewing it in the LCD.

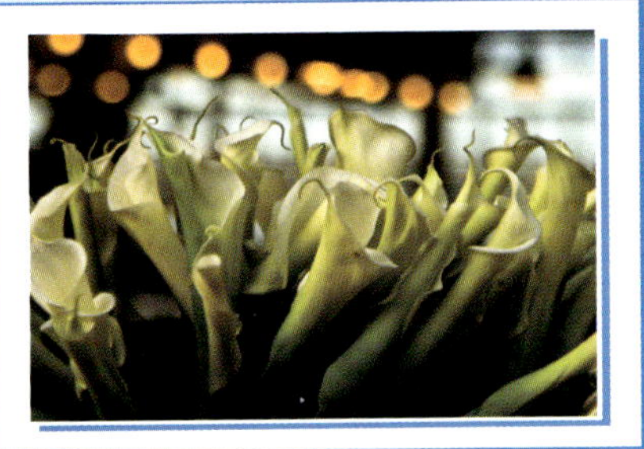

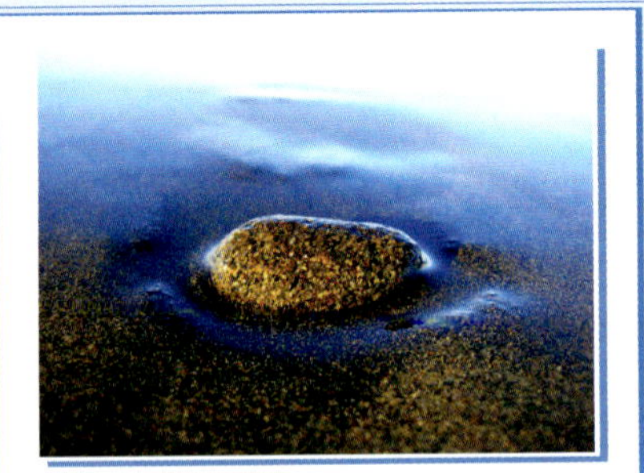

Limits to Control

Sometimes you cannot use the aperture you want because the scene is too bright. In this picture, the bright afternoon sunlight did not allow the use of a wide aperture to limit depth of field. Because the water on the rock creates a lot of reflection from the sky, by putting a polarizing filter on a dSLR camera, you can help tame the amount of light coming back into the camera, which also allows the use of a larger aperture. The result is a decreased depth of field, singling out the subject from the background.

Get the Effect You Want

The pictures on this page show how small, midrange, and large apertures affect depth of field, or the zone of sharpness from front to back, in a picture. In this picture, taken at a rocky beach on the Pacific coast, the zoom was used at its widest setting, and with the camera mounted on a tripod, a small aperture helped create a wide depth of field, allowing both the closest stones and the farthest seastacks to be in focus.

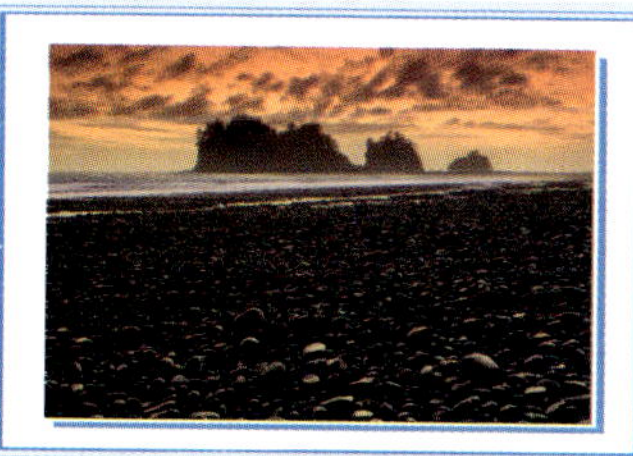

Focus On the Subject

In this picture, the scene mode of the camera was set to Portrait. This scene mode causes your camera to produce a short depth of field, producing a soft, blurred background. When doing any sort of portrait, make sure the eyes are in focus, and when doing a portrait with many people, make sure all the faces are in focus. When in the portrait mode in close proximity to the subject, sometimes the depth of field is so shallow that focus becomes very critical. In this case, the puppy's eyes are in focus, but her nose is already out of focus and the background is totally soft. Make sure you get the focus right.

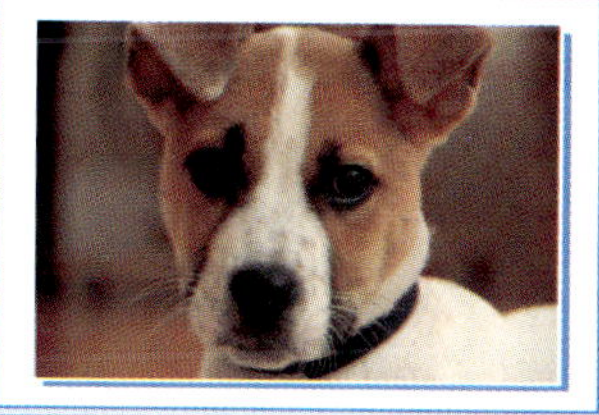

Classic Landscape and Portrait Apertures

A general rule of photography has been as follows: For landscape pictures, use a narrow aperture to create extensive depth of field. For portraits, use a wide aperture to decrease depth of field. Today's cameras generally do this for you automatically. Using the portrait mode changes the camera settings to produce a narrow depth of field. Many cameras also have a landscape scene mode that turns off autofocus and sets the focus to infinity, producing the greatest depth of field possible. It usually is not necessary to use this mode because the camera's autofocus mechanism detects the range and changes the focus to infinity. In many cases though, a moderate aperture of f/5.6 or f/8 is enough to get plenty of depth of field in your photographs.

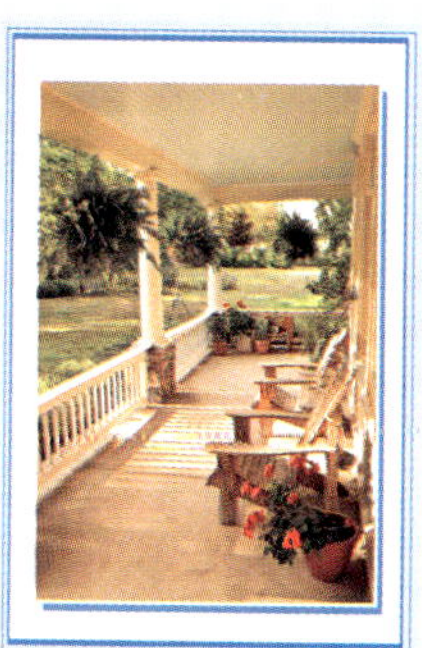

Use Aperture Priority to Learn

A good way to learn how depth of field works with your photography is to set your camera to Aperture Priority or A. Then take several shots at different apertures, letting the camera make the decision on the shutter speed and see how the difference in apertures changes how the photos look. In some cases, because of how wide or long the lens is and how close you are focused, it may take a large change in f-stop to make a large viewable difference, and other times, even a 1-stop difference will make your photos look very different.

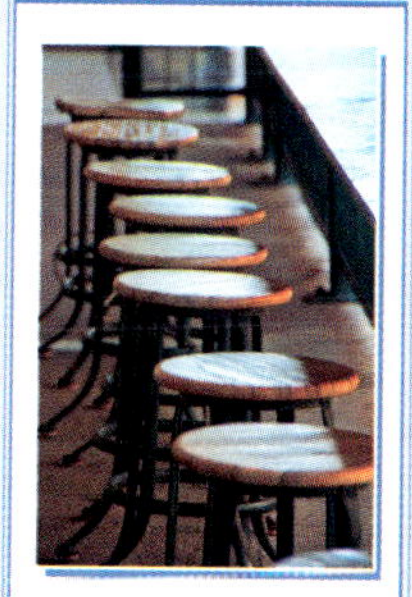

Mix and Match Settings

Now that you know how depth of field affects pictures, you can apply this knowledge to create different specific effects or to find an acceptable exposure in difficult scenes.

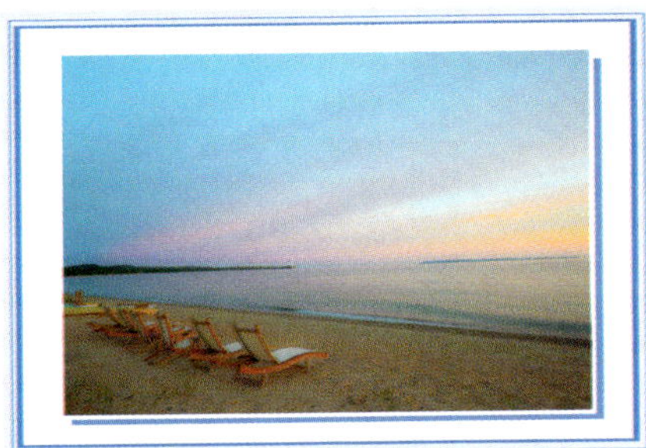

Maximize Overall Sharpness

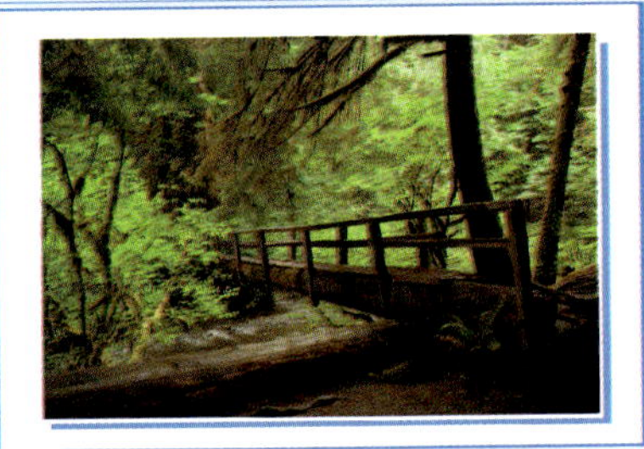

For maximum detail from front to back in a picture, use the widest setting of your camera's zoom lens that still allows you to keep the composition you envisioned. Next, if your camera allows it, change the aperture to the narrowest setting (largest number). As you increase the f-stop number and decrease the aperture size, you notice that the camera automatically changes the shutter speed to compensate for less light coming through the lens. Do not let the shutter speed drop below 1/60 second if you are hand-holding your camera. Below that speed, the camera movement or the movement of the subject may blur the photograph. To increase the chances that you will have sharp pictures at slow shutter speeds, you can use a tree, wall, or fencepost to help to stabilize you. For the sharpest possible photos, stabilize the camera on something solid, optimally a tripod, and use a remote to eliminate the shake from depressing the shutter.

Maximize Sharpness Up Close

You can use the macro scene mode of the camera, and a close camera-to-subject distance to get acceptable sharpness up close. The macro setting of most digital cameras works within a fixed range of the zoom lens setting. Read your manual to find out how the macro setting works on your model, although it is usually controlled by pressing a button with a flower icon. Be aware that most macro settings have a very narrow depth of field. As shown, both the front and back of a small flower can be out of focus. The only way to ensure that the entire subject stays in focus is to carefully review the image in the LCD after shooting a few test shots.

Get a Limited Area of Sharpness

You can combine a telephoto lens, a wider aperture, and a closer camera-to-subject distance for the ideal portrait setting. To emphasize a detail of the subject, move closer to the subject. This allows you to place your people into a scene, but still keeps the focus on your subject and leaves the background just that — background.

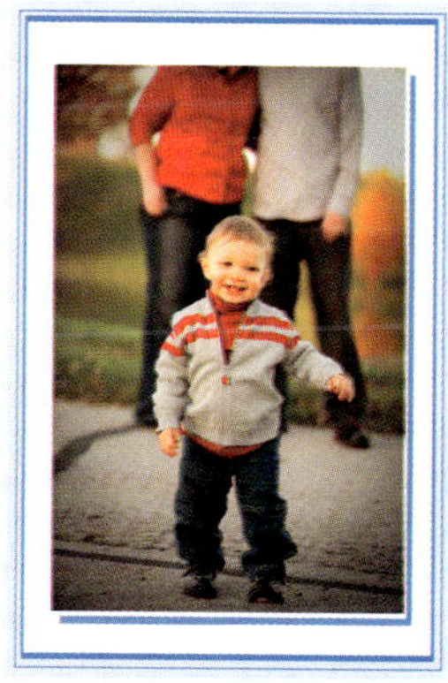

Get Maximum Sharpness in Extreme Close-Ups

If your camera does not have a dedicated macro scene mode, you can combine a telephoto lens, a narrow aperture, and a close camera-to-subject distance when you want to photograph close-up, or *macro*, photos. Because the working distance is close, you can get better depth of field by choosing a narrow aperture, but the closer you get the less will be in focus. All these things combine to reduce the amount of light entering the camera. When shooting a photo in early morning or late afternoon light, the reduced light may affect the autofocus, making it necessary to use manual focus. To compensate for the reduced light, the camera reduces the shutter speed, so be sure to use a tripod to ensure a sharp picture.

Get Sharp, Everyday Pictures

The key to getting sharp everyday photos is to ensure that the camera is set to the right mode, that the autofocus indicator shows that the subject is in focus, and that the camera is focused on the subject of the image and not something else in the frame. For everyday shooting, using the auto settings will usually get you great results with good sharpness.

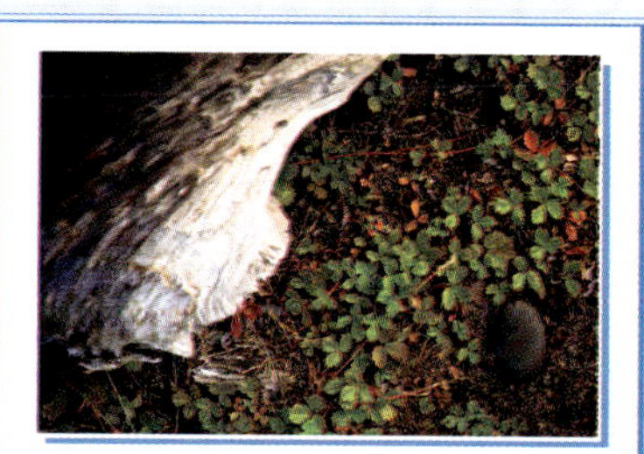

Change Shutter Speed for Effect

The shutter speed on most digital cameras ranges from shutter times of several seconds to up to eight thousandths of a second. Your camera can automatically select the optimum shutter speed based on the available light in the scene. You can select different shutter speeds to stop action or to show action or motion as a blur. You can also experiment with shutter speeds to create unexpected and interesting results.

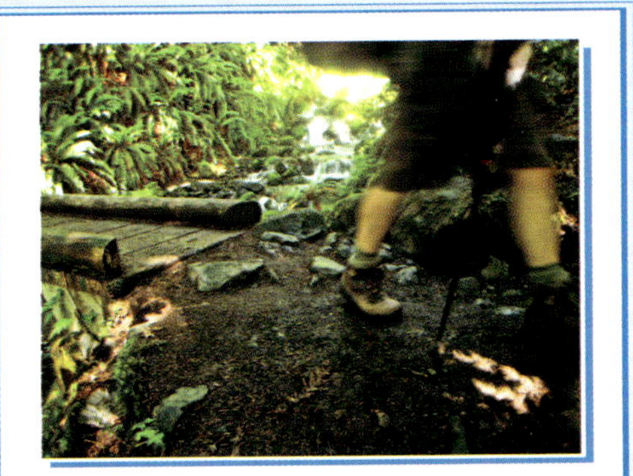

Stop the Action

You can stop action at shutter speeds faster than 1/125 second. Faster shutter speeds work well for capturing an athlete in midair, or for showing subtle action such as a spinning top that looks as if it is standing still. The problem with freezing images using high shutter speeds is that the feeling of motion is lost. The photo of the jet skier has its trail of water spray frozen in time where you can see each individual water droplet.

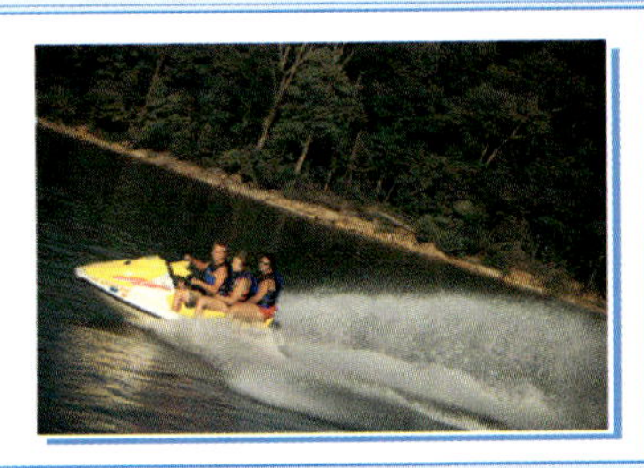

Show the Action

At 1/30 second and slower shutter speeds, you can show action as a blur. With a faster shutter speed, the water looks frozen. By using a slower shutter speed, you can capture the sense of the speed and excitement as the jet skiers skim across the water. Slow shutter speeds are also used to capture moving water, and light trails created by passing traffic at dusk, or for creative light compositions.

Learn with Shutter Priority

In Shutter Priority, you select the shutter speed and the camera uses the meter setting to automatically set the f-stop. You do this by selecting "S" or "Tv" on your camera. Try different shots with several different shutter speeds to determine how fast or slow your shutter speed needs to be to get the effect that you are looking for. Look at the photos on the computer when you get home and use the EXIF data to check the shutter speeds.

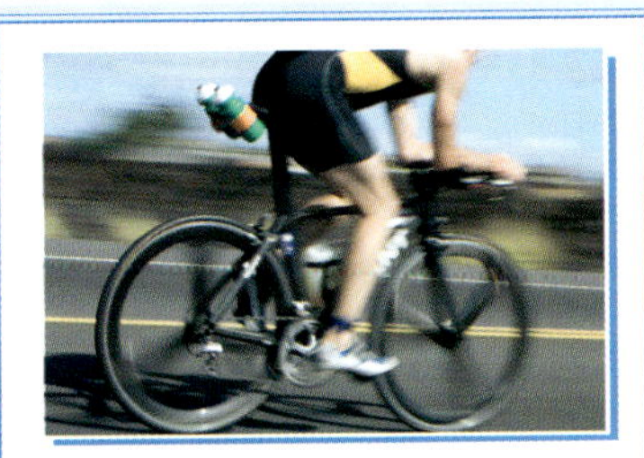

Focus Selectively

You can use focus as a way to direct the attention of the viewer to the most important or a single element in a picture. In close-ups, you can switch to manual focus to get the best focus.

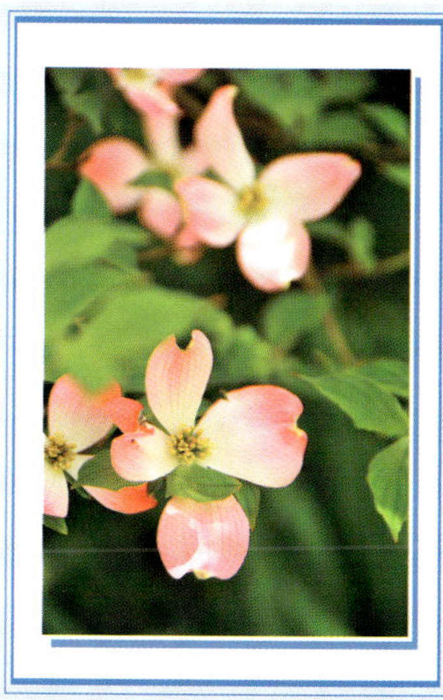

Combine Selective Focus with Distance

To show a small area with fine detail, use a selective focus. In this picture, a narrow aperture of f/16 and sharp focus emphasize the fine details of the flowers on the left, and yet still show all the detail of the stone and cactus.

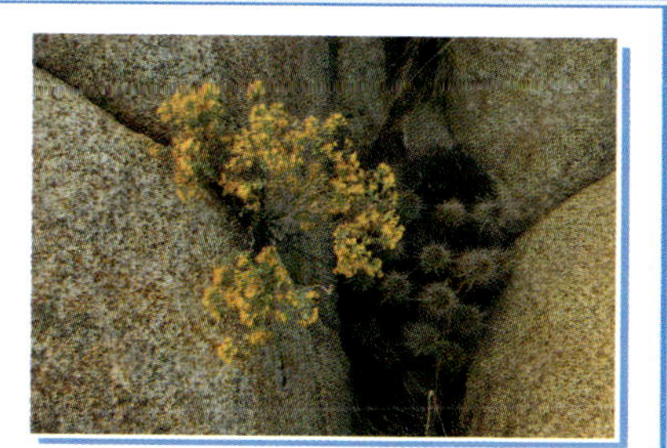

Combine Selective Focus, Focal Length, and Aperture

When you combine a wide aperture setting with a telephoto lens, and focus carefully, you can narrow the focus even more. As shown in this picture, a telephoto lens and an aperture of f/4.5 create a very specific focus.

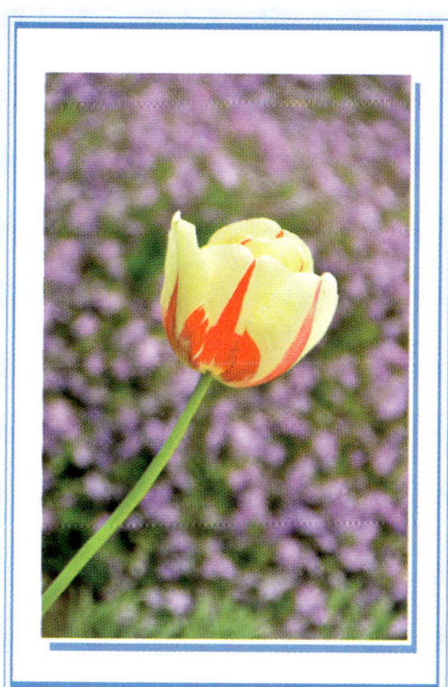

Compose Creatively

You cannot use all these techniques every time you take a photo. As you practice the techniques in this book over and over again, they will become second nature to you. You will get a feel for not only how but when to use them. At that point you can combine exposure, focal length, and composition to take creative pictures that convey a message or tell a story.

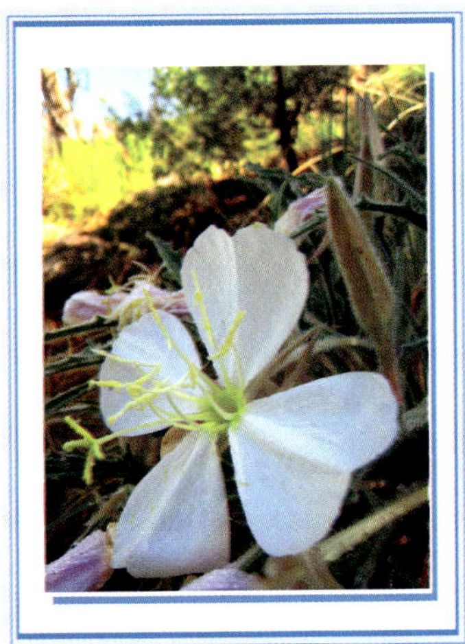

Get to the Point

In this image, the focus of the composition was the nearest wine label with a view of the number of bottles and awards. By using a wide aperture and the zoom lens pushed out toward the telephoto end, it was possible to isolate the front bottle and soften the background at the same time, both giving the importance to subject, but also revealing the environment that contains the subject.

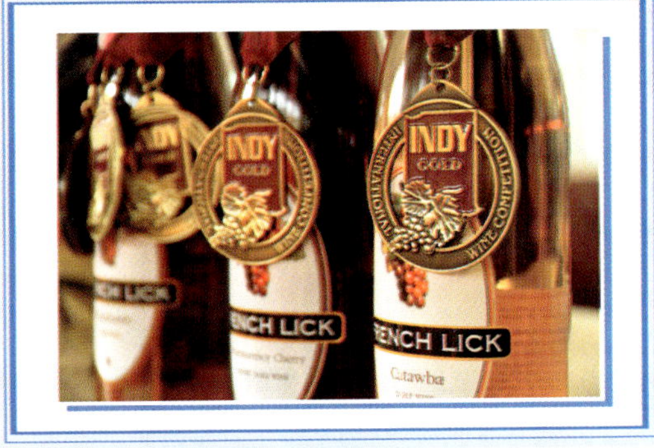

Draw the Viewer In

Here the composition guides the viewer through the flowers toward, and into, the rest of the scene. A narrow aperture creates good detail throughout the flowers to the mountains, despite the close camera-to-subject distance.

Capture the Action

In this image, a wide aperture and a slight telephoto were used to create a narrow depth of field, putting a focus on the subject. This allows for enough shutter speed to stop the action of the dad spinning around with his son, and capture the moment of the boy's laugh.

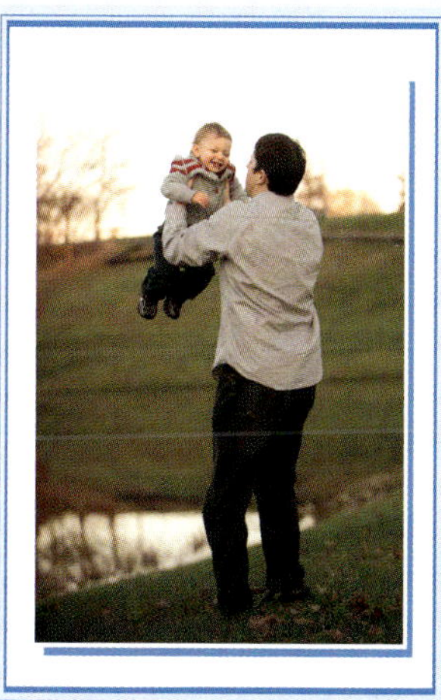

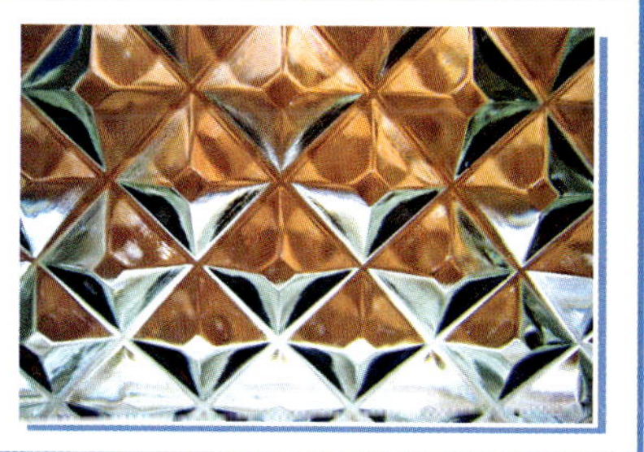

Create Abstract Images

Interesting compositions can come from all sorts of things. In this case, the cut glass window creates interesting shape, texture, and color in the image. Look everywhere around you for interesting abstracts. Sometimes you can use your macro setting to move in close to get an interesting point of view.

Motion Is Good

To show the power of motion, you can combine a slow shutter speed and small aperture, as shown here. To really capture the movement of a race, this image is captured at 1/10 second. This imparts a feeling of time and provides a sense of place.

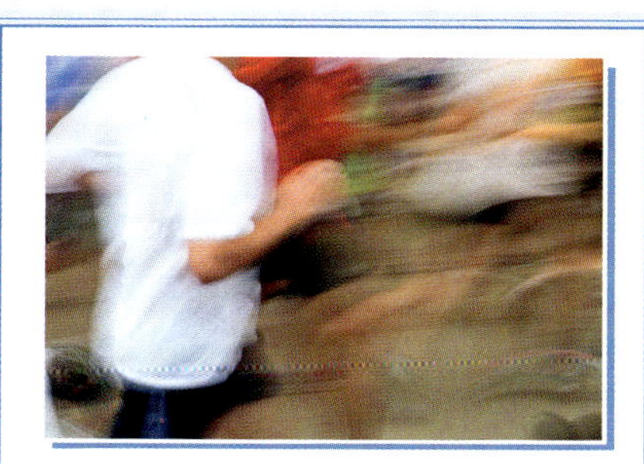

Explore Different Lighting Options

In most cases, the goal is to have sufficient lighting to produce an optimum exposure. Modifying light not only overcomes common problems, like blur in typical scenes, but it can also give pictures a dramatic flair.

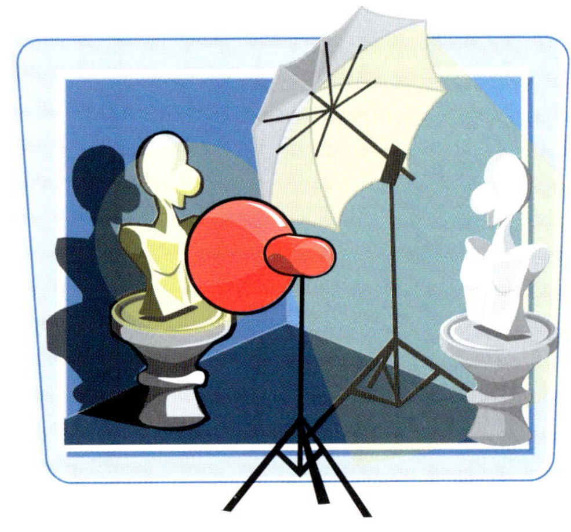

Experiment with a Flash

A built-in flash provides the quickest and most convenient way to alter scene lighting. Experiment with the various sync modes, such as slow, front, and rear curtain synchronization sync modes. In the image shown, the light of the fire is mixed with the light from the flash and then captured using slow sync mode. You can use these modes to obtain good exposures at night and to create front or rear light trails of traffic in dimly lit scenes.

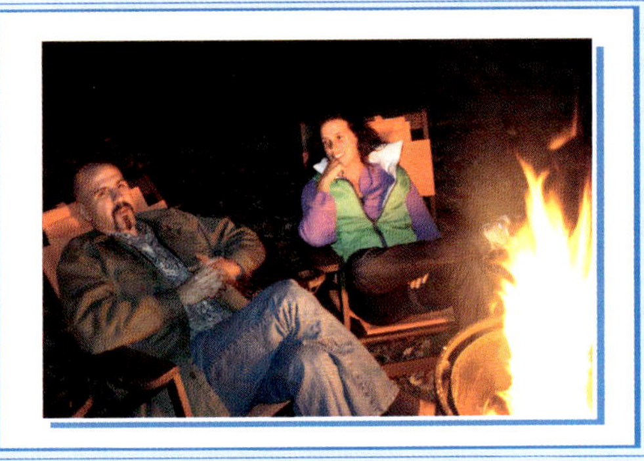

Use Fill Flash

Although fill flash works well for portraits, you can use fill flash for other subjects as well. For example, you can use fill flash outdoors to fill in the shadows coming from the sun. For indoor still-life pictures, fill flash reduces deep shadows caused by daylight from windows.

Use a Reflector

You can use a reflector to catch natural light and reflect it back into a scene. In this picture, a gold-colored reflector adds light to the face of the subject and creates a warm glow. Experiment with the position of the reflector; it takes some practice to get the light quality and quantity right with a reflector, but once you get going, it can really help create some fantastic images. You can purchase small, collapsible reflectors at any camera store, and with a little bit of thinking, plenty of household items can be used as a reflector.

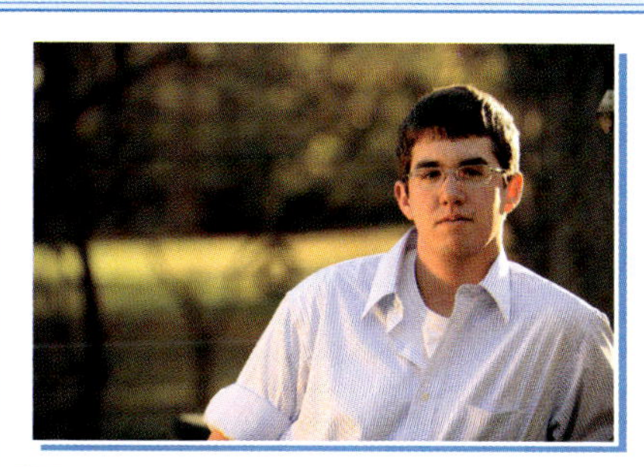

Wait for Flattering Light

To get the best pictures, you should wait for the best light of the day. In most cases that means shooting in the time just after dawn and just before sunset. The light at those times of the day is much warmer, and with the sunlight being much lower in the sky, the angle of the light really creates some beautiful drama with your scene.

Watch for the Best Light Plays

It is a good habit to always have your camera with you to capture some of the beautiful plays of natural light. Using a hazy sunset, you can place people and things in front of the light, creating fun silhouettes. Watch for interesting contrasts of shapes and light in your subjects.

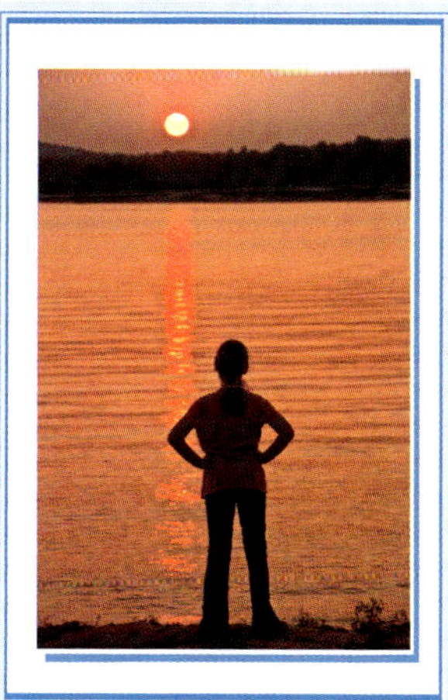

Try Creative Techniques

After you practice using standard photography techniques, you can use other variations that can be fun and create interesting images.

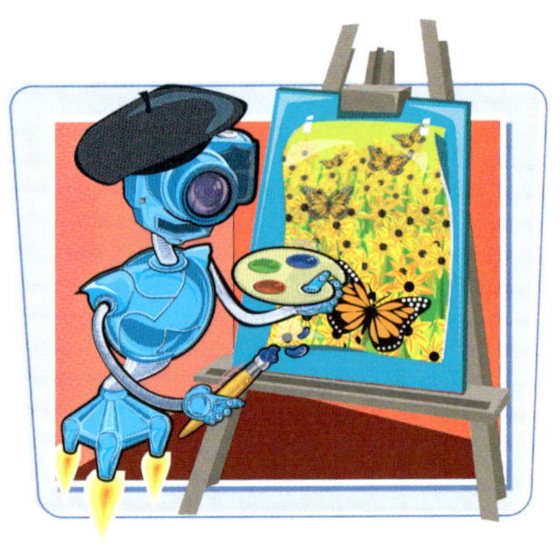

Pan Using a Slow Shutter Speed

At a shutter speed of 1/30 second or slower, you can pan with a subject as it moves, making the background appear blurred. To do this, focus on a place where the subject will pass. When the subject enters the viewfinder, follow the subject with the camera, and then take the picture when the subject reaches the point on which you focused. To maintain a smooth blur, keep the camera in motion as you press and release the shutter.

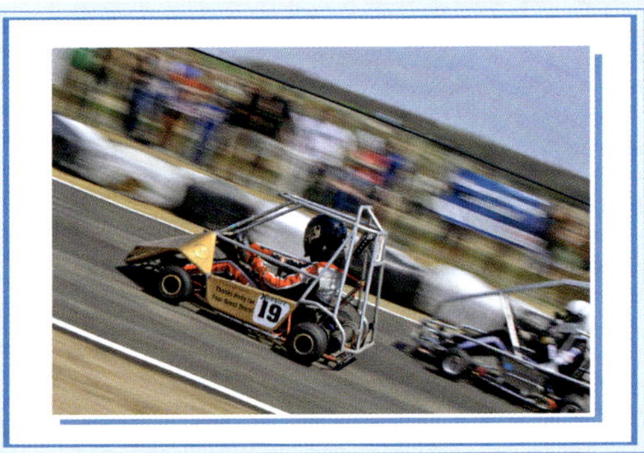

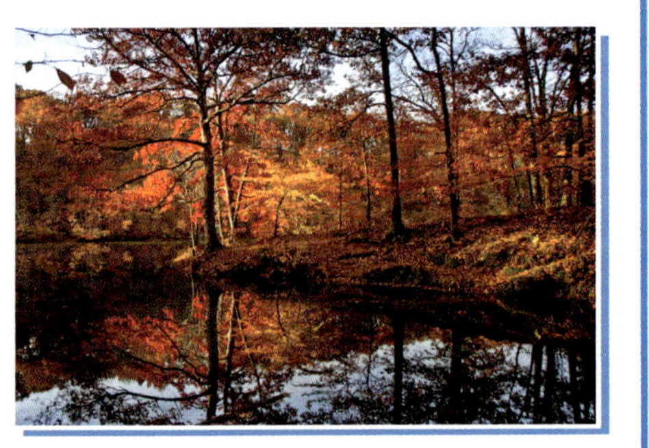

Use Backlighting

In harsh light, you can sometimes turn the light to your advantage by using it to create silhouettes or to enhance vivid color. In many cases, foliage turns to a fiery glow as light passes through it on the way into the camera. Backlight creates some of the most exciting and dramatic photographs, but beware, because it is also the trickiest to tame because of the extreme contrast and tendency to catch lens flare in your images as the light strikes the lens.

Capture Light Trails

You can create cool low-light and night images by switching to low-light or night scene mode. The camera uses a slow shutter speed to capture subjects, such as moving car headlights as streaks of light. If you do not have scene modes, select a shutter speed of 1/30 second or slower, use a tripod, and for shutter speeds of 1 second or greater, use the camera's self-timer to trip the shutter, avoiding any motion to the camera caused by touching the shutter release button.

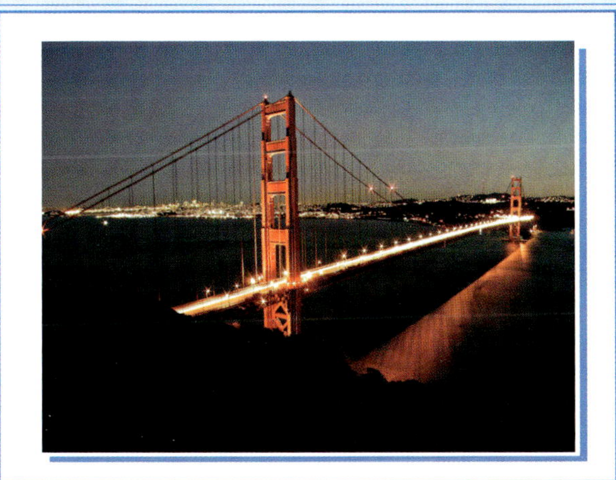

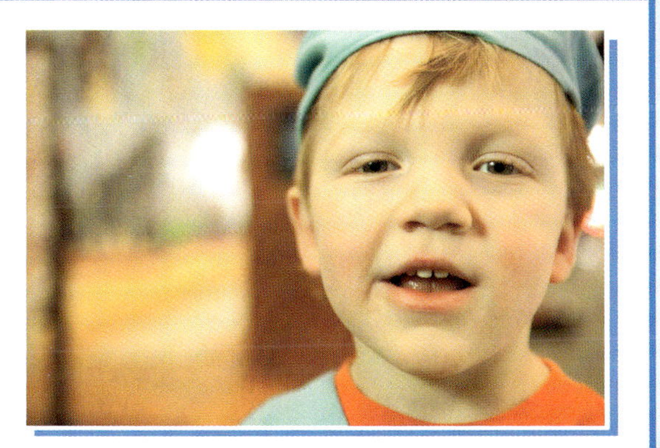

Warm Up Flash Pictures

Some digital cameras compensate for the cool colors produced by the internal flash. You can also use the preset flash white balance to make sure your flash color does not look too blue in your photos. If your flash does not correct the color imbalance, you can warm up the color of your camera flash by placing colored transparent gels or films over the flash.

Chapter 8

Taking Your First Digital Photos

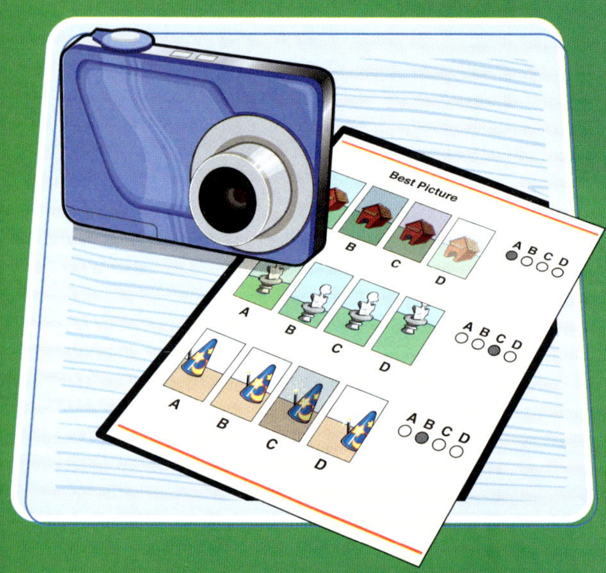

Learn the specifics of setting up a digital camera, and taking, transferring, and evaluating your first set of digital pictures.

Quick Steps

Set Up a Digital Camera 86
Take Test Pictures 88
Troubleshoot Problems 90
Transfer Pictures to Your Computer 92
Evaluate Your Photos 94
Fine-Tune Camera Settings 96

Set Up a Digital Camera

To get off to a good start with a digital camera, take time to read the manual and set camera options to ensure that you get the best image quality. Most digital cameras' manuals are now pretty easy to read, although they used to include a ton of information. Spend some time right away going through your manual with your camera next to you to familiarize yourself with all the advanced features now included. If you need to get started right away, read the quick-start guide, if available, or read the quick-start section of the user manual.

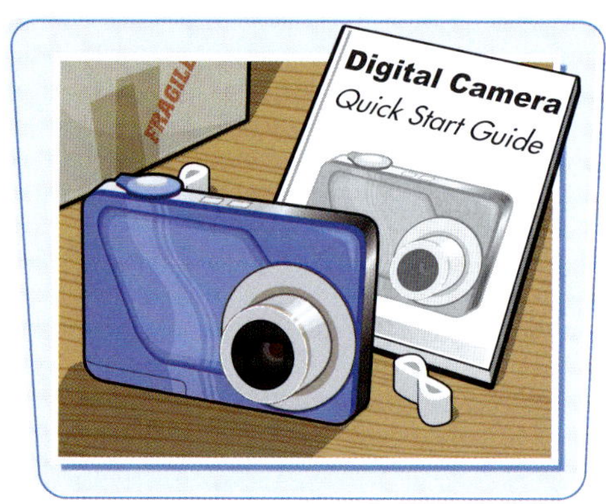

Charge Batteries

As a first step, read the instructions in the quick-start guide or the manual on charging the battery. Some batteries require an overnight charging cycle, whereas others charge in a few hours. Be patient and make sure the battery is fully charged before beginning to use your new camera. While the battery is charging, you can read your manual.

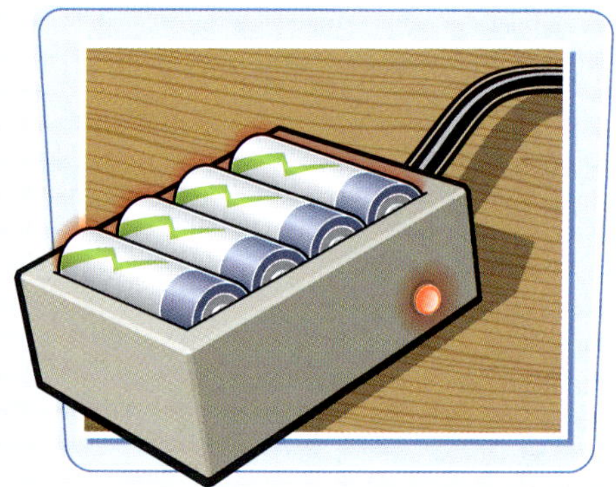

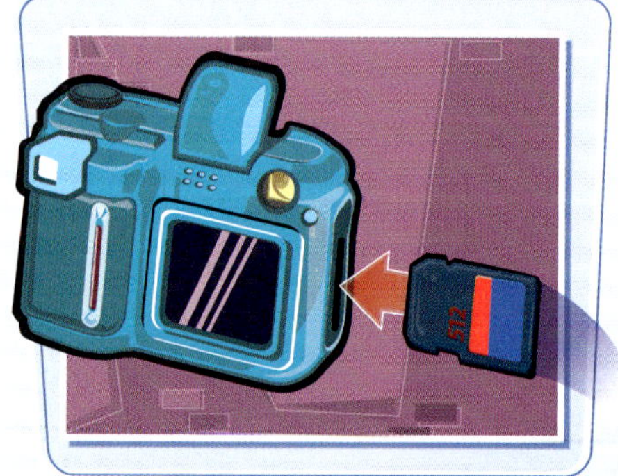

Insert and Format the Memory Card

All digital cameras use a removable memory card to store images. If your memory card has a write-protect (locking) mechanism, unlock the card before inserting it into the camera. Then locate the slot for the memory card, which often includes a diagram showing the direction that you insert the card. Most cameras do not accept a memory card if inserted incorrectly, so never force it. After inserting the card, you should make a habit of formatting it, especially if you have used the card before, to remove any old photos or other digital information it may contain. Some cameras also have built-in memory that saves some photos without a card. Make sure to refer to your camera's instruction manual for more information on how to use the built-in memory.

Set the Date and Time

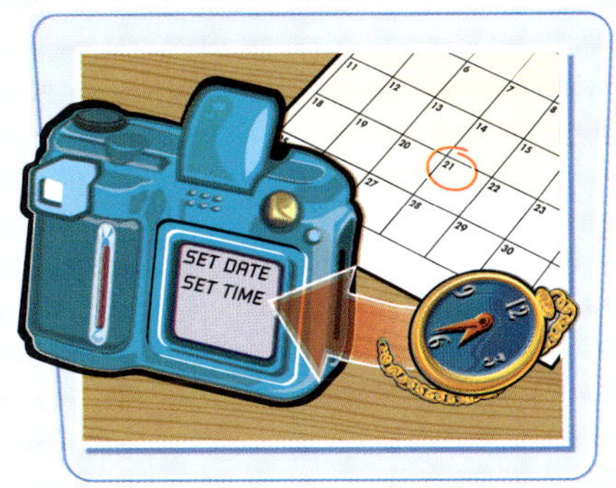

After you have charged the battery, turn the camera on, and then set it to record or picture-taking mode. Follow the instructions on the LCD to set the date and time. You should set the date and time because they become part of the shooting information that the camera stores with images — metadata information that is helpful for organizing and retrieving images later. The term *metadata* describes a large collection of data that the camera produces and includes with each photo each time a picture is taken. In addition to time and date information, metadata includes the camera settings used during exposure, or the camera make, model, and serial number. More than 200 types of information can be included as metadata, depending on your camera.

Set the Image Quality and Format

You can set image size, quality, and format on a camera menu. For best quality, set it to the largest size and highest quality JPEG. It is much easier to make the photo smaller later, but nearly impossible to make it larger. The higher quality settings provide improved quality but the images require more memory card space. On more advanced digital cameras, you can also choose an image format: JPEG, TIFF, or RAW. Although TIFF is a popular format in graphics design, beware of it filling up your card and slowing down the camera. RAW, a format that stores images with no in-camera processing, provides powerful post-capture options, but you must use manufacturer or third-party software to view and save the images.

Set the White Balance

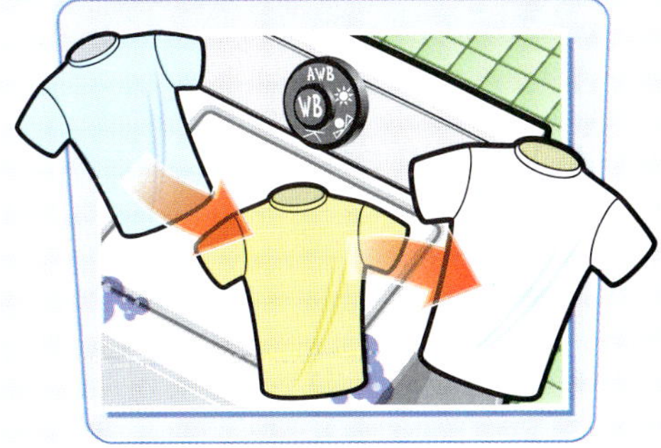

Most modern cameras now produce acceptable color just using the automatic white balance settings. Auto White Balance does a great job in most cases. When doing a lot of photography under a specific type of lighting, you can set the white balance to match the light in the scene to keep the color consistent. Evaluate the light in your scene and then set the white balance appropriately. If using a flash, in most cases leave the camera in its default automatic mode or whatever mode you normally use. Take some time to try different white balance settings in various situations to determine if these settings make your images even better or more interesting.

Take Test Pictures

The first pictures you take provide a great baseline for evaluating the performance and characteristics of your camera. Because no film is consumed, the only cost is the time it takes you to evaluate the results and delete the unsatisfactory ones. Identifying camera characteristics tells you what camera settings to fine-tune to get consistently good pictures. In addition to identifying the camera's characteristics, it is most helpful to become familiar with the camera controls and operation.

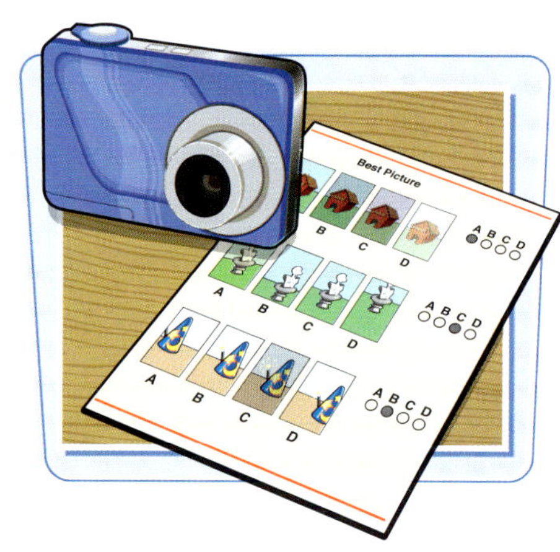

Learn the Basic Controls

Most digital cameras offer a large selection of controls, dials, buttons, and features. Begin by acquainting yourself with the basic controls used for taking and reviewing images. The controls use abbreviations and icons to indicate their function, so learning them is helpful. Several buttons and dials are used for more than one purpose, depending on the camera mode that you select. Locate the zoom control and learn how to use it for composing images. You should also learn to review images and make selections from the camera menus.

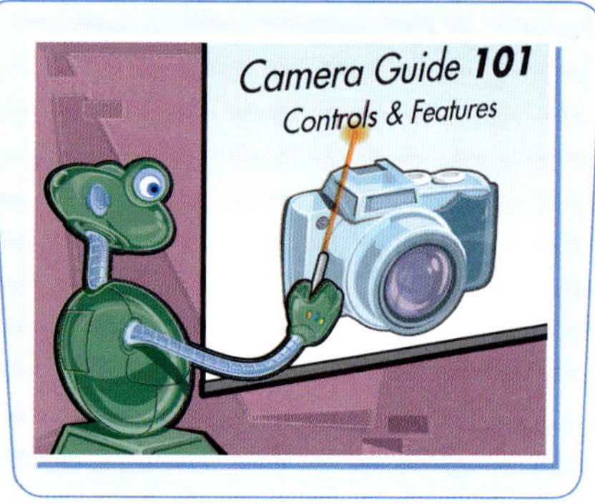

Take Pictures

Get started by taking familiar kinds of pictures of family and friends, indoors and outdoors. Also take pictures with and without the flash, both indoors and outdoors. These pictures establish a level of comfort when using your camera, so you can take photos without having to open the manual.

Adjust to a Digital Camera

Although each generation of new digital cameras gets faster and better, you still may need to become accustomed to slower start-up times that some cameras exhibit, and *shutter lag,* which is the delay between the time you press the shutter release button and the time the exposure is made. Image recording time depends on the size of the image file being used and how many photos you take quickly. Larger image files, such as RAW, take longer to save to the card. If an image is still being written to a card when you turn the camera off, the camera continues to record the image until it is complete before shutting down.

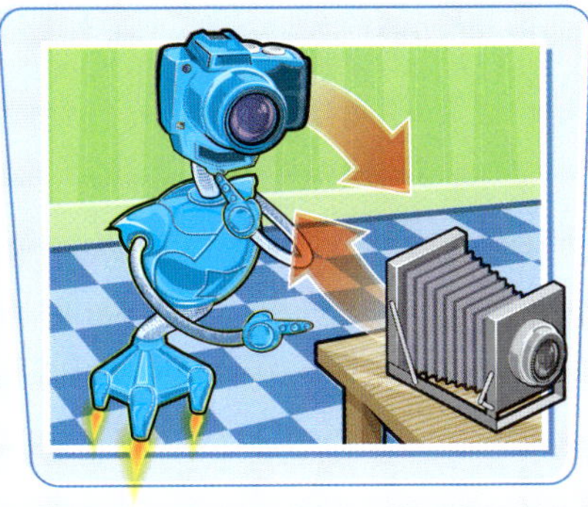

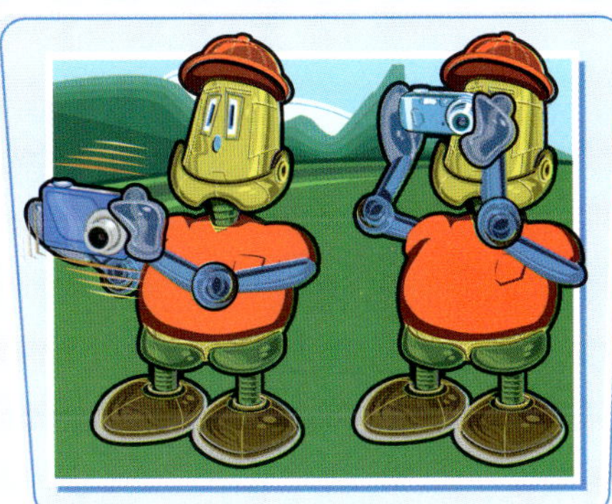

Compose Shots in the Viewfinder and LCD

For close subjects, use the LCD to compose images with your compact digital. *Parallax* is the slight offset between what you see in the viewfinder and what you get on the image. Parallax becomes more apparent for subjects closer than 3 feet, and is more pronounced the closer you get, but can be seen in many situations. Use the LCD for getting the camera into more interesting positions. At other distances, you can use the viewfinder to compose images. On a dSLR or a compact digital camera with a viewfinder, you have more stability and better chance for sharp photos if the camera is pressed to your eye as opposed to viewing the camera at arm's length.

Verify Pictures

As you shoot, be sure to check the pictures on your LCD monitor. The LCD indicates obvious composition and exposure problems. If you are planning to take several photos quickly, do not stop to review each one. Check the first one to make sure your settings look good, try different compositions and settings, and then review, reshooting if necessary. Most cameras can be set to display the picture on the LCD immediately after you take it, but to browse through multiple images, switch to a playback mode.

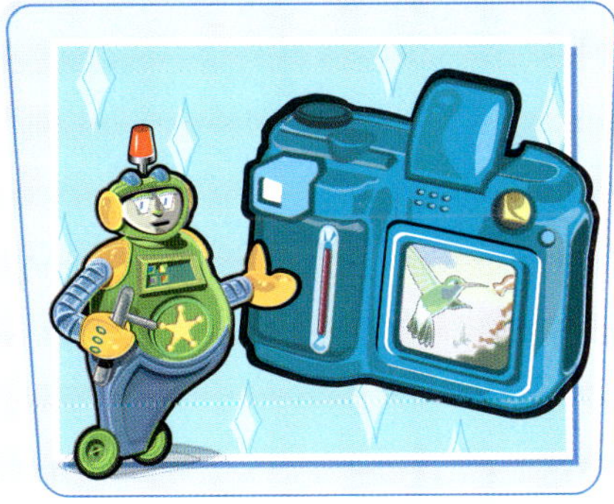

Troubleshoot Problems

Error messages on a digital camera can interrupt your first photo session. However, you can solve the most common problems quickly and easily.

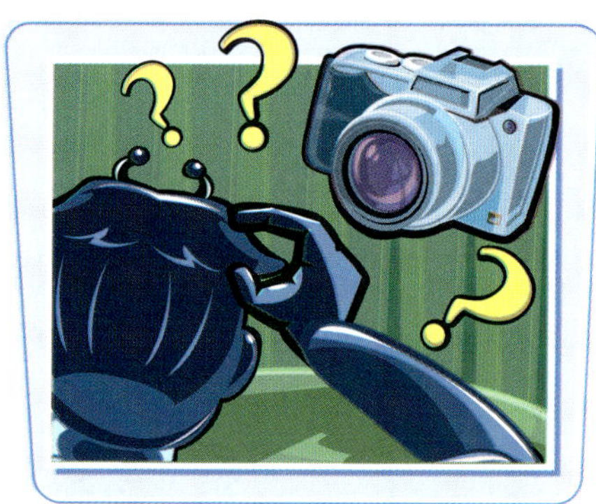

The Shutter Release Button Does Not Take Photo

Several things may cause the shutter release button not to work. The most common is that the camera's autofocus has been unable to determine the correct focus. Another cause is that the memory card is not in the camera or is locked. Take out the memory card and switch the lever or tab to the unlocked position. If you are shooting a lot of images quickly, the camera will not fire when the camera's memory buffer is full while it writes all the photos to the card. If the card is full, the frame counter status usually flashes. You need to replace it with another card, format the card, or delete some images to increase the amount of room on the card. On a dSLR, the lens may not be properly attached to the camera.

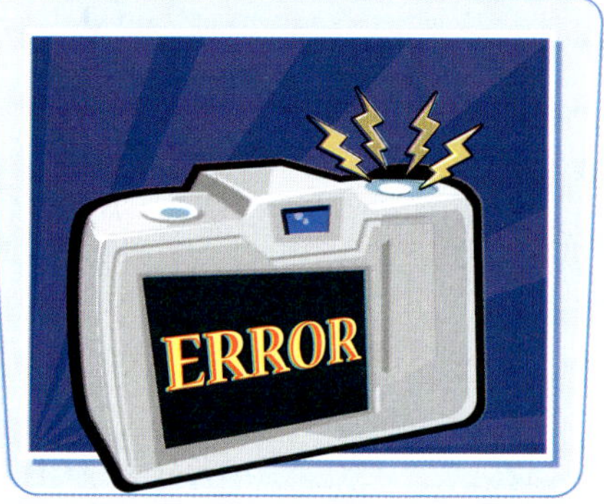

The Camera Is On, but the Status Bar Is Blank

To conserve battery power, most cameras go into sleep mode when they are not in use for a while. You can press the shutter release button to wake up the camera, or you can turn the camera off and then turn it back on. Also, check to see if the memory card is full, or if the battery needs to be recharged or replaced.

You Cannot Save Images to an Empty Memory Card

Sometimes, when a memory card is formatted by a computer using a card reader or if the card has images from another camera, the card is formatted incorrectly. The matter is simple to correct. Simply use the camera to format the card by selecting the Format feature (usually from a menu selection). Formatting the card in the camera deletes all the images on the card, so make sure that the photos are saved on your computer.

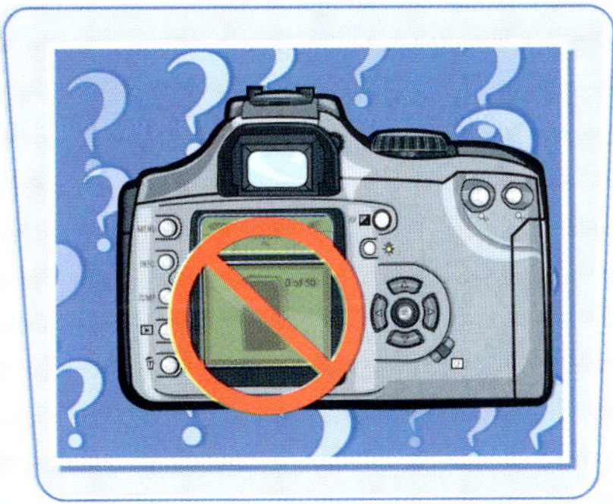

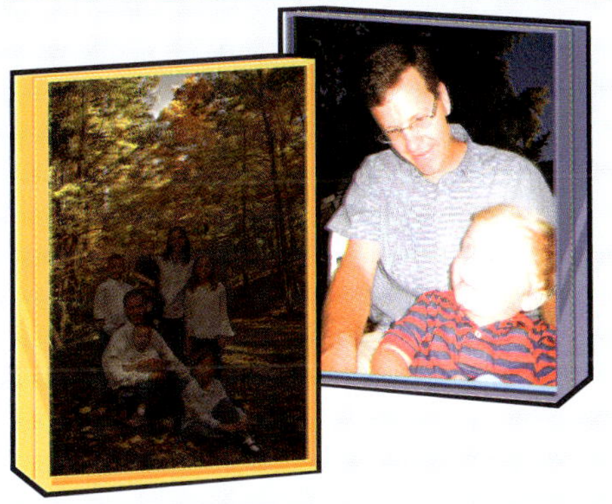

Flash Pictures Are Too Dark or Too Light

All built-in flash units work within a range specified by the manufacturer, usually up to 15 feet. If flash pictures in the LCD look too dark, the subject may be too far away. Move closer to the subject and check the camera manual for the flash distance range. If the photo is washed out, you may be too close or you may be covering the flash sensor with your finger when taking the photos. A finger or other item closer to the camera can obstruct the flash and flash sensor, preventing it from correctly reading the amount of flash. Check your camera manual to learn where your flash sensor is located.

Pictures Are Blurry

Digital cameras include a focus indicator on the back of the camera or in the LCD status display. Always be sure the focus indicator is placed on your subject and shows that the autofocus is set. A common cause is the autofocus is locked on the wrong subject or is focused past the subject. An indication would be if only one part of the photo was in sharp focus. Place your focus indicator on the subject, press the shutter halfway down to lock focus, and then recompose. Check the scene mode settings; pictures can be blurry if you take a landscape shot with the camera set to macro mode.

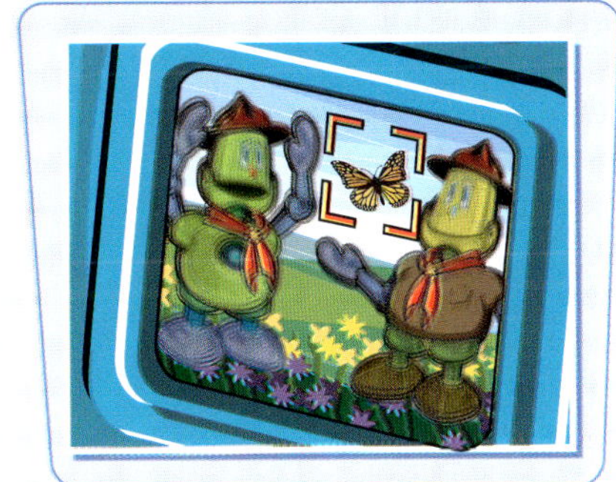

Transfer Pictures to Your Computer

When the memory card is full of pictures or after your vacation or event, you can transfer them to your computer for evaluation. By learning the options for transferring and viewing your images, you can quickly and easily move images from your digital camera to your computer.

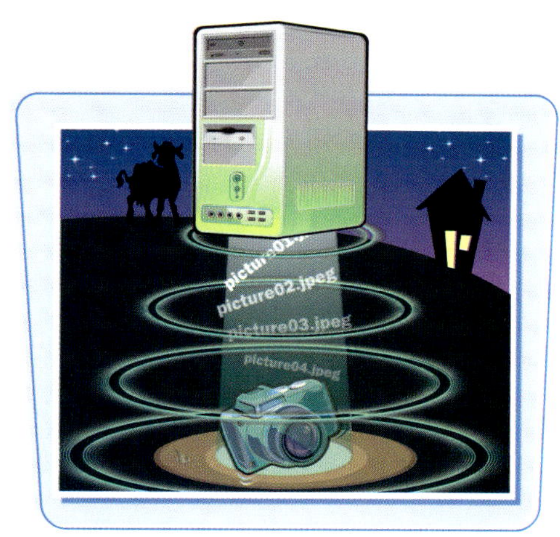

Why Transfer Pictures to Your Computer?

Even on the newest, best digital cameras, the LCD screen is relatively small. By reviewing pictures on the larger screen of your computer, you can decide whether the camera settings that you used need changing. You can use the software that came with the camera on your computer to view the pictures, or an image-editing program, such as Windows Live Photo Gallery, iPhoto, or Photoshop Elements.

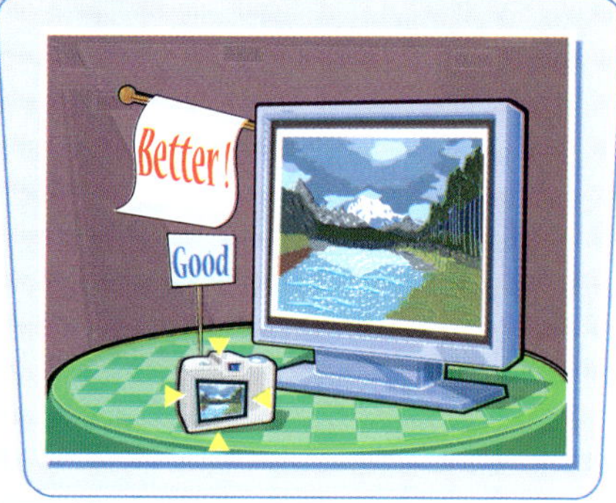

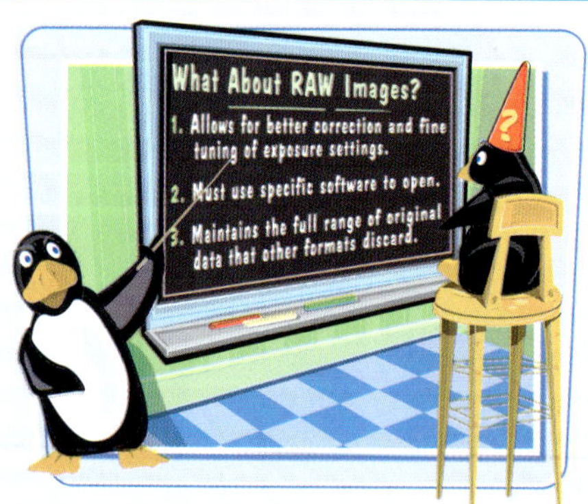

What About RAW-Format Images?

The Raw conversion program allows you to correct or fine-tune exposure settings including aperture and white balance — the RAW files are the true "digital negative" and give the most image file information and image quality. Not all cameras allow you to shoot RAW files. If you take RAW-format pictures, you need to use the manufacturer's software or the Camera Raw plug-in feature of Photoshop Elements to view and edit your images. After you save the images in TIFF or JPEG format, you can open and continue editing images in programs such as Photoshop Elements, Lightroom, or Microsoft Digital Image Pro.

Transfer Options

How you download images depends on your camera. Your camera may have a dock that plugs into your computer. You can also use a USB cable that connects directly to the camera, a separate memory card reader, or a PC adapter card. Computer operating systems recognize most digital cameras or the memory cards, and then your image software takes you through the transfer process using a step-by-step wizard-style interface automatically; some allow you to just "drag and drop" the files from the camera to the desired folder on your computer.

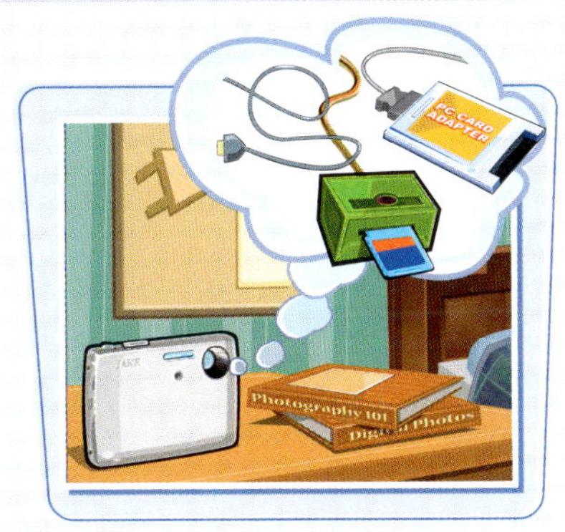

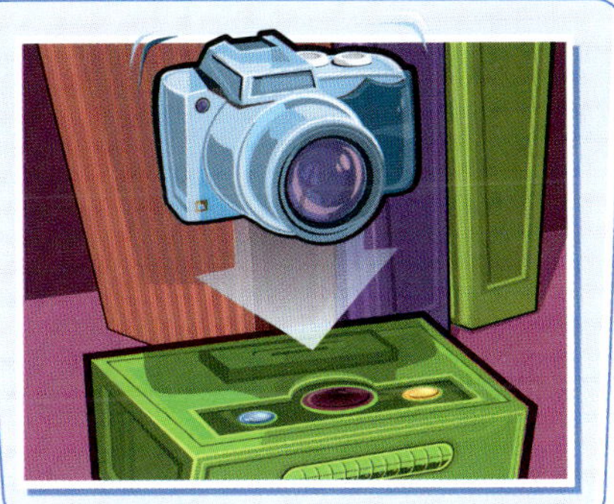

The Easiest Transfer Technique

If your camera has a docking station, the easiest way to transfer images is to place the camera directly into the cradle of the docking station. The computer to which the station is attached detects the camera and begins the download. If your camera does not have a docking station, the next fastest way to transfer images is to use an inexpensive memory card reader.

Disconnect Your Camera and Clear the Card

To disconnect your camera or card reader from your computer, first ensure that the access indicator light is off, and then click the **Safely Remove Hardware** icon ( ) in the Windows taskbar. Then unplug the USB cable. On a Mac, Control +click the camera or memory card icon and click **eject disc** from the menu that appears. You can also drag the icon to the trash and then disconnect the card or camera.

To clear the card, turn the camera on. You can delete the pictures from the memory card by choosing the **Format Card** option on one of the camera menus. Ensure that the images have been transferred safely to your computer before reformatting the memory card.

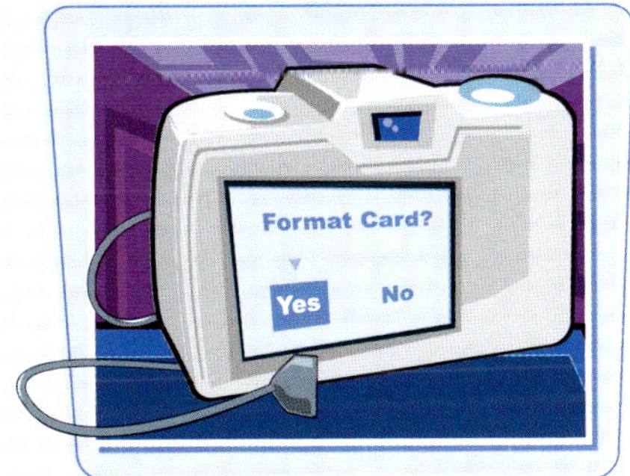

Evaluate Your Photos

You cannot tell how good your test pictures are until you see them on a computer. This is your chance to identify any camera settings you may want to change.

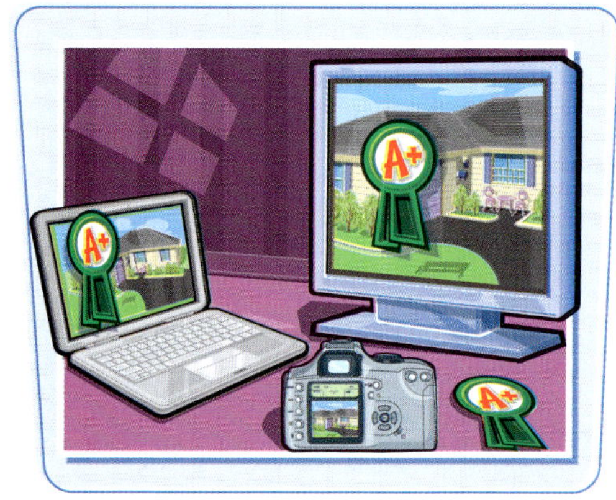

Identify Recurring Issues

Evaluating your first images allows you to determine any recurring problems that require a change in your camera settings. Most problems are related to using incorrect settings for a particular shooting situation. In a few cases, the problems you see may represent a consistent pattern of behavior that requires correction in the camera settings to overcome. Make sure to take a look at the exposure info in the metadata in conjunction with your photos. This will best help you to see how changes in the camera affect your photos.

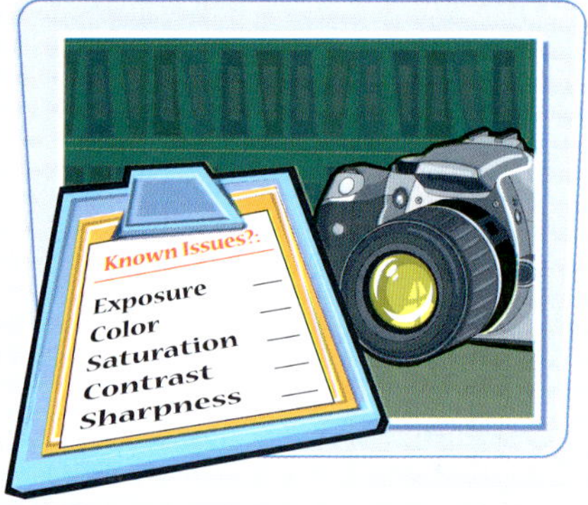

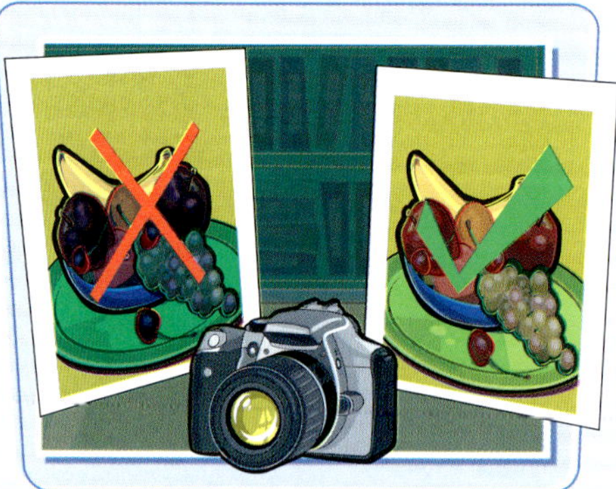

Evaluate Exposure

Different cameras can exhibit different exposure characteristics. If all the pictures look consistently too dark, then the camera may underexpose the images, provided that you use the correct settings when you take the picture. If the pictures consistently look too light, then the camera may overexpose images, or the flash intensity is too strong. Make sure to take a look at the exposure info in the metadata in conjunction with your photos. This will best help you to see how changes in the camera affect your photos.

Evaluate Color

Most cameras evaluate and adjust for white balance correctly. Providing that the camera white balance is set correctly, look for unnatural colorcasts in photos taken on a bright sunny day. The easiest way is to see if the whites really look white, or at least, if they look the way you want them. If you find that the photos consistently produce a colorcast, you can often fine-tune the white balance settings, described later in the section "Fine-Tune Camera Settings."

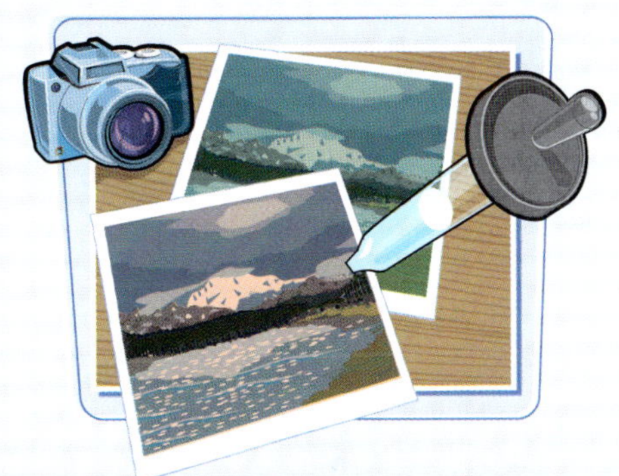

Evaluate Saturation and Contrast

Go through your pictures and evaluate the saturation, which is the intensity of color, and the contrast, which is the difference between light and dark tones. Evaluate whether the colors are too intense or unnaturally vibrant, or make sure they are not too dull and washed out. To get the most accurate color, make sure to calibrate your monitor frequently.

Do Not Worry About Sharpness

When you look at some digital pictures on a computer monitor, they may seem *soft*, not as crisp as film prints. Although you can adjust sharpening settings on most cameras, resist the urge. You can sharpen images as the last step in editing. You sharpen images based on the final image size and whether you want to print the picture or use it on the Web.

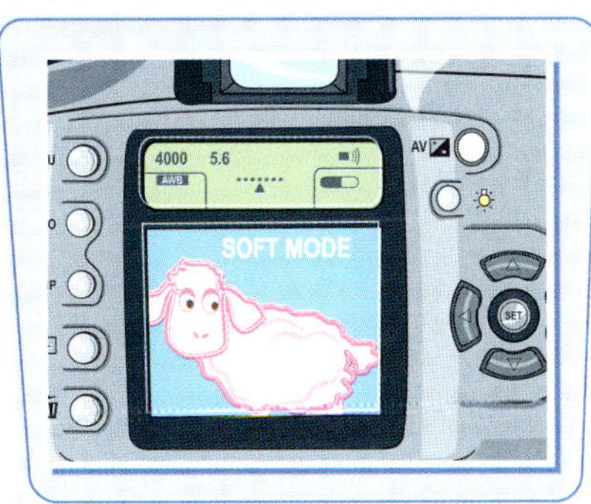

Fine-Tune Camera Settings

Most digital cameras today produce excellent exposures with good color accuracy. In some cases, fine-tuning your camera settings helps you get better photos without the need to make corrections on your computer.

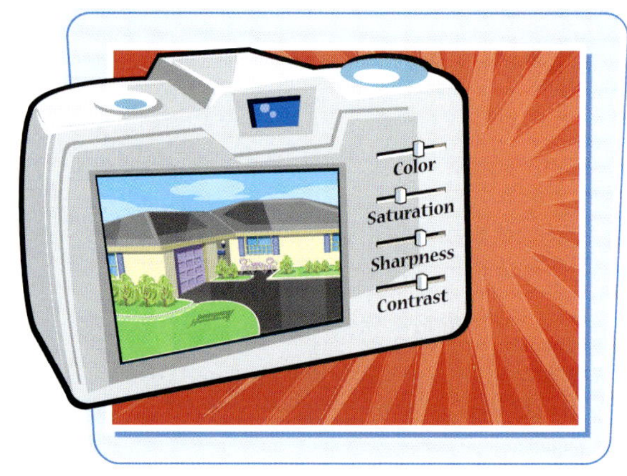

Make a List of Settings to Fine-Tune

Your first foray into using the digital camera provides an overview of the camera's capabilities in normal shooting situations, using the default settings. Now you know which settings to adjust and which ones to leave as they are. Make a list of the settings you want to adjust, and begin by making small adjustments. Then evaluate the results. Modern cameras typically produce good results, and so you may not need to make any settings adjustments at all.

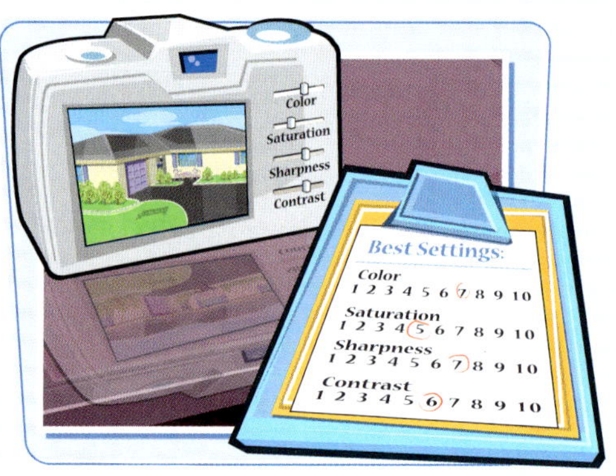

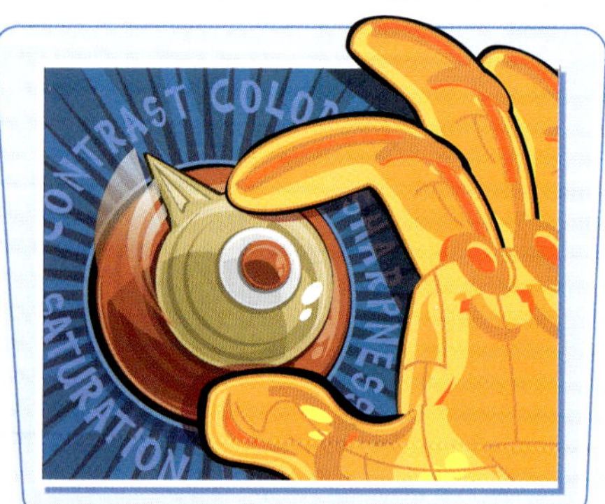

Why Fine-Tune Your Camera Settings?

Each situation that you come across in your photography is different, and when taking different sorts of photos you will want different feels and looks for these situations. A landscape photo might need some additional saturation and contrast, whereas that same saturation setting on a portrait might tend to produce ruddy, unnatural skin tones. Fine-tuning your camera helps make things go more quickly and smoothly when you start editing your images on the computer.

Fine-Tune the Flash

If flash pictures are overexposed or too light, and the cause is not a finger obstructing the flash sensor, you can adjust the flash intensity by lowering the power with flash exposure compensation. If you do not have a flash adjustment option, you can set a minus exposure value (EV) when you take a flash picture. You can experiment to see which setting produces the best flash photo.

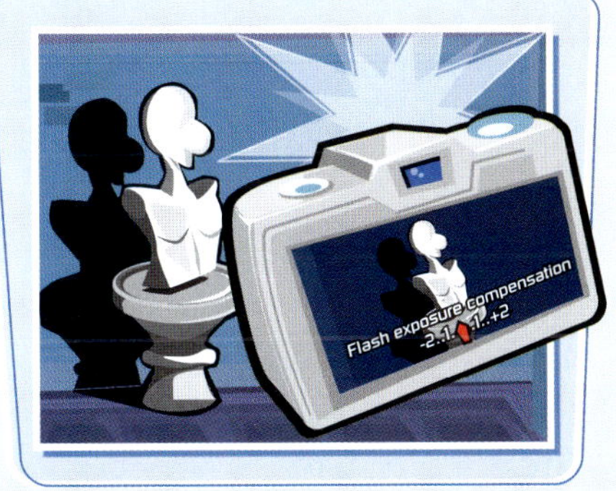

Fine-Tune the Exposure

Scenes with large expanses of very dark or very light areas can fool the camera meter so that pictures are overexposed and underexposed, respectively. You can set exposure compensation, or a plus or minus exposure value (EV), to get a picture with normal tonal values. Sometimes you may even want to use the exposure compensation to more creatively affect your images' exposure in the automatic setting.

Fine-Tune Color, Saturation, and Contrast

Newer digital cameras offer options to increase color, saturation, and contrast. Never adjust settings based solely on the LCD screen on your camera, which, even as they increase in size, is still too small to accurately show all the characteristics. Instead, evaluate a large sampling of representative pictures on a computer and as prints. If the color, saturation, or contrast is not what you want in your photographs, then adjust in small increments until you get the pictures you do want.

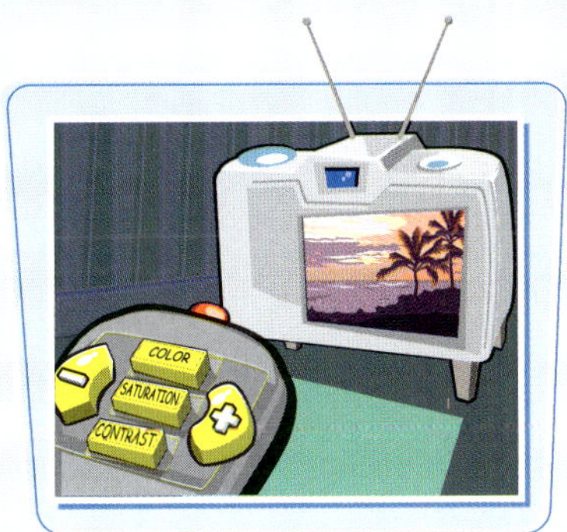

Taking Advantage of Your Camera's Settings

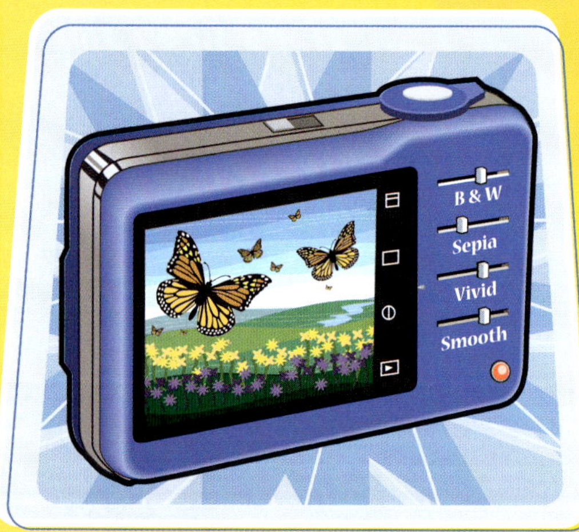

Today's digital cameras are better than ever at helping you to take superior photos easily. With just a twist of a dial or quick run through the menu, your camera can automatically adjust your camera's exposure settings to help you get the photos that you envisioned.

Quick Steps

Match the Scene to the Setting 100
Be Aware of In-Camera Settings 101
How Do the Scene Settings Change the Images? 102
Use the Settings Creatively 104
Evaluate Your Photos 106
Better to Change Things Later? 107

Match the Scene to the Setting

To help in creating the best photos possible, digital camera manufacturers offer what are commonly called ***scene settings***. These aid you in learning about photography and how your camera works as well as help you create better photographs than the standard automatic settings would give you.

When to Use Scene Settings

Many digital cameras have a series of "scene settings" which automatically change the settings of your digital camera in accordance with the scene in front of your camera. These settings help to take some of the guesswork out of your picture-taking when the scene or the lighting might be somewhat unusual or difficult.

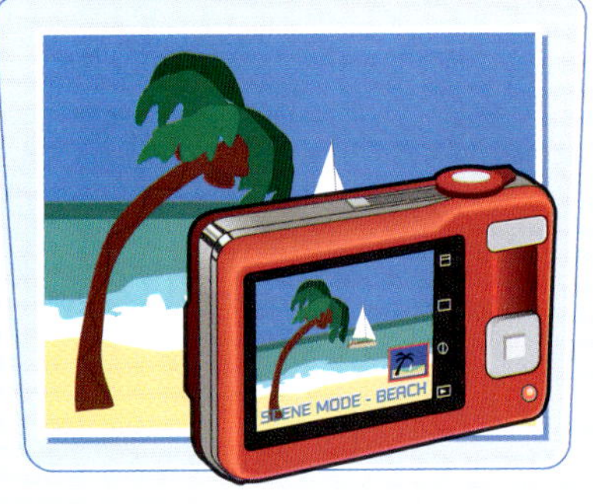

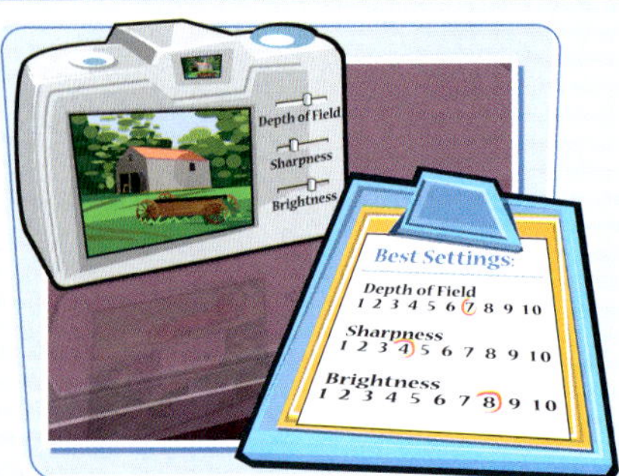

Match the Scenes

Because more than one combination of exposure settings can get the same exposure, the scene settings help you to get the best one mostly by optimizing your shutter, aperture, and ISO. Some cameras' scene settings even affect focus, flash, white balance, and color settings.

Visualize the Scene

These settings should be easy to recognize when you are taking photos, with most of them having the basics: portrait, landscape, sports, and macro. Many digital cameras now have 10 to 20 different scene settings, such as kids, nighttime flash, fireworks, pets, underwater, sunset, party, snow, and beach. Simply set your camera to the scene setting that corresponds to the scene you are shooting, and let the camera do the rest automatically.

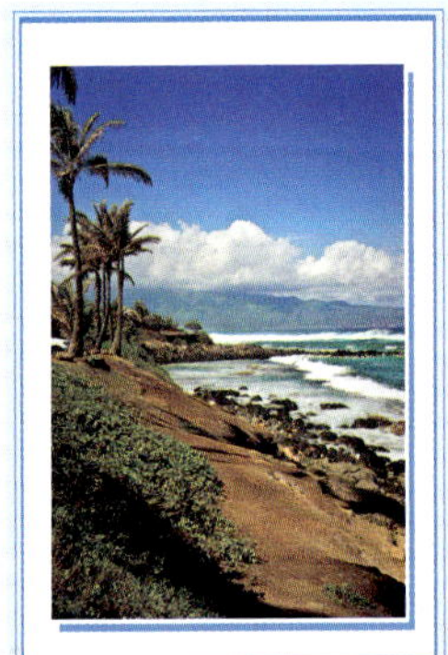

Be Aware of In-Camera Settings

Sometimes the settings you make in your camera can be detrimental to your photographs — for example, the more you raise the sharpness level, the more noise you introduce into the image.

Real or Unreal

Any time that you make big changes to the settings in your camera, the effects may become exaggerated. This may lead to extreme contrast and colors that could look artificial. This might be okay at times, but be careful especially with people pictures — skin tones can quickly look unflattering when effects are overdone.

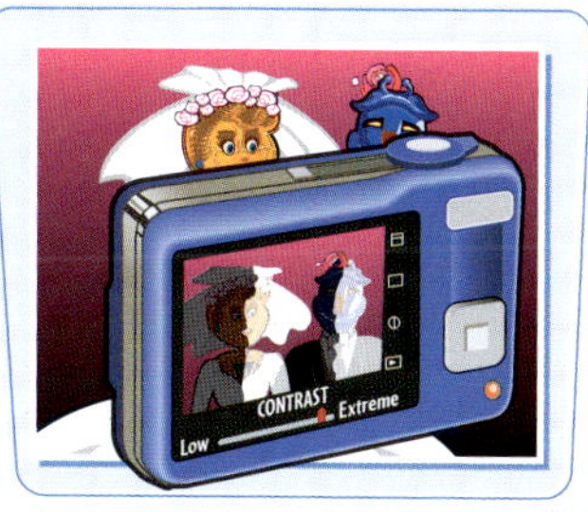

Be Realistic

Because the LCD monitor on your camera is small, you do not always get an accurate idea of exactly what the photo will look like when you make a print. If you are trying to get the most realistic-looking image, it may be better to set your camera to its most neutral settings and then make changes on the computer.

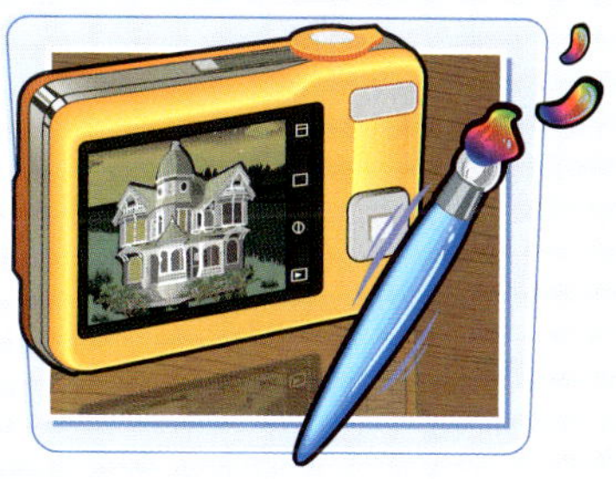

Happy Accidents

Sometimes you take a photo at some random setting — too dark, too light, too much blur, wrong color setting — and it ends up being great. Do not just delete an image because the camera was not set right; wait until you get home and really check things out before you decide that it needs to be deleted. It might be a technically perfect photo, but it might be something that moves you nonetheless, such as this image which was shot 2 stops underexposed.

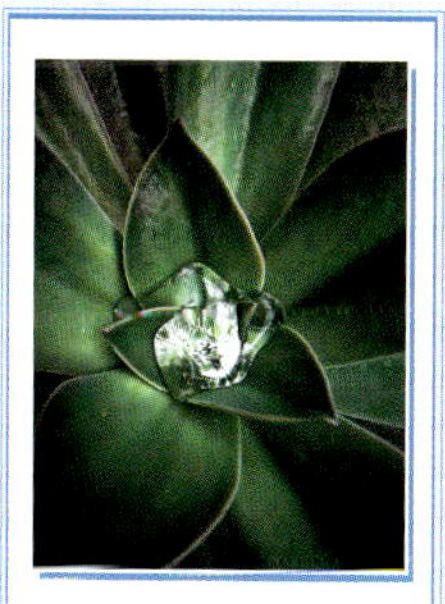

Have Fun!

With all the settings you have, and all the rules of exposure and focus and testing to make sure everything looks the way you want it, just make sure that you are having fun with your photos. All these different automatic settings are there to help take some of the guesswork out of things so that you can just take great photos.

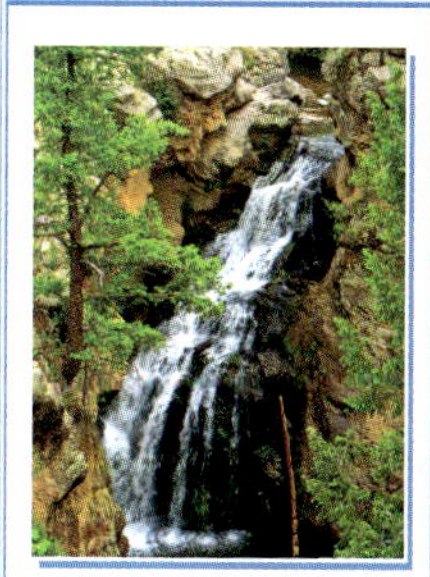

How Do the Scene Settings Change the Images?

Your automatic scene settings make visible changes to the photos. You can maximize these scene settings by matching the icon or name of the setting with the photograph that you want to take.

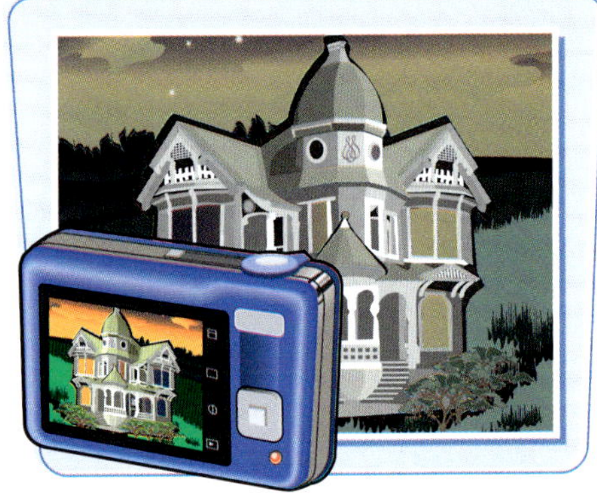

Change the Exposure

Using the different apertures and shutters changes the look of your photos even when the exposure is the same. So if you are taking photos of your kids playing sports and are using the Sports scene setting, the camera tries to get the fastest shutter speed it can to make sure that it stops the action of the event. For some of the other scene settings, such as the Landscape setting, the aperture is adjusted for maximum depth of field, whereas the Portrait setting uses the aperture to minimize the depth of field.

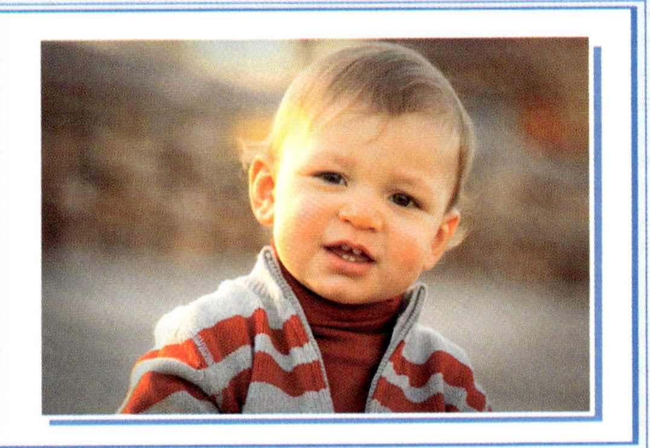

Make Bigger Changes

When you change the different scene settings, your camera also changes the type of focus, white balance, and color settings. For example, a "party" setting might set the camera's focus setting to face priority where the camera automatically focuses on the faces in your scene. A "sunset" setting may use a warmer white balance along with a more vivid color style to accentuate the color in the scene you are going to photograph.

Are They Always Right?

Matching the scene to the setting might not be foolproof, but the technology built into today's digital cameras gets you excellent results in most situations. Try different scene settings when shooting different situations, and if the photo that you are taking is a once-in-a-lifetime situation, make sure the setting and scene match and the photo is the way you want it before you put the camera away.

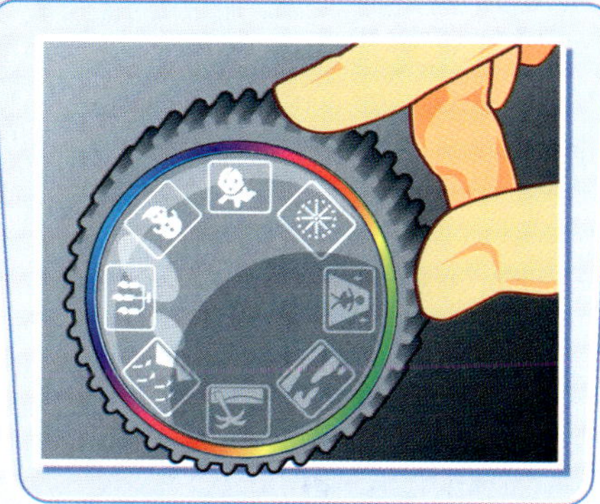

Take Time to Prepare

Spend some time with your camera's manual to learn what all the different settings are and how they affect your photos. Learning what these settings do and do not do might save time, and you might even realize that the scene settings do even more than you thought. Even when you know what you are doing, the scene settings can be great timesavers.

Use the Scene Settings to Learn

After you take your photos using the scene settings, take some time to look at your photos on your computer and check out the EXIF data. Even though these are all fully automatic settings, the exposure information is still there for you to see what the camera thinks makes the best photo out of the scene settings. Compare the information between different photos and different settings to learn how to create the looks you are looking for.

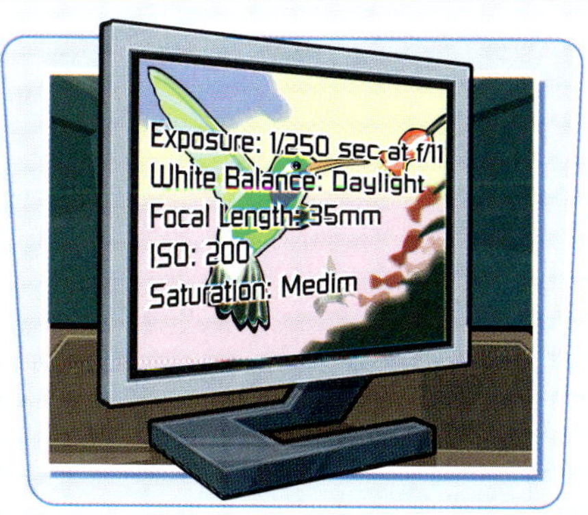

Use the Settings Creatively

Digital cameras also offer additional settings that allow you to make even more interesting images. Use these settings to alter color and contrast to build interest and excitement in your photos.

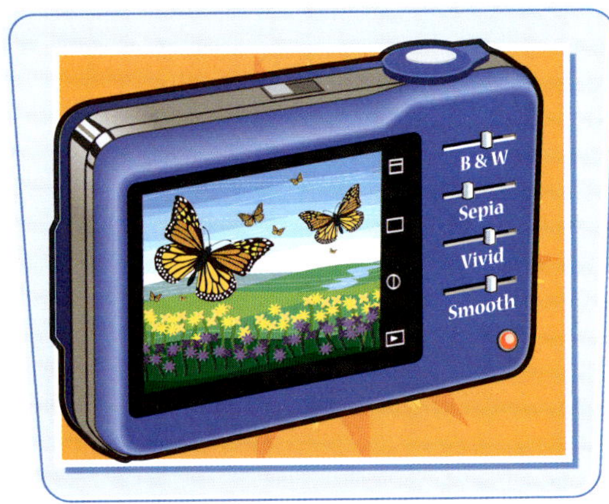

Use the Presets Creatively

Taking photos in a scenario where you can use one of the presets gives you the freedom to just take photos and compose creatively and not have to worry about the camera settings. Not only do the scene settings allow you to create better photos in certain situations than the standard auto settings, but once you learn what the settings can do, you can try those settings in different situations to see if you like the effects on your photos.

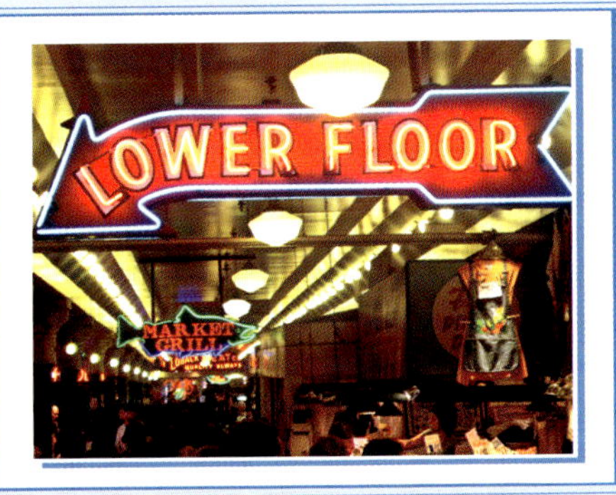

Try Different Color Settings

Most digital cameras have several different creative color options. These are usually accessed through the menu, and can be anything from adding a fun colorcast to the entire photo, to replacing certain colors for others, creating an abstract look, or even making your images look like old or antique photographs.

Digital Film Settings

Many film stocks have their own unique color characteristics. Your digital camera may be able to emulate some of those looks. If your camera has a setting for "positive," it gives your photos the punchy color and contrast of slide film. Other settings might give the soft contrast of the negative film that wedding and portrait photographers might use.

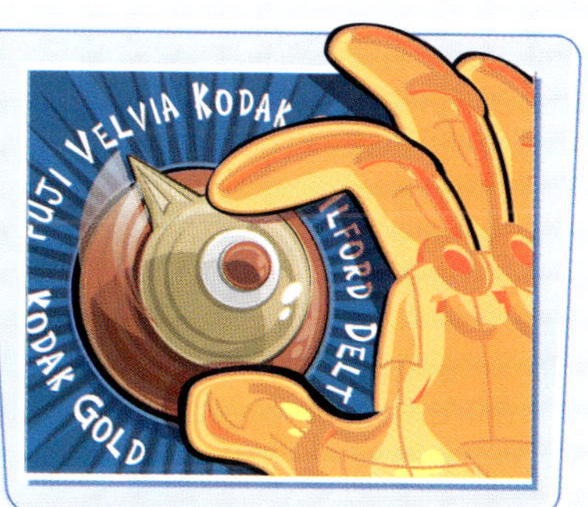

Black and White

Black and white is still a favorite look for many photographers. Creating your images in B&W can often simplify a scene, add a contemporary or nostalgic look, or add a mood that simply would not be available in a color image. B&W allows you to focus on just the essentials of your photography, yet often creates images that are beyond your hopes. Many digital cameras even have multiple B&W settings, each having different levels of contrast.

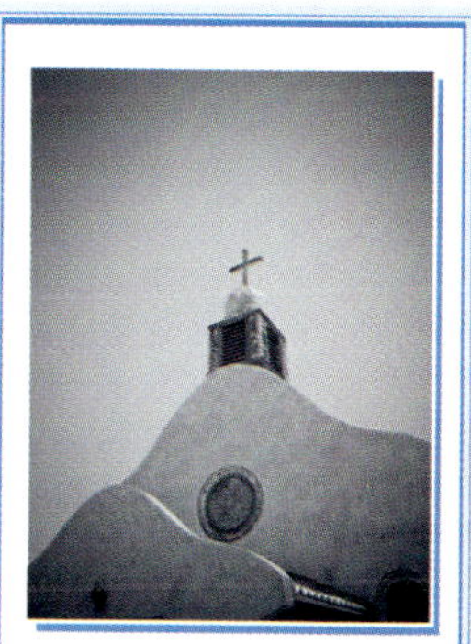

Saving Your Favorites

You may spend time going through all of the many options, mixing color, contrast, focus areas, and exposure settings to get exactly what you want for your photography. Many digital cameras have ways to save those settings so that you can easily access them whenever you want. These are usually designated with a name like "Custom" or "My Settings."

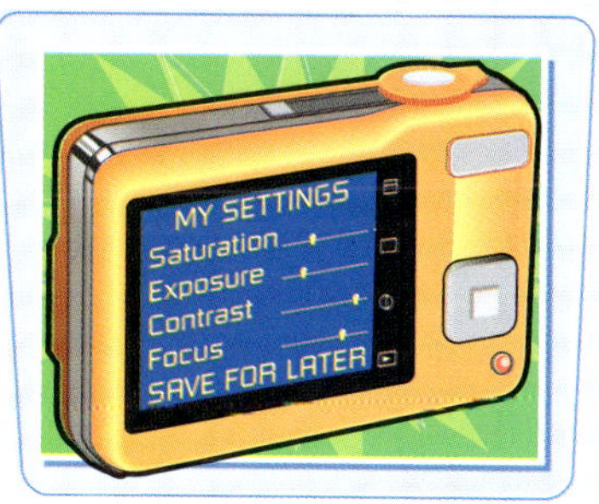

Spend Time with a Good Book

Once you have gotten comfortable with your camera, it is probably time to revisit your camera's manual. What seemed like an overwhelming amount of information when you first got your camera probably is much more manageable now. Take some time to go back and see what you forgot or did not understand before. Your camera has so many options that you might have to jog your memory to spark some new creativity in your photo-taking.

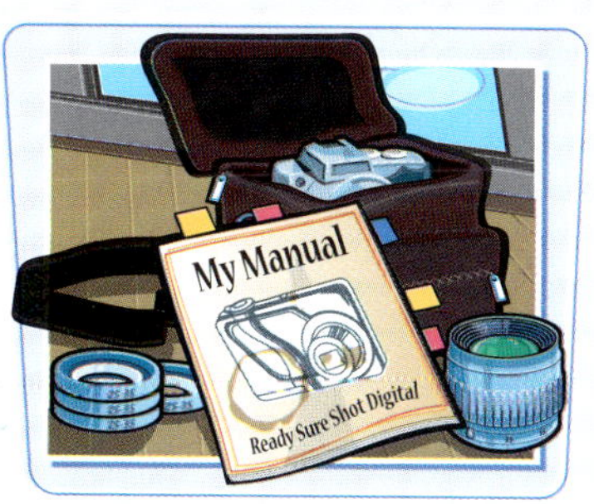

Evaluate Your Photos

You have many great options to make sure that the photos you take are the photos you want. Take advantage of all these to get your photos exactly the way you want them.

Check the Image on the LCD

It might seem obvious, but make sure to take some time to check that the image you are shooting is how you want it. Is it composed and exposed the way you want it? Use the LCD zoom to confirm focus if you are unsure. Make sure to check before things change. If you are taking a lot of photos, do not feel like you need to check each one — get your settings right, take several images, and then make sure they are what you want; then either take more or move on to the next photo opportunity.

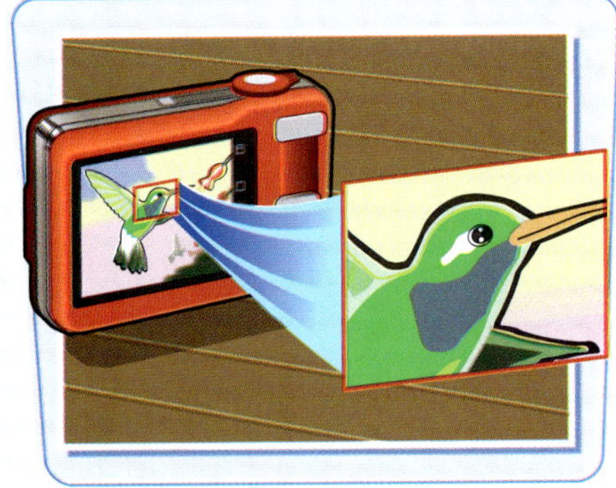

Download for Scrutiny

As good as today's LCD screens are, they do have limitations. To really scrutinize focus and exposure, you need to look at your images on your computer's monitor. Make sure that you are comfortable with all the settings and functions of your camera before you head out to photograph that once-in-a-lifetime event.

When to Delete

When you delete a photograph off the card while it is in the camera, it is gone forever. Do not delete in a hasty moment or when you are not paying attention and accidentally delete something you cannot reshoot. Deleting images that are obviously no good is fine, but make sure to evaluate them confidently.

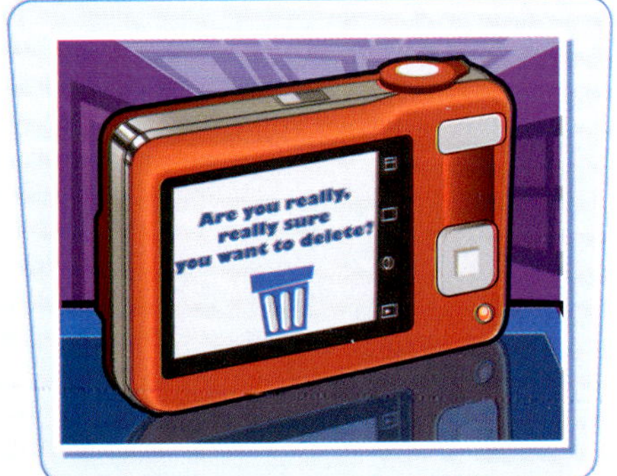

Better to Change Things Later?

With all the options available to you with your digital photography, take some time to decide if making creative decisions with your camera or with your computer is better.

Camera or Computer

Just as there are many ways to make changes to your photos with the camera, there are even more ways to affect your photos with the power of your computer. You have more control and can do much more when you make changes with your computer, and those changes can be reversible. The changes that you make to photos in your camera are permanent and limited.

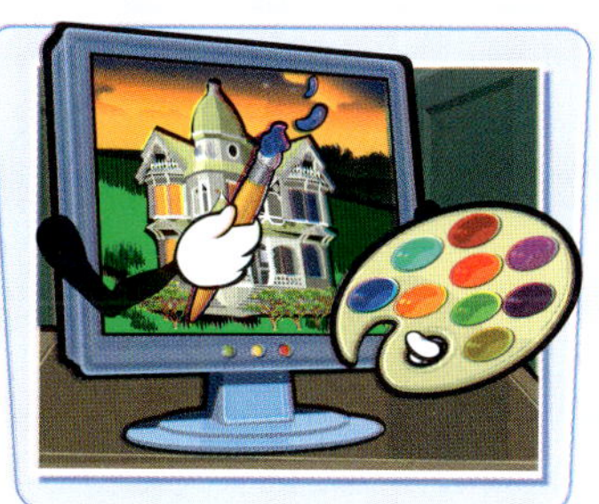

Comparison Viewing

Take the time to make some photos with and without the camera's effects and compare them on your computer so you can see what you want and what you do not. Use the software on your camera to make changes to the straight photos and see if you like them better than what the computer does.

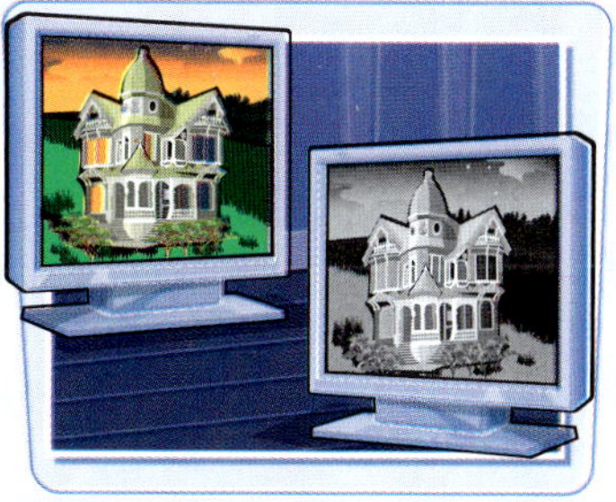

How Much Is Too Much

Many times the settings that you can apply to your photos in the camera can be heavy-handed and overdone. What looks good and cool on the back of the camera may look cartoonish on your monitor or a print. That might be okay, but make sure to try several different things if the photos are important.

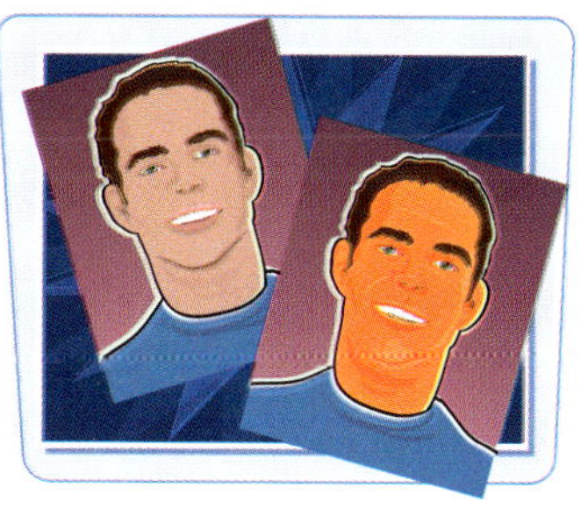

Best of Both Worlds

The RAW file has all the photo information, and that file has to be "processed" on your computer. By shooting RAW and JPEG photos with advanced digital compact cameras and dSLRs, you can take a JPEG file with any settings that you want, and still have an untouched RAW file as a blank slate, ready for your changes to be applied on the computer.

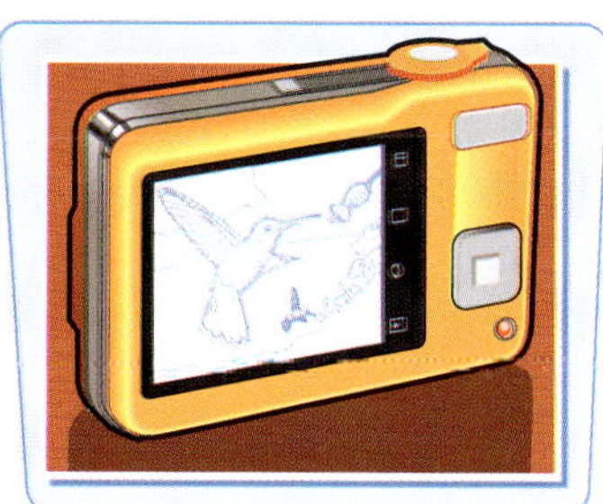

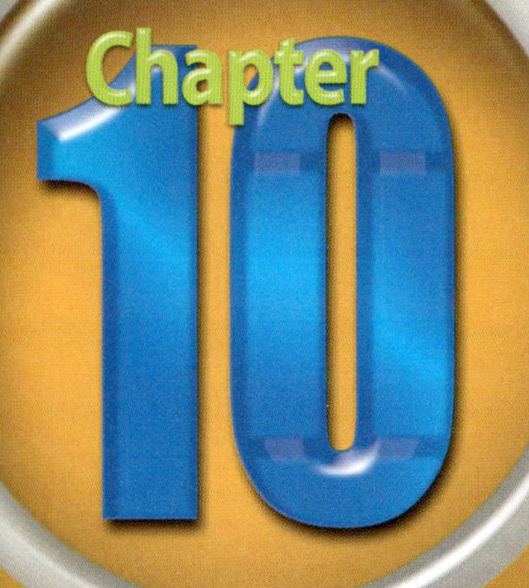

Avoiding Digital Photography Pitfalls

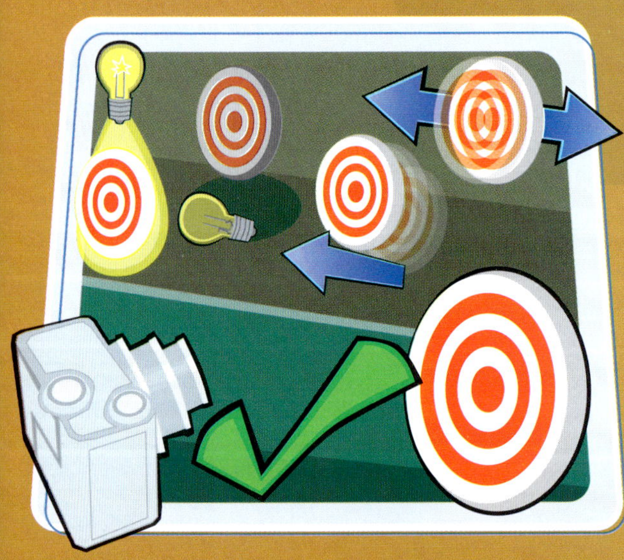

In this chapter, you learn how to recognize and avoid the most common problems in digital photography.

Quick Steps

Avoid Taking Unfixable Pictures ... 110

What Is a Histogram? ... 111

Use a Histogram as You Take Pictures ... 112

Compensate for Shutter Lag ... 114

Avoid Blowouts ... 115

Keep Your Camera Steady ... 116

Avoid Undesirable Colorcasts ... 117

Never Use Digital Zoom ... 118

Reduce Digital Noise ... 119

Avoid Taking Unfixable Pictures

With all the automatic features in today's digital cameras, you can still take digital pictures that have problems that no amount of computer image-editing can fix. You can learn the most common digital photography problems and how to avoid them.

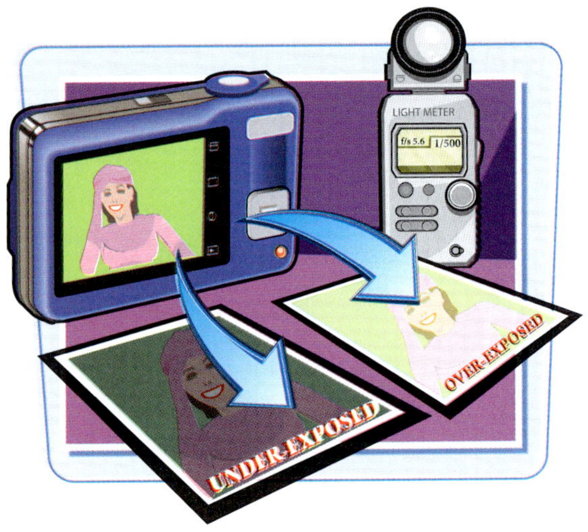

What Are Unfixable Photo Problems?

Unfixable digital photo problems include excessively overexposed or underexposed pictures, pictures with excessive *digital noise* — unwanted multicolored pixels throughout the image — and blurry, out-of-focus pictures. Use the tips in this chapter to avoid taking unfixable pictures as well as to learn about other common digital photography problems.

Many people think that a lot of problems in photos can be solved in the computer with software such as Photoshop Elements. When problems are small, this may be the case, but trying to fix large problems usually ends up in photos that just do not look good.

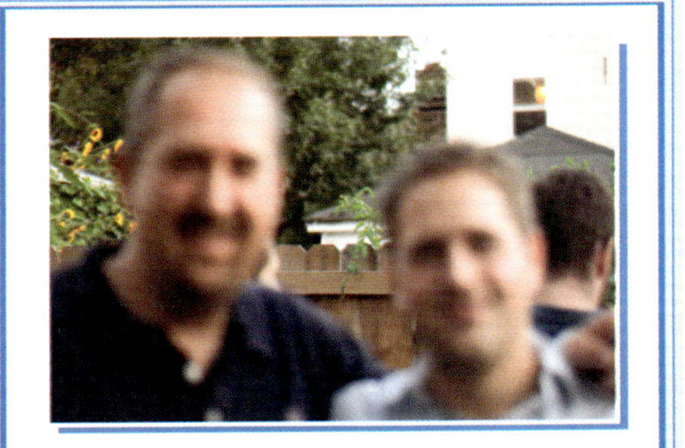

What Is a Histogram?

Your histogram is a graphic representation of the tones in your photo. You can tell if an image is properly exposed by looking at the distribution of light, medium, and dark tones shown on the image histogram on the camera or in an image-editing program. This graph can usually be seen when you are reviewing the images on the LCD screen, and some cameras even have it as part of the live view before you take the photo. The histogram is a tool; it only tells you how the image is exposed. You do not change the histogram because you might change your exposure, which would affect the histogram.

Not all digital cameras offer a histogram feature. Refer to your manual for details.

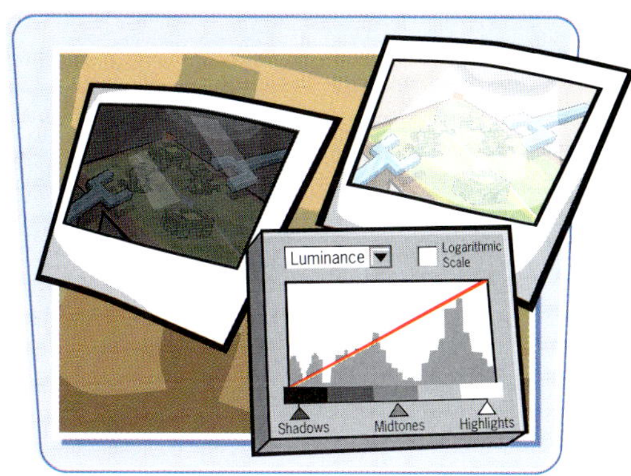

What a Histogram Shows

A histogram shows the distribution of tones, or the *contrast*, in an image. Brightness from black (on the left) to white, appears on the horizontal axis. The vertical axis shows the number, or weight, of pixels at each brightness level. In an average scene, a well-exposed image shows tonal distribution and weight distributed fairly evenly, like a flattened bell-shaped curve across the entire histogram.

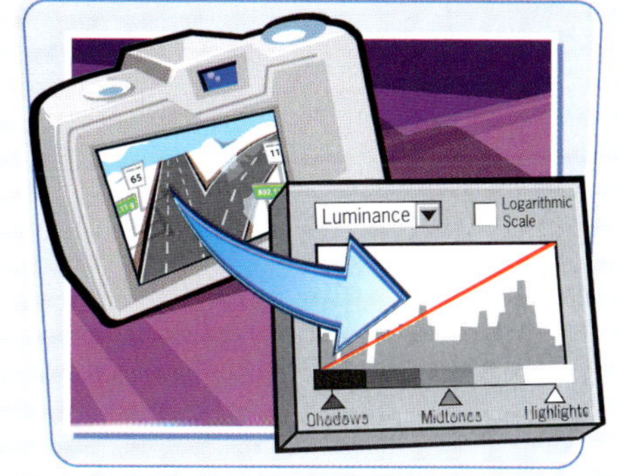

How to Identify Problem Pictures

When examining a photo's histogram on the LCD of your camera, you are looking to see if the pixels drop off sharply at either end of the histogram. A steep drop-off is called *clipping*, and it indicates that some of the pixels in the image are either overexposed (right side) or underexposed (left side). When pixels are clipped, they are either pushed to pure white or black and lose all detail.

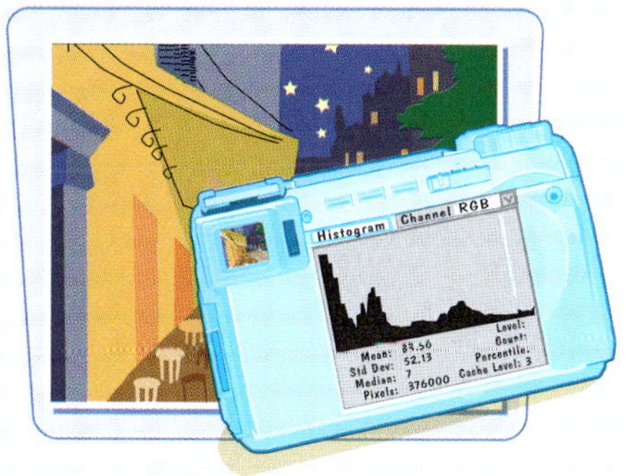

Use a Histogram as You Take Pictures

Even under the best conditions it may be difficult to evaluate a photo on the camera's LCD screen, but it is especially difficult under harsh sunlight. On digital cameras that display a histogram, you can judge whether or not a picture is properly exposed by checking the histogram immediately after you take the picture.

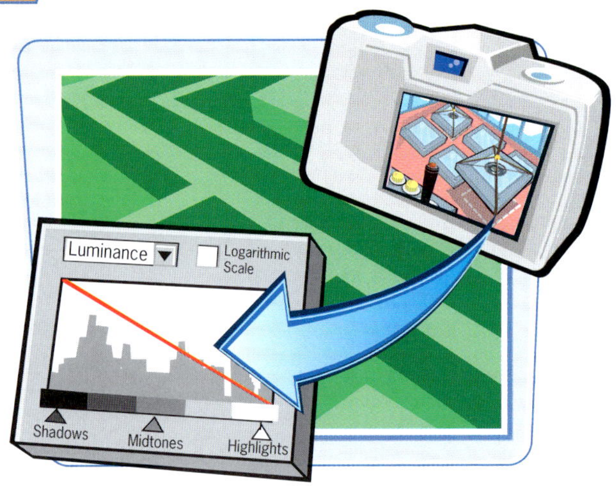

Turn On the Histogram Display

To see if your camera offers a histogram display, check the playback display options, or check the camera manual. Sometimes you may need to scroll through the image information menu to get to the histogram in playback mode. In some cameras you can even select histograms that show the red, green, and blue color distribution along with the exposure tones.

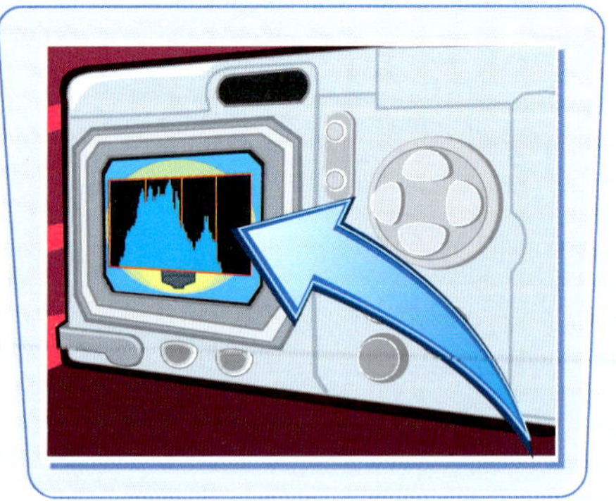

Use Overexposure Warning

Some cameras offer an LCD display mode that flashes the overexposed parts of the image. Some areas of an image, such as a bright, overcast sky or a white fence, can be overexposed without affecting the quality of the photo. If your camera offers a histogram display, areas of the photo that are too light appear bunched up on the right side of the display.

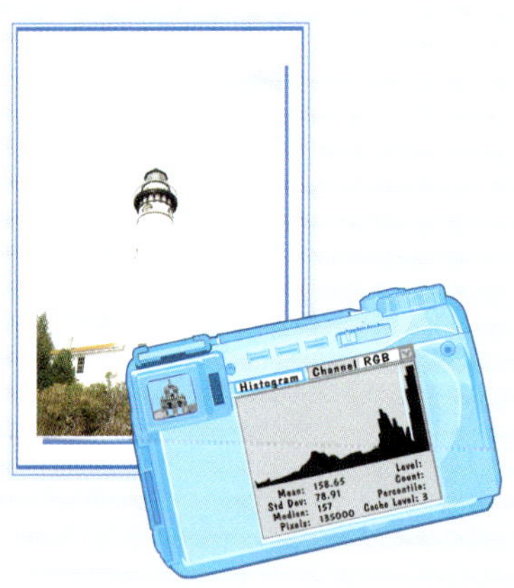

Does the Overexposure Warning Flash?

If the overexposure display flashes in certain areas, note the exposure settings shown. You can then move the subject to a less bright area, or choose an exposure compensation setting, such as –1.0 EV, that lets half as much light into the camera. Take the picture again and check the histogram.

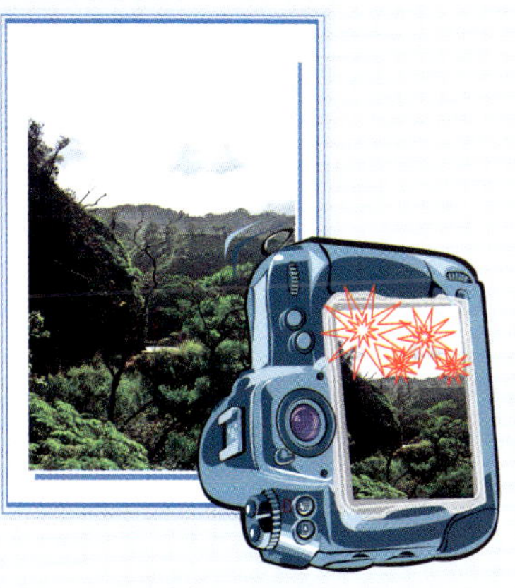

Non-Average Scene Histograms

When scenes are predominately dark or light, the histogram reflects the predominate tones. For example, if you take a picture of a bright or backlit scene, the pixels fall on the right side of the histogram. In a darker situation, the pixels fall on the left side of the histogram.

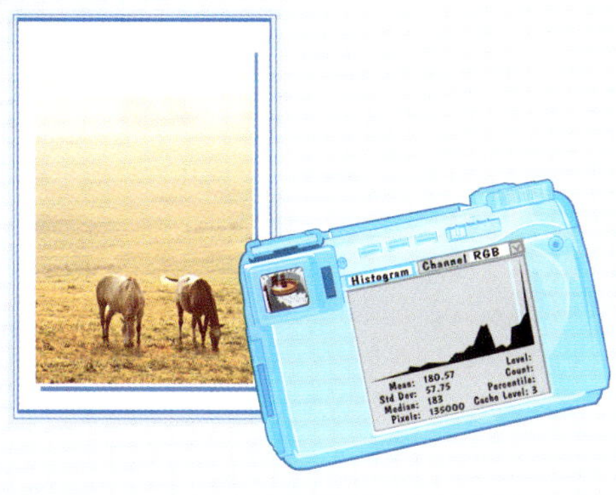

High-Key Histograms

In *high-key* scenes, with mostly light tones, most of the brightness pixels fall to the right of the histogram, even with an accurate exposure, as shown here. High-key photos are popular in advertising these days, but you need to ensure that areas in which the details are to be preserved are not so bright that the camera records no detail in the picture.

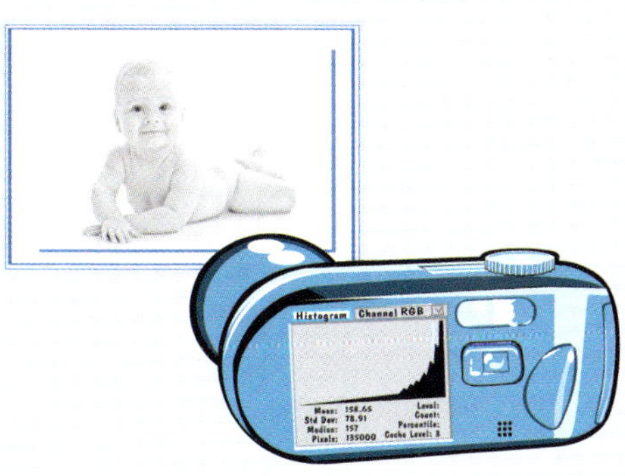

Low-Key Histograms

In *low-key* scenes, with mostly dark tones, most of the brightness pixels fall to the left of the histogram, even with an accurate exposure, as shown here. In low-key scenes, try to ensure that darker shadow areas retain detail by checking that the scene is not overexposed. You can also regain some shadow detail using the midtone adjustment in the Levels dialog box.

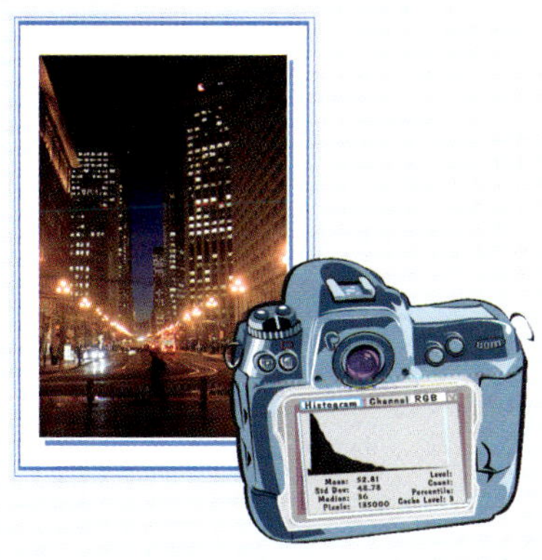

Compensate for Shutter Lag

Unlike film cameras that instantly take a picture when you press the shutter release button, many digital cameras delay before taking the picture. With each new model of digital camera, the amount of delay (shutter lag) gets smaller, and with most modern dSLRs, this lag is nearly imperceptible. The fact is almost all compact digital cameras have some degree of shutter lag. Regardless of how much shutter lag your camera has, you can learn how to work around the delay to avoid missing the action.

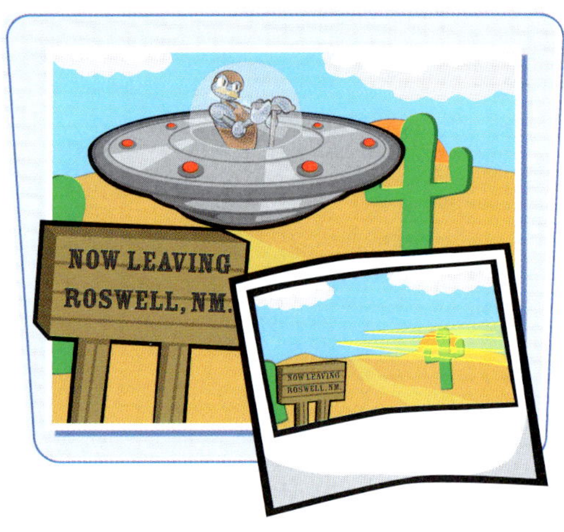

What Is Shutter Lag?

The delay between the time you press the shutter release button and the time when the camera takes the picture is called *shutter lag*. Shutter lag happens because of the time that it takes for things to happen, like charging the image sensor, focusing, or metering. Because of this delay, you can miss capturing the action, such as the moment a family member blows out candles on a birthday cake, or when a basketball player moves a ball down the court.

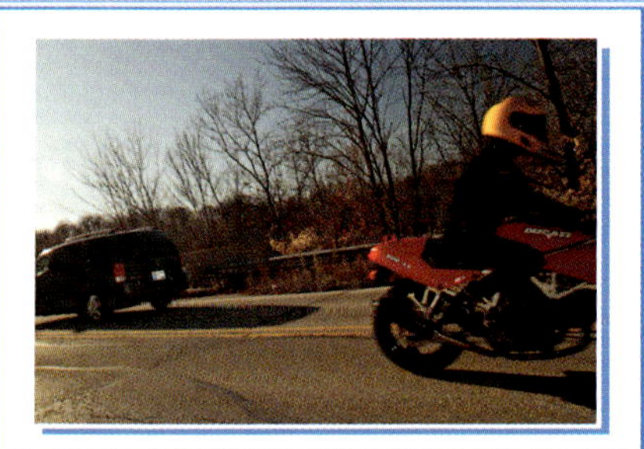

Avoid Missing Critical Moments

To work around shutter lag, you can anticipate the action. Focus on where the action will happen and press the shutter release button halfway down, wait for the action, and then take the picture. Pressing the shutter release halfway down to set the focus and meter cuts the lag time a lot. Making sure that the flash is charged, ready with the red eye mode Off, helps speed things up if you are taking flash photos. Also, if your camera has the capability, switch to burst mode to capture a rapid sequence of pictures with no shutter lag.

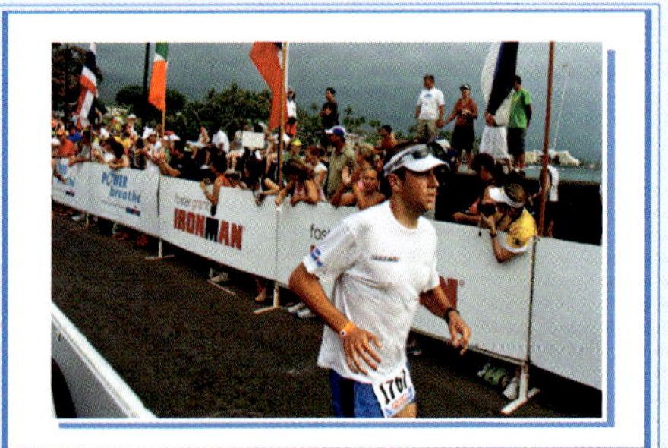

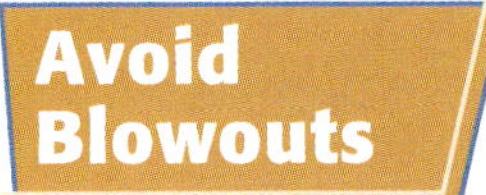

Avoid Blowouts

You can fix many problems in image-editing programs, but you cannot fix areas of the image where the camera records no details. You can learn how to avoid blowing out the highlight details.

What Are Blowouts?

When you take pictures in a scene with very bright and very dark areas, the brightness differences may exceed the camera's *dynamic range*, or its ability to record both very bright and very dark areas. As a result, very bright areas often lack detail and appear as solid white.

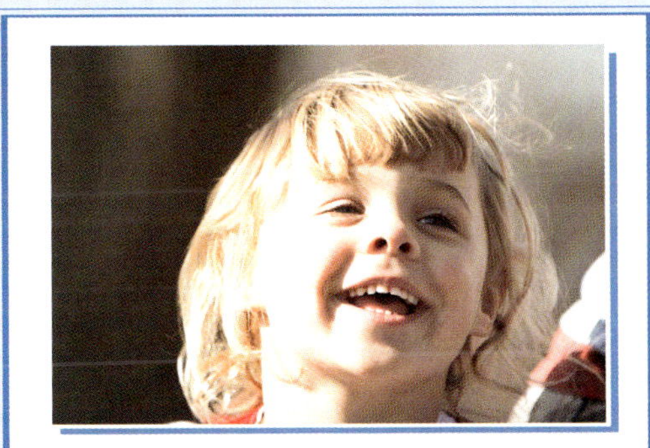

How to Avoid Blowouts

It is particularly important to avoid blowouts in the main subject area. One very problematic subject is a wedding dress on a bright, sunny day. To avoid blown highlights, switch to a semiautomatic or manual mode, and then select spot or center-weighted metering. The camera meter weighs exposure primarily for light falling on the subject instead of averaging the entire scene, ensuring accurate subject exposure, as shown here. If the dress is not properly metered, it blows out and the details of the dress are lost.

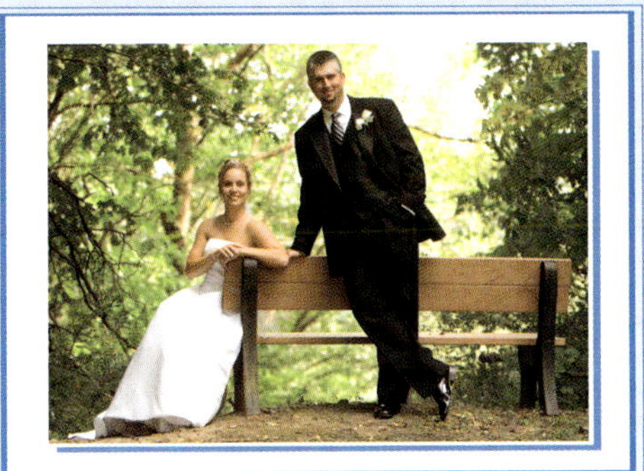

Pay Attention to Your Light

The best way to avoid having blown-out areas on your photos is to pay attention to your light. Any time you have hard sunlight and shadow, the contrast is too much to capture in a photograph. Taking a moment to evaluate what the light is doing in your photograph and turning or moving your subject into some open shade helps with blown-out areas on your subject.

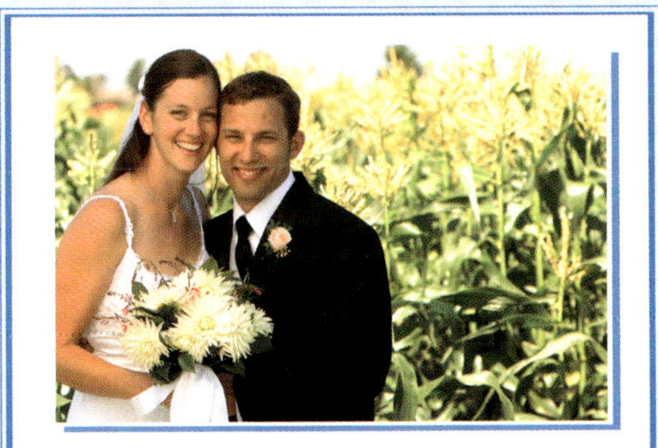

Keep Your Camera Steady

Small, lightweight cameras invite a lot of everyday, impromptu snapshots. But the camera's light weight can also mean blurry pictures. You can learn how to get sharp pictures with small cameras.

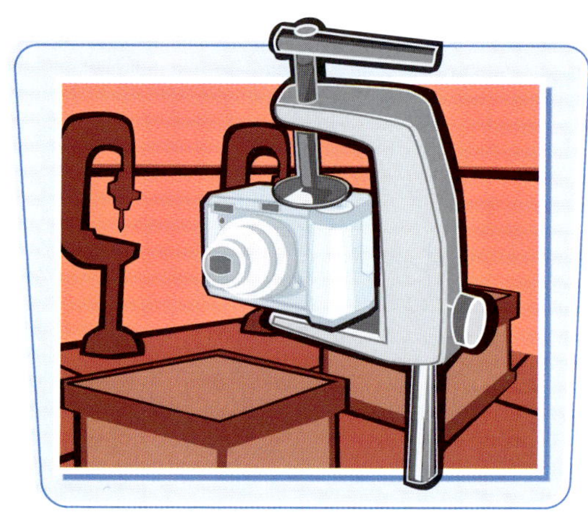

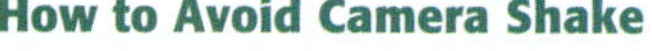

What Is Camera Shake?

Newer pocket- and palm-size digital cameras make everyday snaps inviting and easy. Because of their low weight and holding the camera out away from you to see the LCD, avoiding *camera shake* — blur from hand movement during shooting — can be challenging, especially if the light level gets low. Whenever you have the zoom lens extended to telephoto, the camera is more susceptible to shake.

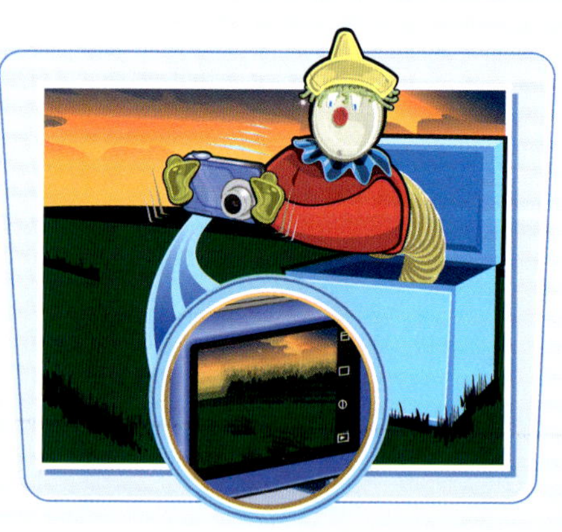

How to Avoid Camera Shake

In all but very bright scenes, you need to steady the camera by leaning against a solid surface such as a wall, or by setting the camera on a solid surface when taking the picture. Alternatively, you can buy a tabletop tripod that ensures sharp images. By keeping your camera close to your face and keeping your elbows tight to your body, you can create a more stable platform for your camera. When you press the shutter release, be sure you press it down firmly and smoothly; do not jab it down quickly.

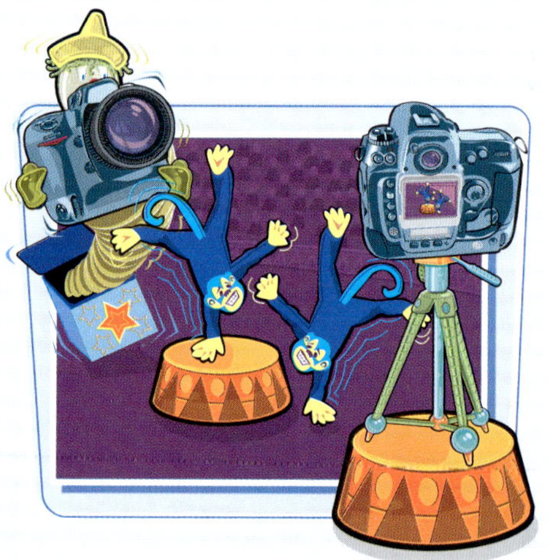

Avoid Undesirable Colorcasts

With digital cameras, you can easily avoid taking pictures that have an unwanted colorcast. Setting the camera to get accurate color also saves time when you edit images on the computer.

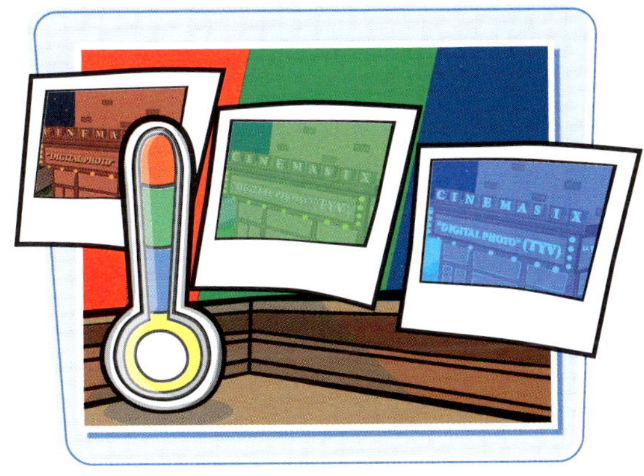

What Causes Undesirable Colorcasts?

Modern digital cameras produce accurate color in photos automatically without using additional settings. Colorcasts occur when you take pictures in one type of light, such as shade, but the camera either cannot determine the color temperature of the light source, or the camera is set to a type of light, such as bright sun. In the photos shown here, one was shot with AWB in the shade, which gives it a cool, blue cast. The second photo was taken with the WB set to shade, giving it the correct tone. To produce accurate colors, the camera must be set for the light in the scene. See Chapter 4 for more information about light.

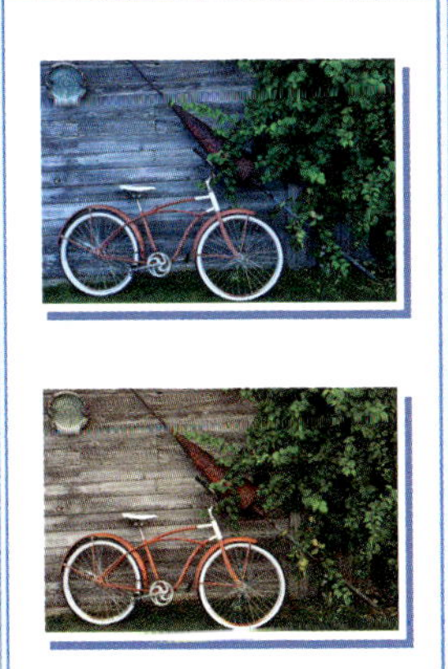

Set White Balance to Get Accurate Color

When shooting outdoors, you can usually use the automatic settings with confidence. However, you may want to experiment with different white balance, or WB, settings, to become familiar with the effect that each setting produces and to help you avoid taking pictures with unnatural colorcasts. To set the white balance, press the WB button and check the menu to find a setting that matches the scene light, such as daylight, fluorescent, flash, or tungsten (common household light). Be careful when you use manual settings: It is easy to forget that by selecting a white balance setting, you have turned off the automatic white balance.

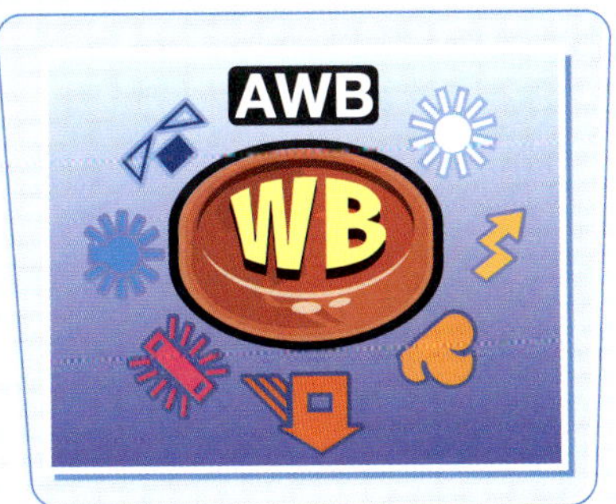

Never Use Digital Zoom

Although all digital cameras often advertise amazing telephoto zoom capability, digital zoom produces a lower-quality picture than just using the lens's optical zoom.

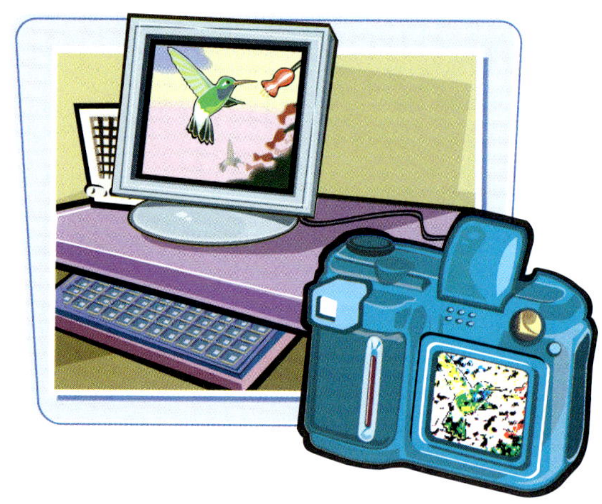

How Digital Zoom Works

With digital zoom, the camera crops into the center of the image, getting rid of the edges, and then expands the center section to full-image size. Some cameras *interpolate*, or add pixels into the image, to bring the image to full-resolution size. Because interpolation guesses where to add pixels to the image, the results are never as good as using optical zoom.

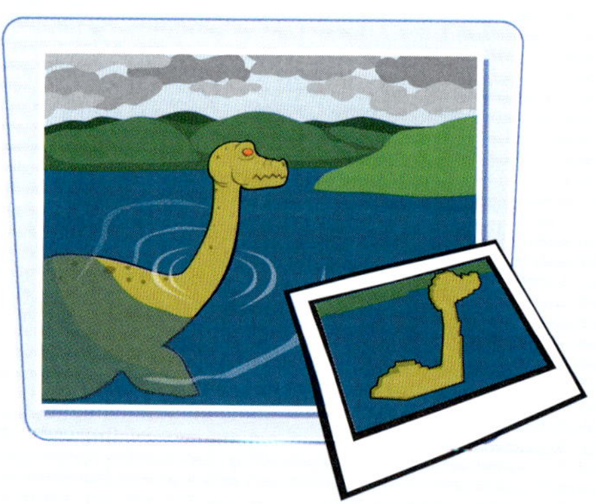

How to Avoid Using Digital Zoom

On all digital cameras that have digital zoom, you can turn off digital zoom by selecting an option on the camera's menus. Most cameras with digital zoom include an LCD indicator or an audible signal to tell you when to move from optical to digital zoom. Use the indicators to avoid activating the digital zoom feature.

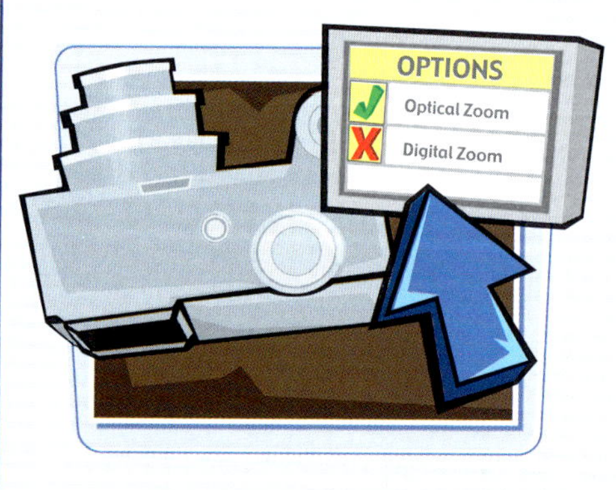

Reduce Digital Noise

Digital noise is multicolor flecks or pixels in dark areas of a low-light picture or areas of solid color, such as a bright blue sky. The noise can make your digital images look like a grainy film image. You can reduce the chances of getting digital noise by following a few simple guidelines.

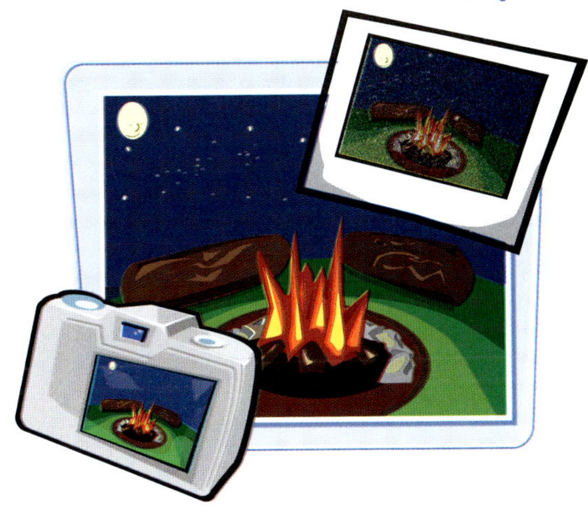

Recognize Digital Noise

When you take digital pictures in low-light scenes, or if the ISO is set to a higher number, you often see brighter, colored pixels scattered throughout the dark and shadow areas of the image. Although you may not see noise on the LCD without zooming in, you will see it on the computer at 100-percent or 200-percent magnification, and in larger prints, especially in large expanses of solid color.

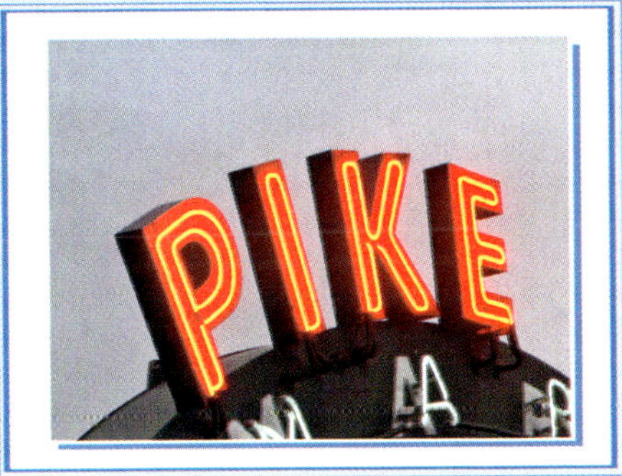

How to Avoid Digital Noise

Both high ISO settings and long exposures contribute to digital noise. To prevent digital noise, select settings such as ISO 400 or lower. dSLR cameras have lower noise in the images than compact digitals. If you have to take photos of moving subjects under low-light conditions, you can turn on digital noise reduction, if it is available on your camera. Digital noise reduction does not eliminate the noise, but it does reduce it; however, it may produce a "smeary" look.

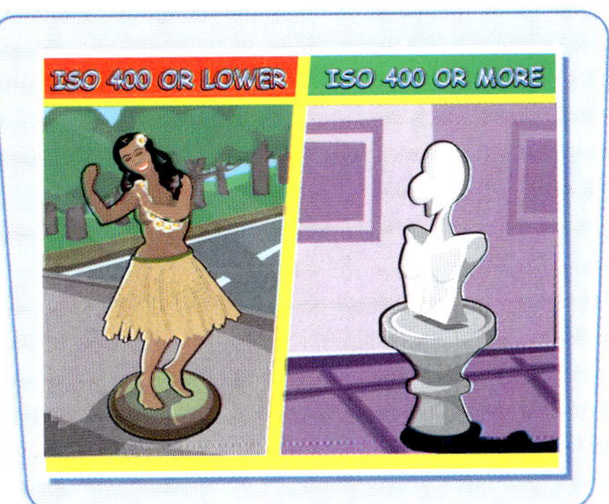

Chapter 11

Capturing Unique Photo Opportunities

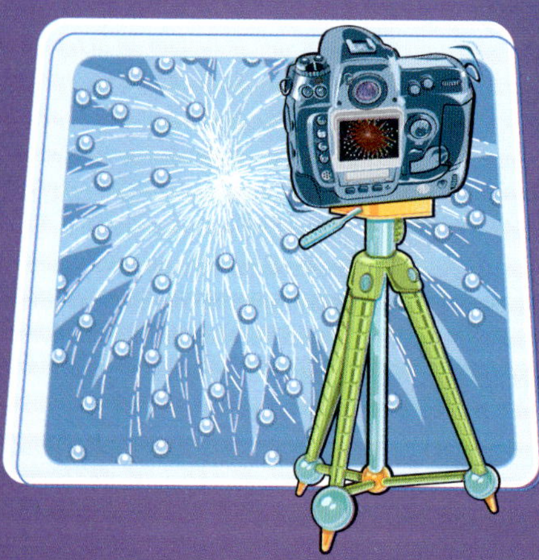

Some photographic situations are not ordinary and require extra effort to get a satisfactory result. Whether you are taking photographs of items to sell on eBay or for insurance purposes, capturing the grandeur of a fireworks display in the evening, or shooting and creating a panorama, you can use your digital camera to get the most out of each event.

Quick Steps

Photograph Products to Sell on eBay 122
Take Great Close-Up Photos 124
Take Photos at Night without a Flash 126
Capture Firework Displays 127

Photograph Products to Sell on eBay

Millions of people sell products on eBay every day. While using an existing product photo is a timesaver, products that sell best are those that include photos of the actual items. Taking your own photo, you can more accurately show exactly what you are selling, and if there is an interesting detail or flaw, you can point that out in a detail shot. In this section you learn the basics about how to photograph your priceless objects to get the best price for them.

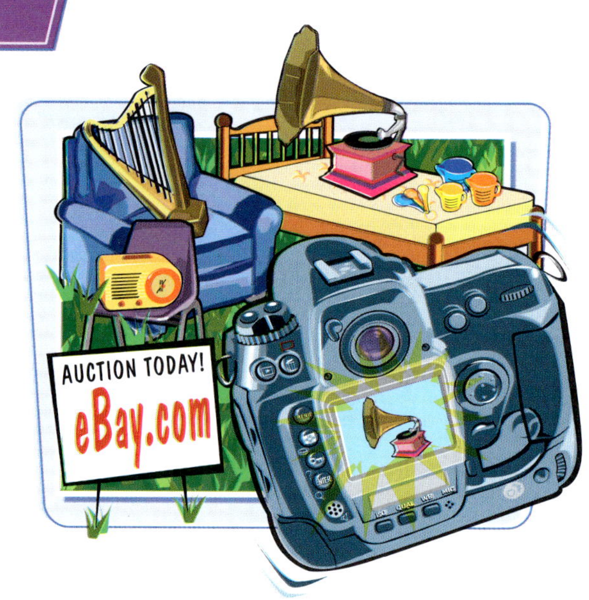

Keep It Simple

Do not take a photo of an object that has a cluttered background or a background the same color as the subject you are photographing. You want the eyes of the potential buyer to focus on the object that you want to sell and not to be lost in the background.

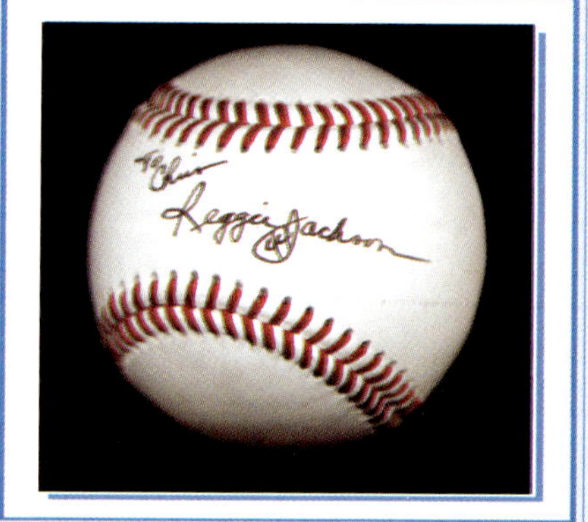

Fill the Screen

Fill the screen with the subject you want to sell. If the object you are photographing is small, hard to see, and potential buyers have a difficult time examining it, they will move on to similar objects for sale. Move in as close as possible and use the macro setting if necessary.

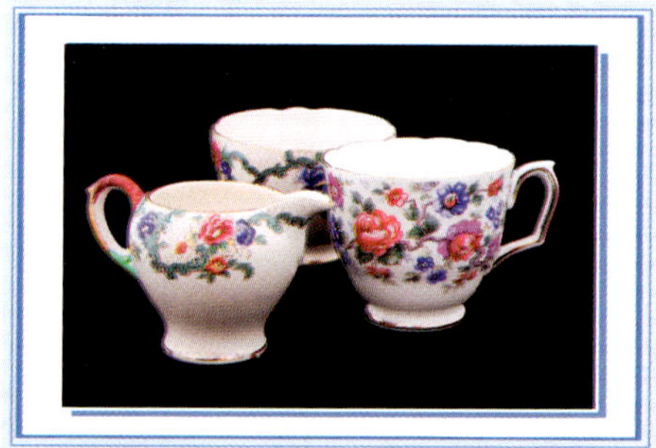

Use Props to Hold Objects Up

If the object is a book or something that typically lies flat, prop it up by putting it in a stand or by putting something behind it; this makes things look more dynamic. For flat items like books, magazines, or art, make sure that you are square to the item, so that the perspective is correct.

Using a tripod is very beneficial in this situation, and will help you to get your camera square to the subject. Additionally, with flat items, you can use tools such as the ALZO Horizontal Mount, which lets you position your camera so that it looks straight down at a subject on a table or floor.

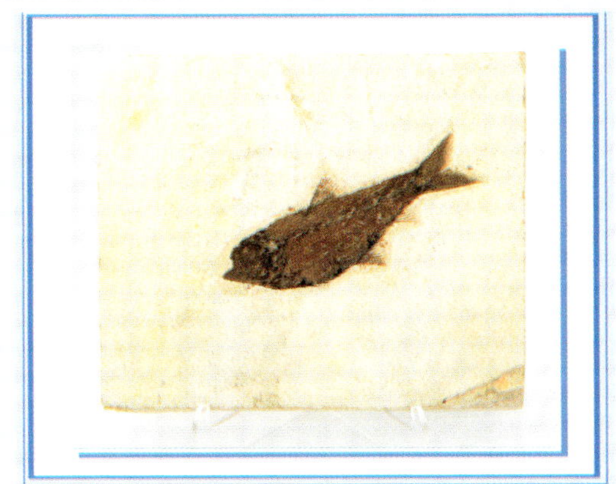

Focus, Focus, Focus

The autofocus (AF) system of a digital camera typically has a difficult time focusing under low light or when the subject is really close. Make sure your photos are in focus by viewing them on your computer or using the zoom function on the LCD screen on the back of your camera. Use the macro setting when appropriate, and make sure there is enough light so you do not have to worry about camera shake or depth of field.

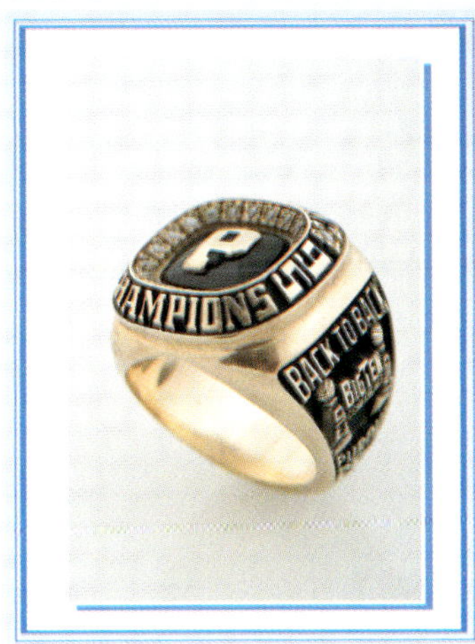

Look At Your Light

Take a few minutes to think about your lighting when shooting for eBay. You can place your subject near a window, outside in the shade, or in some other place that has plenty of light. Use a flash if necessary, and if you can, try bouncing the flash against a neutral wall or ceiling to get a softer light. Many eBay sellers invest a little in getting a small "light tent," which sheds even lighting on any subject.

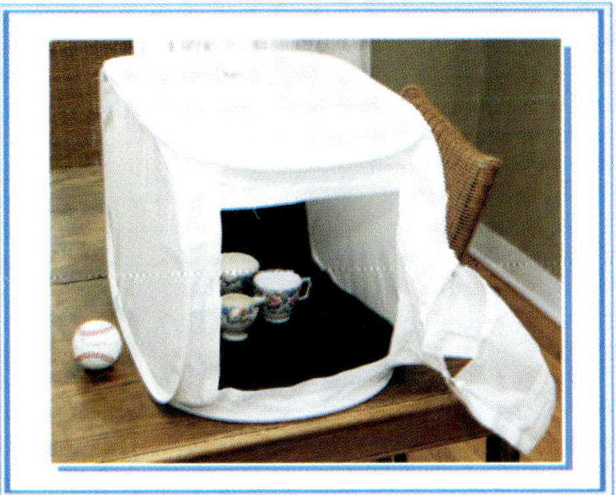

Take Great Close-Up Photos

Close-up photography (called macro photography) opens up a whole new world of detail. Most digital cameras do not require any special equipment because they have a macro mode built in. This section covers some very simple and basic rules for taking macro photographs.

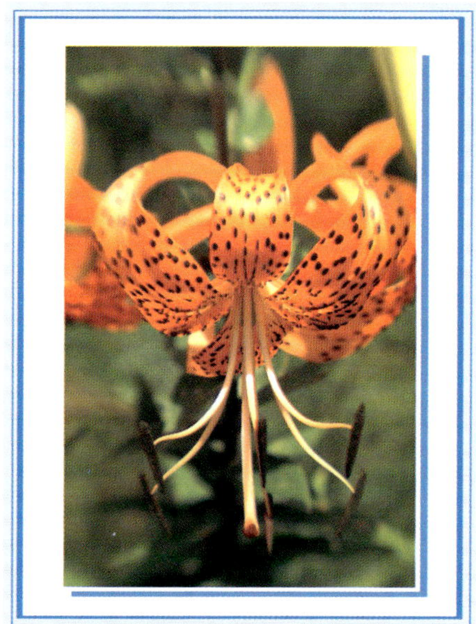

Switch the Camera to Macro Mode

Most digital cameras' macro mode is enabled by selecting the focus mode with a button or from a menu on the LCD screen. When the camera is in macro mode, it can focus on subjects that are as close as one inch from the camera lens.

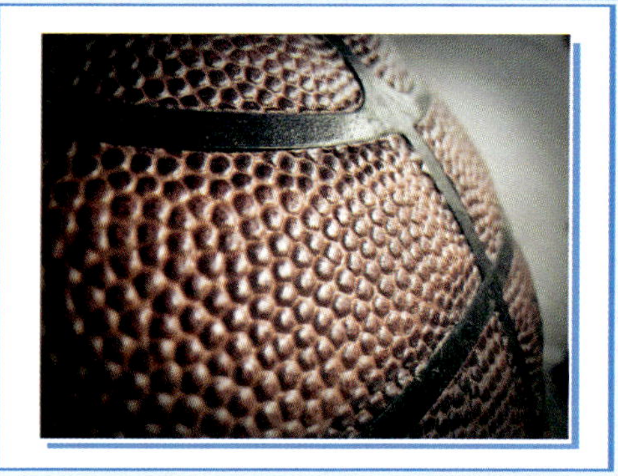

Get Close to Your Subject

Often the subjects of macro photography are at or near ground level. The best way to create a great photo is to get down on the ground with the subject. This allows you to steady the camera with your elbows on something solid, such as the ground.

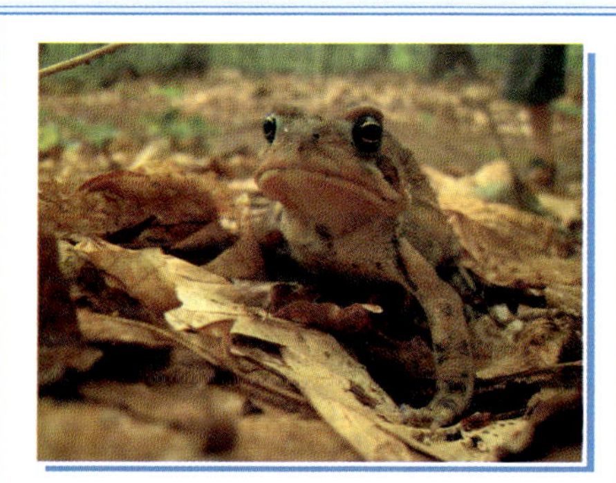

Use a Focus Light

When photographing natural subjects under low lighting conditions, the autofocus, or AF, system of the camera often has a difficult time finding the sharpest focus. Many digital cameras have AF assist lights built in, and shooting in macro is just the place to use this. Other times, the light on your subject may be what draws you to the subject, and some photographers even use a pocket flashlight in the field to help with focus.

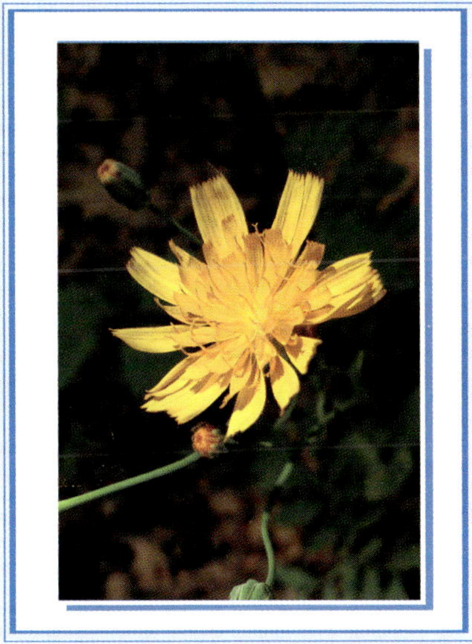

Depth of Field

When a camera is in macro mode, depth of field (DOF) is greatly reduced. This means that something only a few inches behind the subject may be completely out of focus. Reducing the aperture (increasing the f-stop number) can help increase the amount of area in focus, but it will rarely be more than a few inches in macro mode. In most cases it produces a soft background that enhances the photo.

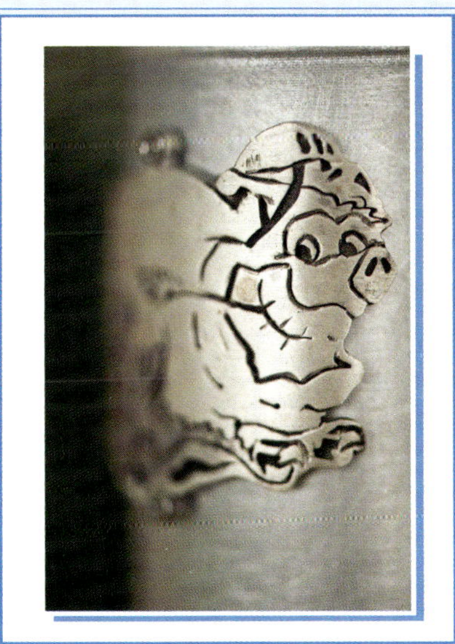

Take Photos at Night without a Flash

Taking photos at night without the use of flash can produce dramatic pictures; the camera changes the way areas of light and dark appear. The necessity to leave the shutter open for long periods of time to get a proper exposure produces streaks of lights as moving cars go past the camera lens. The light produced by high-pressure street lamps changes the colors of ordinary scenes into something surreal. A tripod might be helpful in this sort of photography, or making sure that you have set your camera to a high enough ISO.

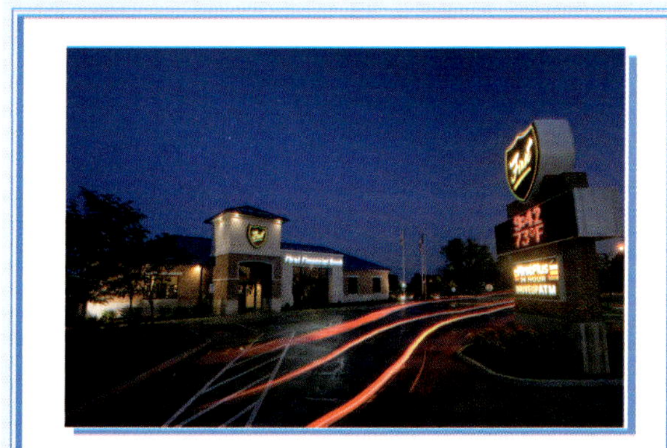

Use Night Mode

If your camera has a night mode setting, you should use it. Usually selected through a dial setting, the night mode usually increases the ISO (sensitivity) settings of the camera to a high level. This higher setting allows you to take photos without a flash, but it also increases the amount of noise in the photo.

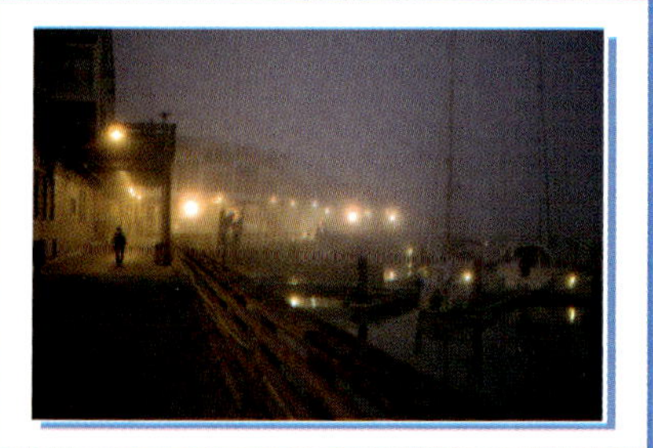

Keep Your Camera Steady

If your subject is stationary, you can take a photo under low-lighting conditions by stabilizing your camera. In most cases this means using a tripod, but a camera placed on a bean bag or something solid works just as well. The only problem with this approach is if the subject moves — your steady camera is of no use then.

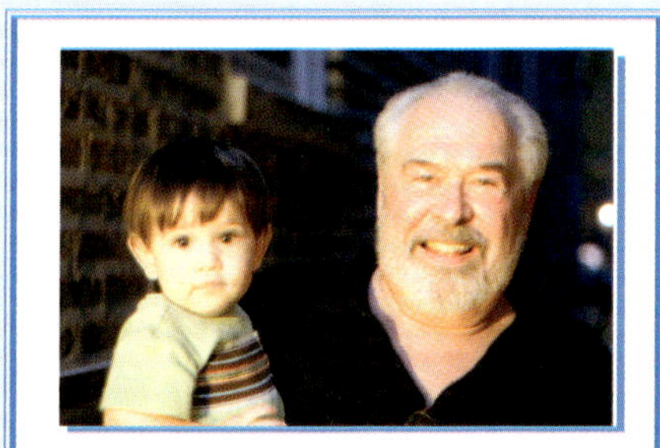

Capture Firework Displays

Firework displays dazzle viewers but can be a real challenge for the digital photographer to capture. Although the lights in the sky are beautiful to the human eye, they are dim to the digital camera and confuse many of the mechanisms in the camera such as autofocus and light metering. Some digital cameras actually have a fireworks shooting mode, but most do not. Here are some basic things to know about photographing fireworks.

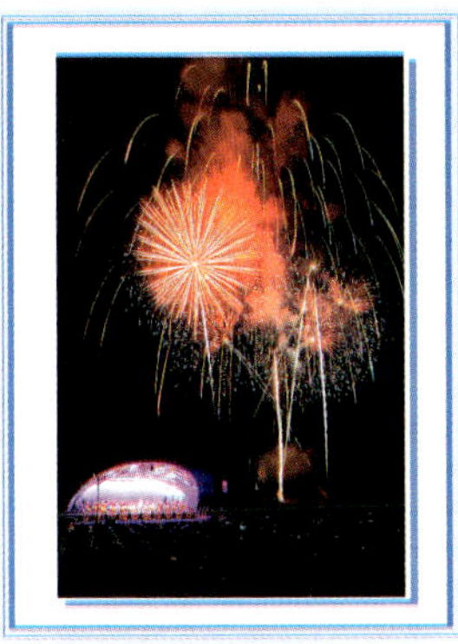

Capture Firework Displays

Set Up Your Camera

1. Set up your camera on a tripod.
2. Turn off your camera's flash.
3. Set the focus mode to landscape.

Note: *This turns off the automatic focus, or AF, and sets the focus to infinity.*

4. Set the shutter speed to bulb.

Note: *If your camera does not have a bulb setting, use a 1-second setting.*

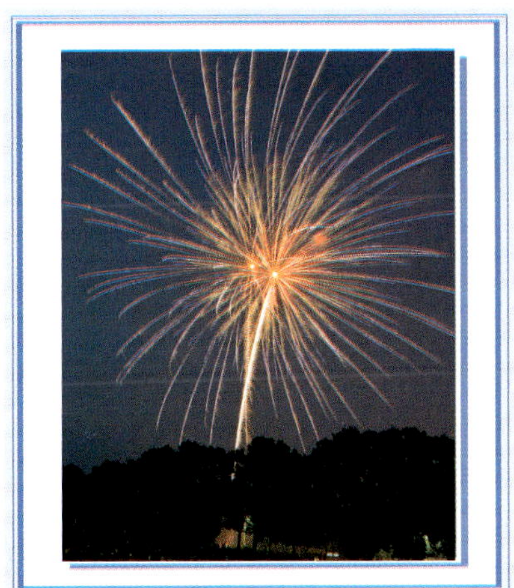

Capture a Burst of Fireworks

5. Aim the camera at the area you expect the fireworks to explode.
6. Wait until you hear the sound of a firework being launched (a dull thump).
7. If you use bulb setting, push your shutter release button down, and hold it.

Note: *If your camera has a remote shutter control, you can use it to prevent any jiggling caused by the pressure from your finger on the shutter release button.*

8. When the burst has completely finished, release the shutter.

Note: *For cameras without a bulb setting, press the shutter release button after the explosion has started.*

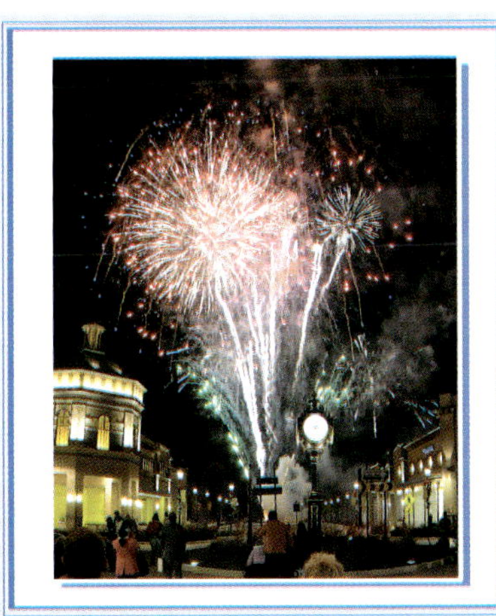

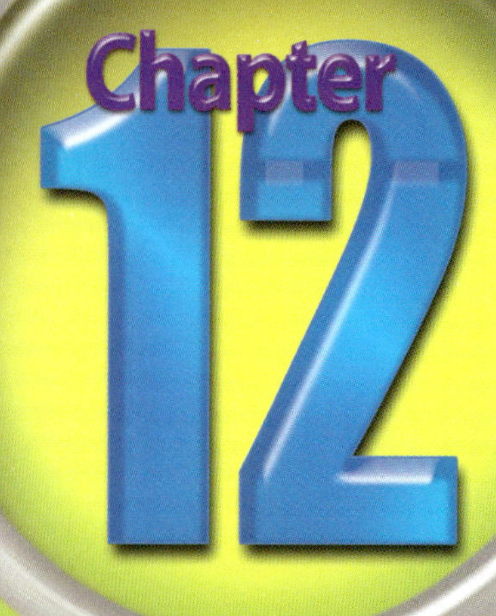

Organizing Your Photos

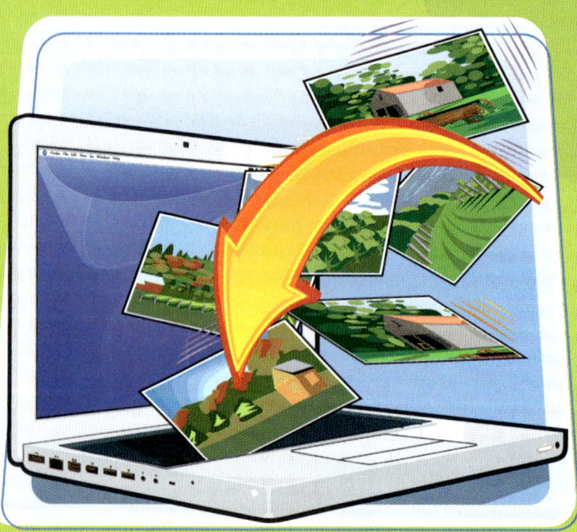

One of the many benefits of owning and using a digital camera is the ability to take an almost unlimited number of photos without incurring additional costs, such as film and processing fees. You can take and download so many photos to your computer that sorting and organizing them is often challenging. In this chapter, we discover how to start organizing your images so that it is quick and easy to view and find a particular photo.

Quick Steps

Why Use Image Editing Programs? 130
What Is a Digital Editing Workflow? 132
Photo Editing Options 134
Understanding Metadata in Your Photos 136
What Are RAW Digital Photos? 137
Import Photos to Your Browser 138
Review, Sort, and Tag Your Photos 140
Tag Photos 142
Find Images Using Tags 146
Use Tags to Sort 148

Why Use Image Editing Programs?

Image editing programs allow you to view and modify photographic images. You are able to open your digital photos, as well as crop, color-correct, and enhance them. With some image editing applications, you can even create special effects, modify elements of the image, add text, and convert images to different formats for various uses.

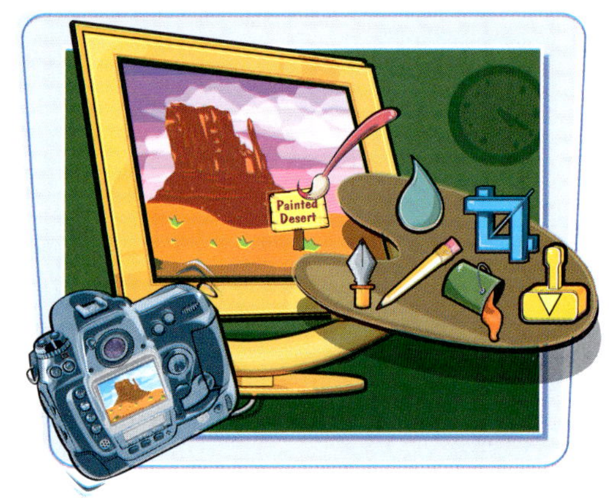

Image Editing Programs

You can choose from a variety of image editing programs. In fact, many digital cameras and photo printers include a simple image editing program. Such bundled programs are usually more limited in scope than those that are purchased separately. Most new home computers also have powerful image software built in that may allow you to do all the photo editing you need. These are easy to use and intuitive to learn and work with in conjunction with other programs on your computer.

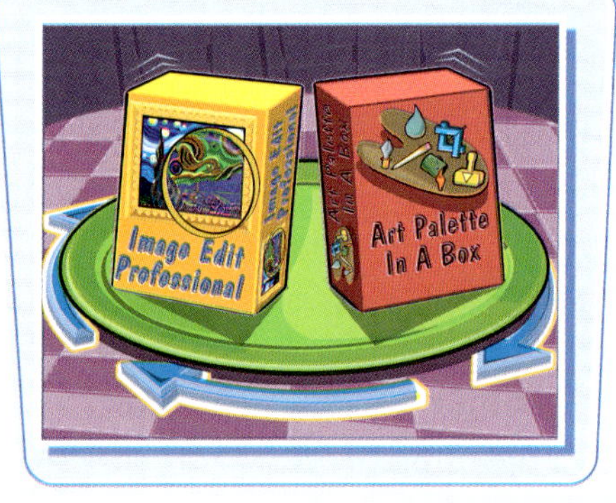

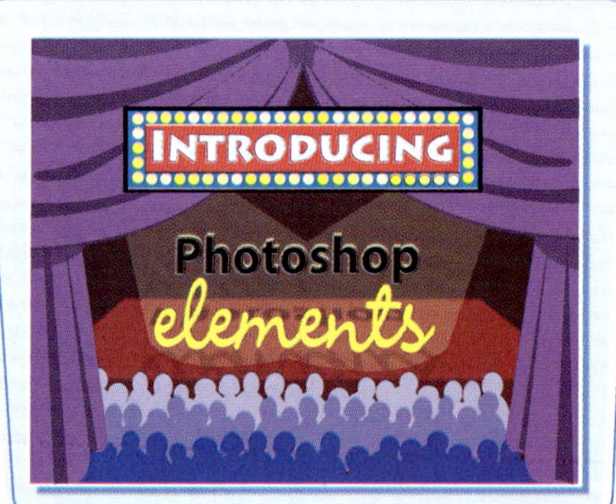

Use a Complete Image Editing Program

For a more advanced user, Photoshop Elements is considered a standalone image editing program. Based on the most widely used professional image editor — Photoshop — Photoshop Elements is very powerful and versatile, and therefore one of the most popular programs available. Photoshop Elements not only allows you to download images to your computer, correct photo problems, and apply special effects; it also includes a photo organizer that simplifies the task of viewing and organizing your digital images.

Change Ordinary Photos into Digital Creations

Using your image editing software you can make extensive changes to your photographs, adding or subtracting color or even subject matter. You may be able to add text to a picture and turn any photo into a greeting card. You can use your favorite photos to create a personalized calendar or create a slide show from any group of photos and save it with music and transitions.

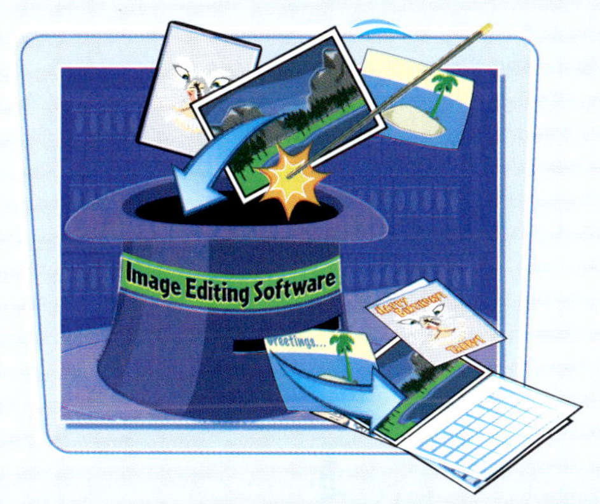

Why Use an Organizing System for Digital Photos?

When you start taking photos with a digital camera, the number of photos you take will increase dramatically. It is not unusual to take more than 100 photos at a birthday party or other event. With so many photos, you need a way to sort, group, and save them in specific locations on your hard drive or external media to keep things from getting lost and forgotten.

Stay Organized

You can import photos from your camera or memory card directly into your image editor's photo browser and categorize or tag them for easy reference. You can then use this photo browser to find and view specific photos while keeping them easily accessible and smartly organized.

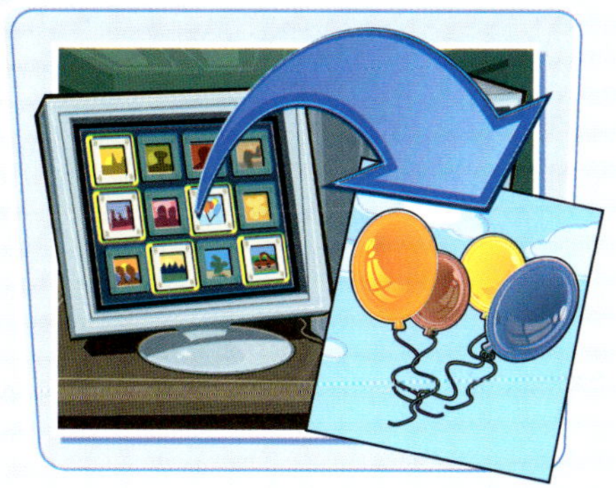

What Is a Digital Editing Workflow?

A digital editing workflow is a sequence of steps for importing, organizing, editing, and sharing your digital images. Following a workflow that fits your particular needs ensures that all your photos are imported, reviewed, organized, corrected, or enhanced, and prepared for sharing in a simple, straightforward manner. Setting up your workflow early helps to make sure that your images are easy to locate and work with now and in the future, saving yourself time and frustration.

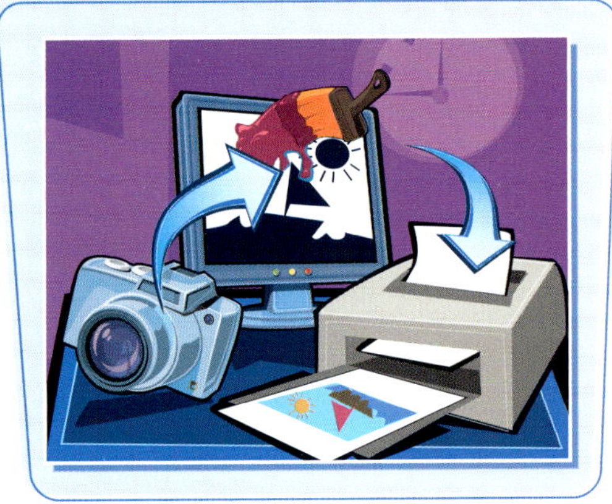

Import and Organize Your Photos

The first steps of the digital workflow include moving the photos from your camera or another folder to your computer, reviewing the photos, assigning tags and keywords that can be used to identify them, and grouping them into collections — which are similar to traditional photo albums with photos grouped by themes.

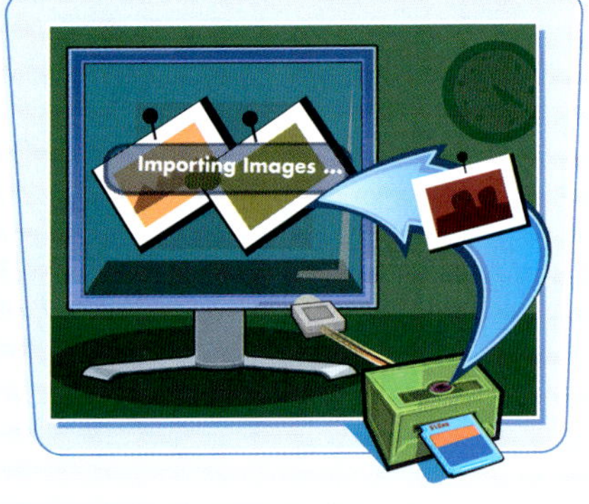

The Editing Process

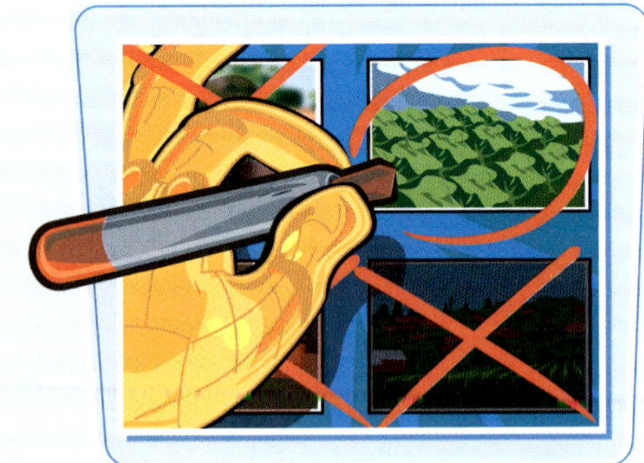

Evaluating your photos to find the best ones is very important. Use your photo browser to select your favorite photos with flags, or rate them with stars. This also gives you a chance to delete unusable images from your hard drive and to focus on your best photos.

Tuning Up Your Photos

The next steps include making changes to the photos to correct image rotation, removing defects such as red eye, and making adjustments to color and lighting. At this stage you can also make other enhancements such as removing objects or people from a picture, creating a composite of several pictures, and adding text or special effects.

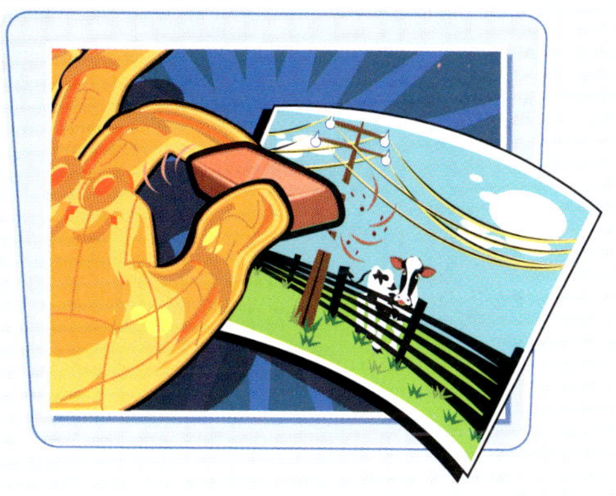

Make Digital Photo Creations

Optionally, you can use any photo to create special greeting cards or postcards, design photo calendars, and put together slide shows and photo albums. Many people create standard prints of these images for things like scrapbooks and traditional photo albums.

Output Photos for Print, CD, DVD, the Web, and E-mail

The final steps of the digital workflow is to print your images or creations or share them by burning a CD or DVD, making a Web photo gallery, or sending photos as e-mail attachments.

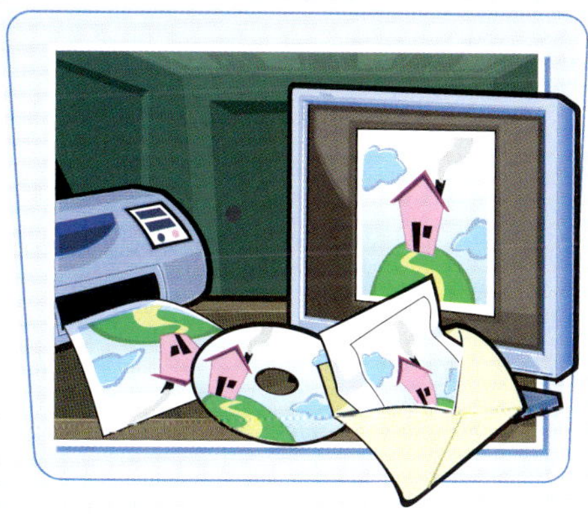

Photo Editing Options

There are many photo editing options, from the software that comes with your camera to expensive professional software. Some easy-to-use, easy-to-learn, and still powerful software is probably already located on your computer.

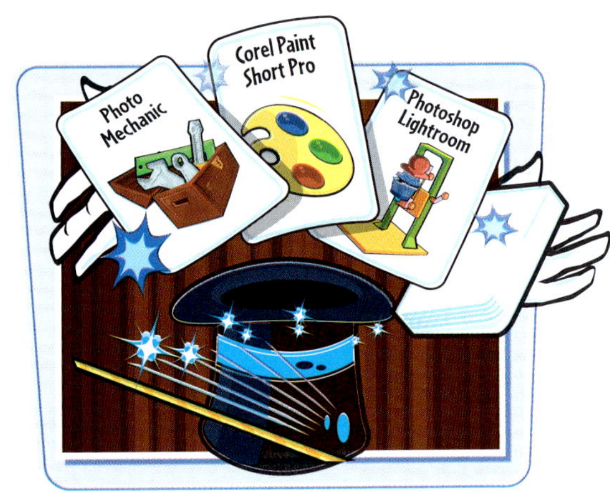

As you begin to go farther in your photography, the software that comes with your camera and the software built into your computer may not be powerful enough to harness your creative vision. Several software developers have come up with very powerful image editing software. Do some research before you spend your money on these, and make sure they do what you want and they work intuitively for you. Most of these allow for a free trial period so you can try them and see how they work for you.

Basic Photo Editing Options

Windows Live Photo Gallery

If you are using a PC with the Windows operating system, you can begin using Windows Live Photo Gallery, which is part of the free Windows Live downloadable software suite. Windows Live Photo Gallery is a photo browser which also allows you to go through and look at your photos, select and edit, and help output your images easily on your PC.

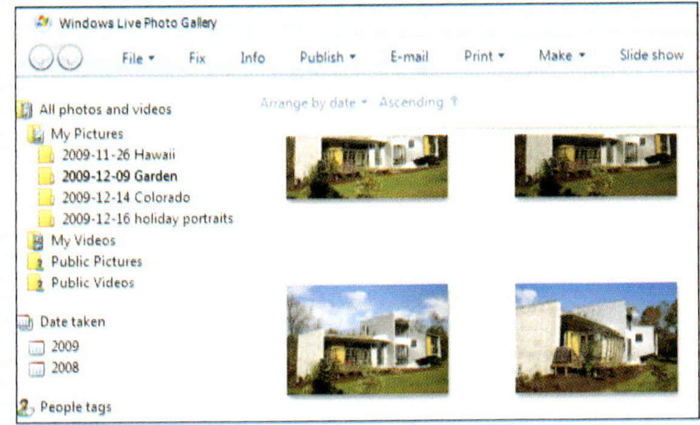

iPhoto

For Mac users, you can take advantage of iPhoto, which is part of the iLife software suite. iPhoto gives you the ability to review, organize, edit, share, and output your images. iPhoto is also designed to be integrated with your Mac and all of the iLife applications such as iMovie, Mail, and so on. iPhoto helps you easily work with your photos in any Mac application.

Advanced Photo Editing Options

Photoshop Elements

Photoshop Elements is the most popular computer image editing program available, and because it is based on the most widely used professional image editor — Photoshop — Photoshop Elements is also a powerful and versatile program. Photoshop Elements not only allows you to download images to your computer, correct photo problems, and apply special effects; it also includes a photo organizer that simplifies the task of viewing and organizing your digital images. Photoshop Elements can be purchased for either Windows or Mac.

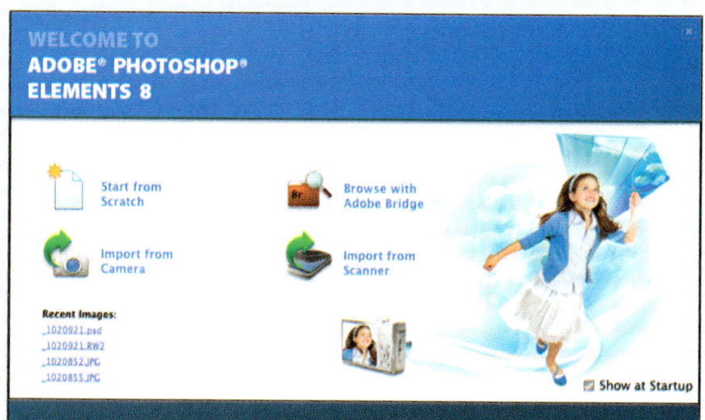

Photoshop Lightroom

Photoshop Lightroom is also based on, and can integrate with, Photoshop, but it is a more powerful image catalog system, browser, and RAW converter. Photoshop Lightroom uses a system of *sidecar* files to make changes to your photos without actually affecting the image files until you output your photos. The catalog system with Photoshop Lightroom is also excellent, allowing both easy access to your folders and the ability to make collections of favorites and events. Photoshop Lightroom is available for both Windows and Mac.

Photo Mechanic

Photo Mechanic is a very powerful photo browser that can be used on both Windows and Mac. It allows for very fast scrolling through images at high resolution. Photo Mechanic is an excellent program for those dealing with batch changes to EXIF data and image resolution. Photo Mechanic is the image editing software choice for photojournalists.

ACDSee

ACDSee is a bundle of image processing software that can be purchased together or separately. It has options that allow for creative framing and card making, help with high quality printing, and image organizing. ACDSee Pro offers many of these options as well as professional-level color and contrast controls and pixel-level editing. ACDSee is available for computers using Windows.

Corel Paint Shop Pro

Ease of use is the hallmark of Paint Shop Pro. This image editing program adds features that allow for 1-click solutions to correct many of your photos' problems, such as red eye, sharpness, and contrast. Paint Shop Pro also lets you add special effects and print and share your photos using its easy-to-learn interface. Paint Shop Pro is available for computers using Windows.

Understanding Metadata in Your Photos

One of the unique features of photos taken with digital cameras is that a lot of information about the camera and its settings is stored with each image. When you release the shutter, a digital camera records more than just the scene you captured. The camera attaches descriptive data known as ***metadata*** to each image file on the digital media card. Many different types of data can be attached to an image. Some cameras even provide a Global Positioning System (GPS) receiver connection, thereby precisely pinpointing the location where the photograph was taken.

What Is EXIF?

EXIF stands for Exchangeable Image File Format. It is the most commonly used metadata. It was developed to standardize the exchange of data between imaging devices such as a camera and software. EXIF is the information that the camera stores with each photo and includes the date and time, the make and model of the camera, the white balance settings, whether the flash was used, and other details about the image capture.

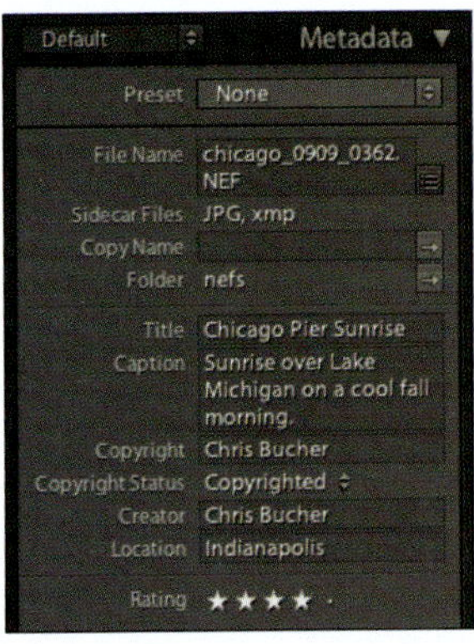

chicagoBDay_0909_A-312.jpg

Camera Data 1

Make:	NIKON CORPORATION
Model:	NIKON D90
Date Time:	2009-09-19T19:56:22.00-04:00
Shutter Speed:	1/400 sec
Exposure Program:	Aperture priority
F-Stop:	f/4.5
Aperture Value:	f/4.5
Max Aperture Value:	f/4.4

How You Can See the Metadata

Photographers and photo students used to have to write down all their exposure information in a log to remember what they did later when they looked at the developed photos. Now you have all that information at your fingertips as you are learning what effect changing your camera has on your photos — and the camera saves the information automatically.

Personalize Metadata

You can add your own information to the file's metadata to help identify and organize your images. When you add titles, tags, and descriptions in your photo editing software, it stores that data with the photo file. In fact, when you edit photos in Photoshop Elements, the edit history is also added to the metadata.

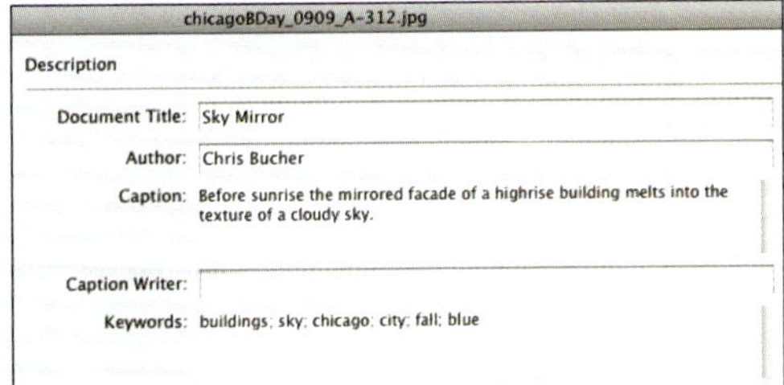

What Are RAW Digital Photos?

dSLRs and most high-end compact digital cameras can save photos in a format called *RAW*. The term RAW is not an acronym. It means that the image data coming off the camera sensor is not processed or compressed before being saved to the memory card. Although RAW format files are larger than JPEG files, they give the photographer more control over exposure, color, and tonal correction of the photo when it is processed on the computer.

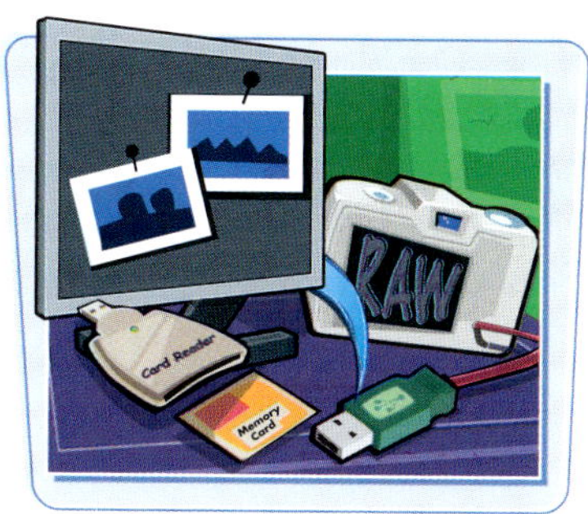

Processing RAW Format Digital Photos

Before you can use a RAW format file on your computer, you must first convert it into a standard graphics format. There are several ways to process RAW digital photos in your computer. You can use conversion software provided by the camera manufacturer, a third-party conversion program, or the RAW file conversion software now included in many popular image editors. Regardless of the process you choose, the end result is an image in a format that can be used with your image editor, such as a JPEG or TIFF.

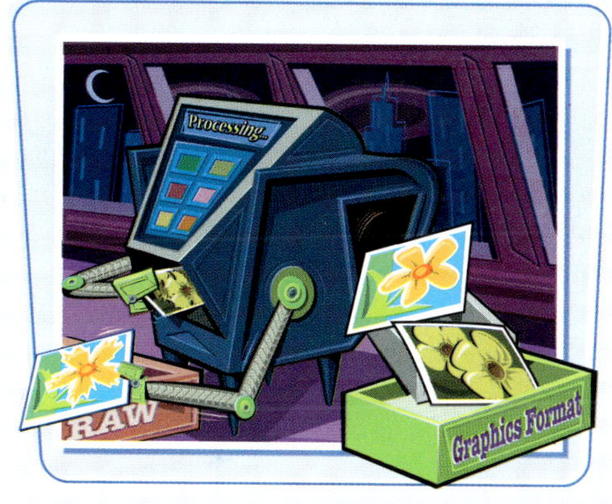

Advantages of RAW Format

When you take a photo using a JPEG format, the image sensor data is processed using the camera's current white balance, exposure, contrast, and saturation settings and these settings cannot be changed. When an image is saved as a RAW file, the actual data produced by the photo sensor is stored on the memory card. As the photographer, you can then visually control the color and tonal corrections as you process the image on the computer. This allows you to maximize your control of virtually every aspect of the image, not to mention get the best possible image quality because you are working with the original image file with the most information.

Import Photos to Your Browser

When you bring photos or any other media files into your photo browser or image editor, you have the opportunity to rename your images; add keywords, events, and dates; and create or build your catalog. Each photo editor does this slightly differently; here are some basics for both Mac and Windows.

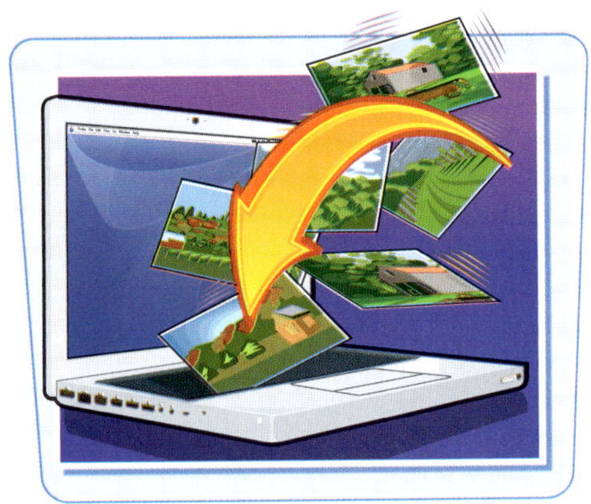

Import Photos into iPhoto

If you already have photos on your computer, it is easy to just drag the folder of photos onto the iPhoto icon in the dock. The photos are automatically imported and sorted by date, and are then called *events*.

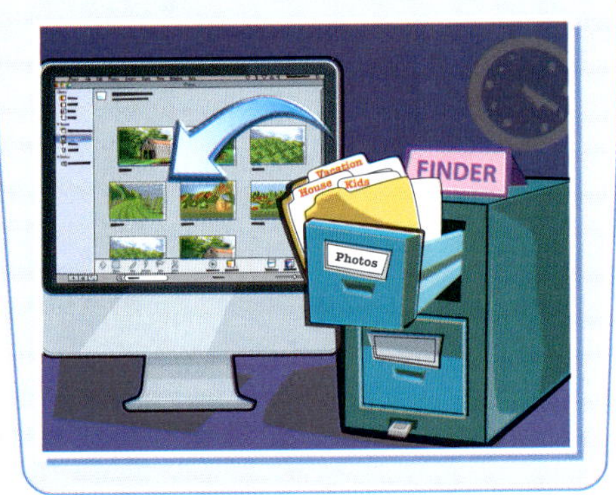

Import Photos from a Camera or Card to iPhoto

When you plug your camera or memory card into your Mac, the photos automatically upload into iPhoto. This is a nearly seamless operation, and by default, iPhoto opens when you first plug in the disc or camera. As above, the photos are sorted initially by date.

Import Photos from a Camera or Card to Windows Live Photo Gallery

1. Connect your card or camera to the computer by plugging it into the USB slot.

   The Import Pictures and Videos dialog box opens.

2. Type a word, phrase, or event that describes the photos.
3. Click **Import**.

- Leave the Erase After Opening box unchecked.

Note: *Remember to format the card in the camera after you are certain you have saved all images.*

The Windows Live Photo Gallery opens and displays your photos.

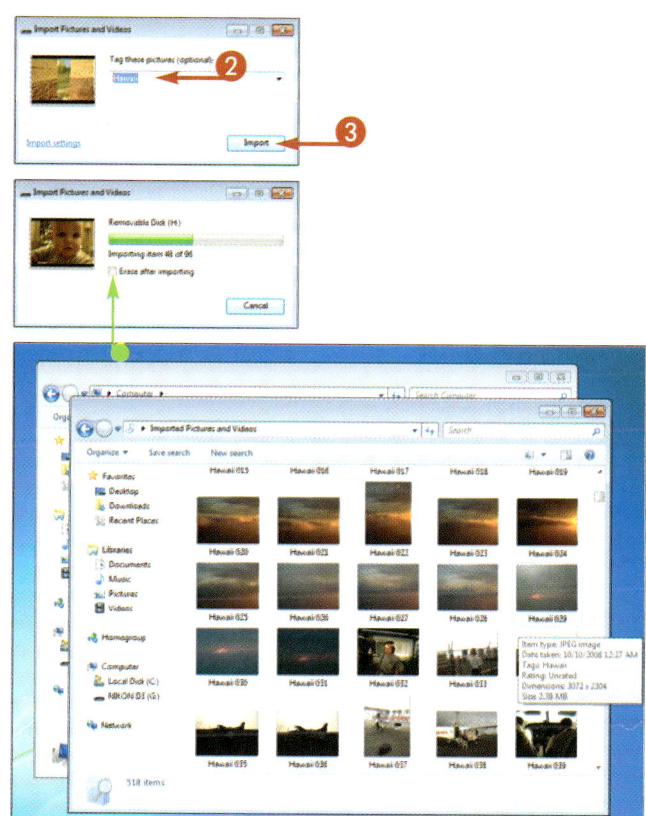

How do I view newly imported photos?

When you are ready to go back to look at the photos, remember that Windows stores the imported digital photos in the Pictures library. Windows Live creates a new subfolder, which is named with the date of the import and whatever word, phrase, or event that you typed into the Tags box before importing. So if you downloaded the photos on November 29, 2010 and you typed **Colorado** in the Tags box, the subfolder will be named 2010-11-29 Colorado.

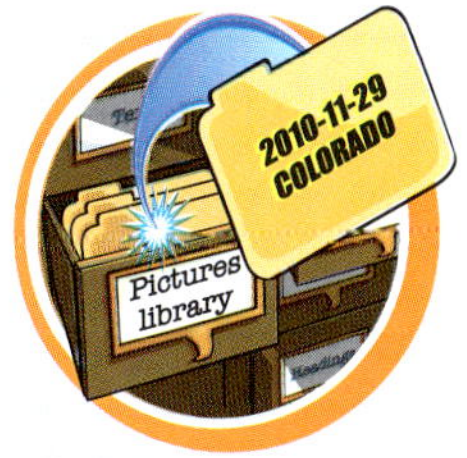

Review, Sort, and Tag Your Photos

After the photos are in your computer and have been added to the catalog, the next step is to carefully review them, compare similar images, and decide which ones should be kept and which should not. Why not keep all of them? Photos take up space on your hard drive, so keeping photos that you do not need wastes your time — when looking through the catalog — and occupies space on your hard drive.

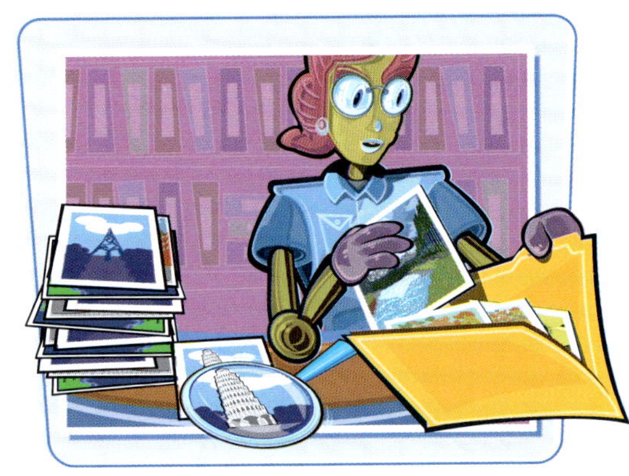

Review and Tag Your Images

With all the new technology available to us we are now able to access our images and the people in them like never before. In both Windows and Mac, you can "tag" your photos, assigning them keywords, descriptions, and people's names so that they may be found, and so that they may be grouped together. These new technologies also allow you to use facial recognition software so that you can easily find photos of family and friends among the many photos stored on your computer.

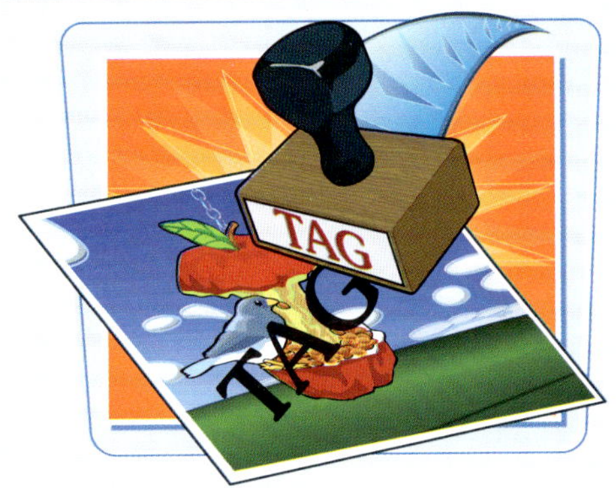

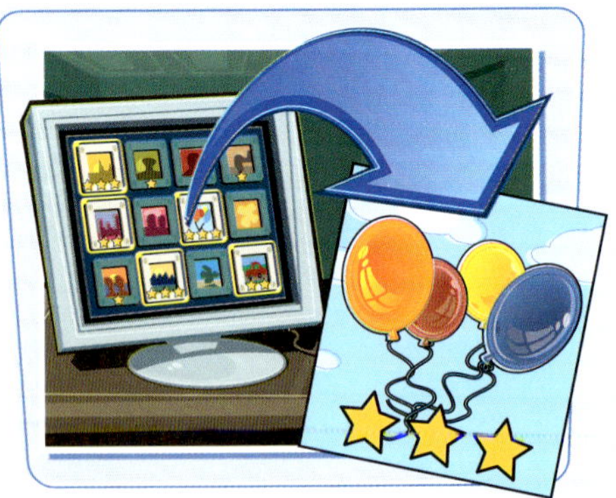

Rate Your Images

Many photo browsing software programs have ways to rate your photos, usually by giving the photo a star rating. Rating your photos is a great way to help refine your editing choices. Giving your favorite two or three photos from a shoot five stars lets you know that those are probably ones that might go on the wall, four-star photos might go in the photo album, three-star photos might go into the long form slide show, and, well, you get the picture.

Flag in iPhoto

Besides using star ratings, iPhoto also uses flags to denote favorite photos.

In the large view of a photo, simply click on the flag to mark that photo as flagged. In the browser view, a small flag (●) appears at the upper left corner of the photo. The flag is easily seen, but unobtrusive, so that you can find your favorite photos quickly.

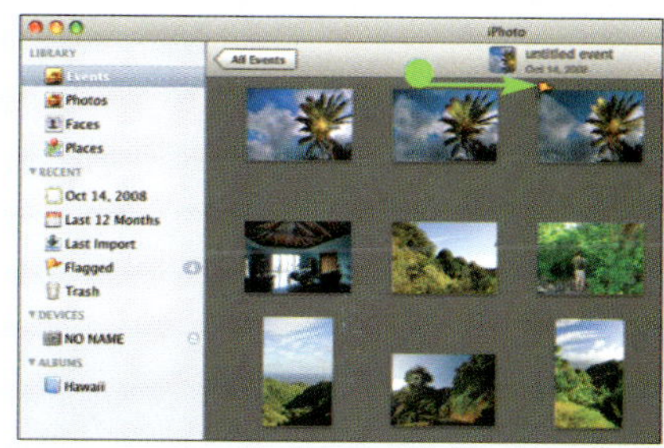

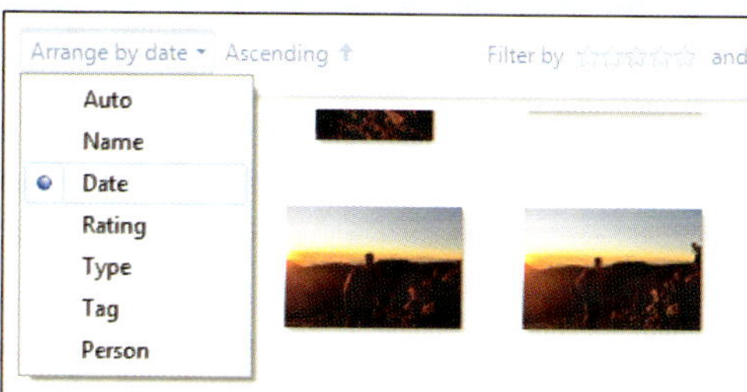

Arrange

How the photos get arranged on your screen is entirely up to you. Some people set their photo browser to show images via date or name, whereas others are constantly changing their viewing options. Typically you can arrange by Date, Name, Filename, Rating, Type, Flag, or Tag, and generally you can set them to ascending or descending order, depending on what you are looking for.

Reviewing in Windows

In Windows Live Photo Gallery, you can quickly scroll through your photos to see which photos you like or dislike. Positioning your cursor over the image (●), but without clicking, creates a larger thumbnail, which allows you to make sure the photo is in focus without leaving the browser.

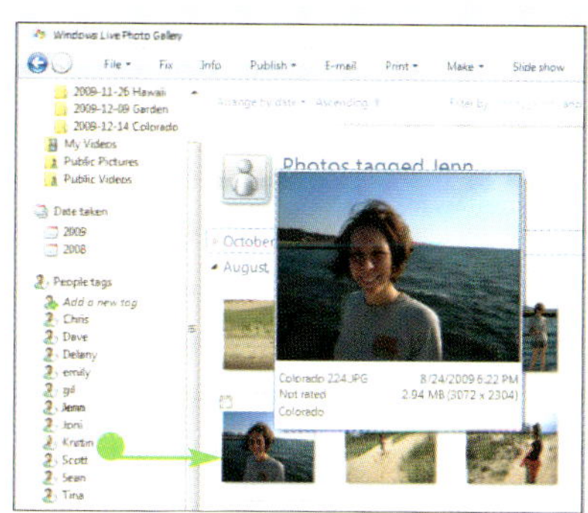

Tag Photos

Tagging your photos is a quick and easy way to find and recognize the people in your photos. This is the digital equivalent of writing the names of the people in the photo onto the back of photo prints. It is fast and easy and fun!

Clicking the photo takes you to a larger version of the photo. Click Info for the Tags Window to pop out.

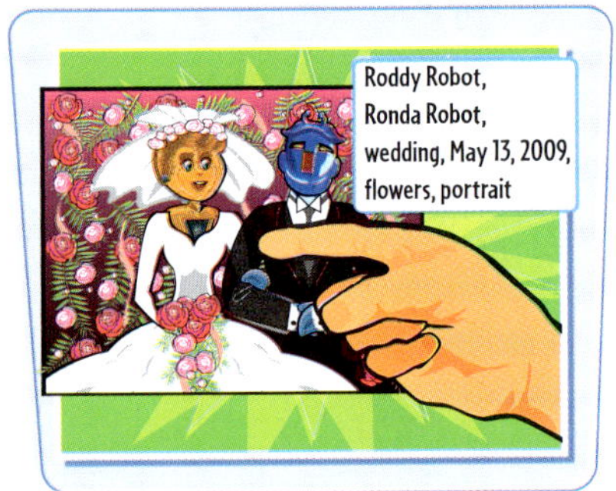

Tag Photos

Tag Photos in Windows Live Photo Gallery

1. Click **Tag someone**.

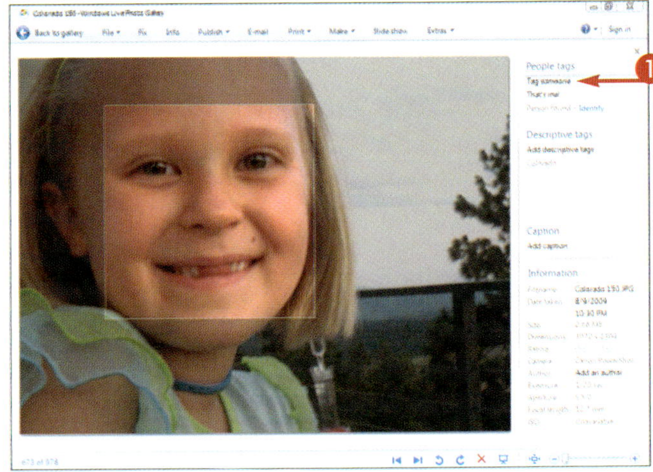

2. Click that person so that his or her face is highlighted.
3. Type that person's name.

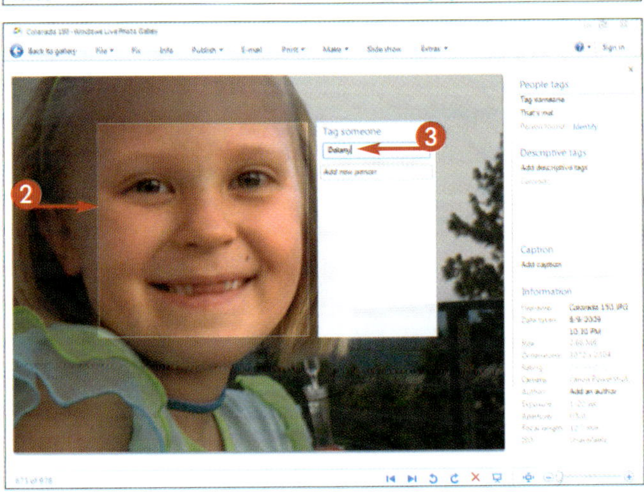

4. Click **Descriptive tags**.
5. Type any words, names, or descriptions of the photo that would help you remember them or group the photo with others.
6. Click **Caption**.
7. Type a caption of what is going on in the photograph.
8. Click a star rating for the photo for reference and grouping later.

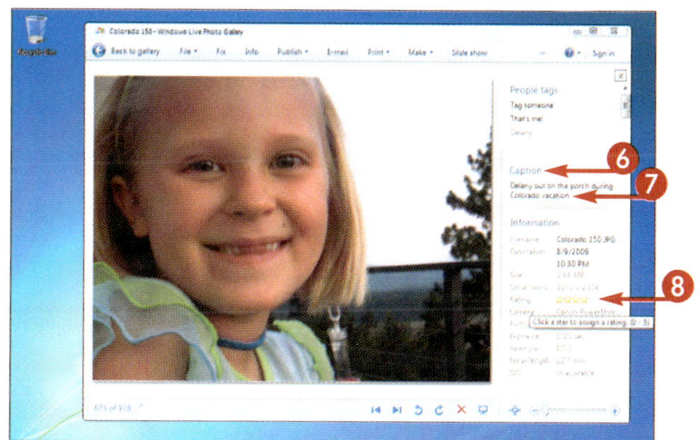

What if I want to tag something else besides a person?

In some cases you may want to tag a building, mountain, tree, or other inanimate object so that you can find it in a search later. Go ahead and click the **Tag Someone** button and then just use the cross-hair tool to tag your object and then name it as needed. You now have a tag for that object, but obviously any facial recognition will not work on a building or tree.

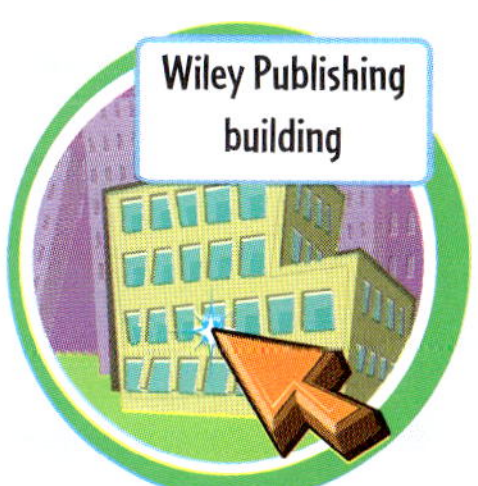

Tag Photos *(continued)*

In iPhoto, you can tag photos using the Faces tool, which is essentially the same as in Windows, but the interface is slightly different. iPhoto can locate people using built-in facial recognition type software, so tagging someone helps you find all the people with that face.

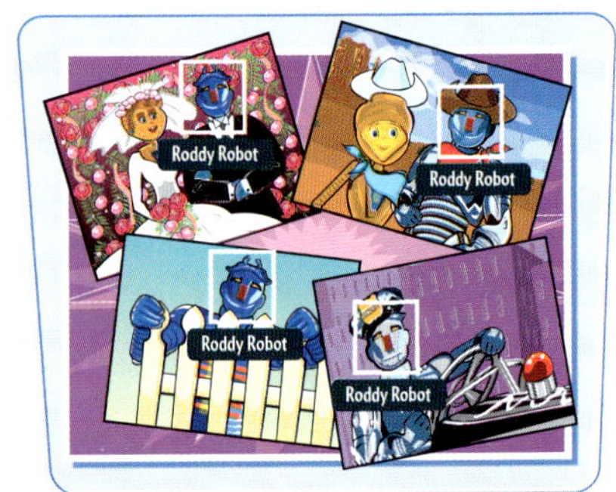

Tag Photos *(continued)*

Tag Photos in iPhoto

1. Click once on a photo of a face to select it.
2. Click the **Name** button (👤).
3. Click ***unnamed*** in the text box.
4. Type the name of the person.

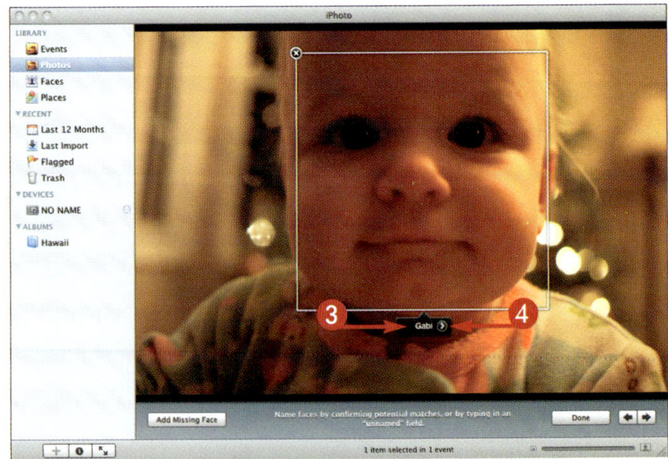

5 Click the arrow next to the name.

6 If a face is unrecognized, click **Add Missing Face** to put a selection box on the face.

iPhoto searches for other faces that might be the same as the one you just named.

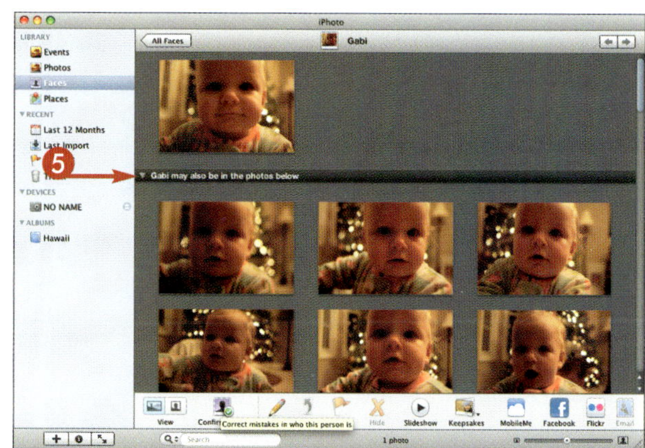

7 Click each face to confirm that this is the right name for the face.

You can ignore any faces that do not match the name.

8 Click **Done** to finish tagging that face.

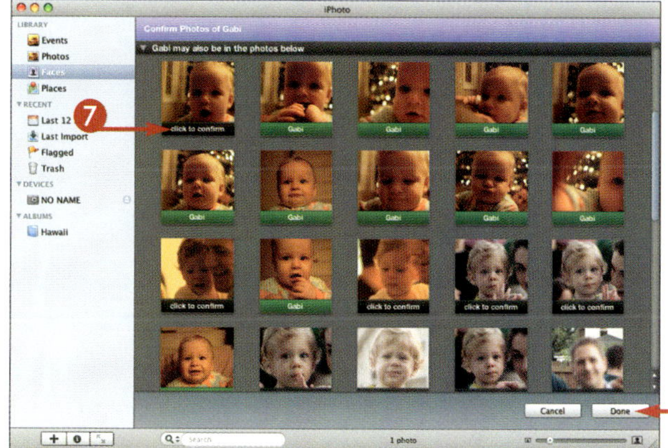

What if iPhoto does not recognize a particular face in one of my photos?

iPhoto may not have scanned through the photos yet for the face that you are looking for, or there may be some obscuring of the face which would make it unrecognizable to Faces. You can easily click the **Add Missing Face** button to make the positioning box appear so you can continue with the Faces process.

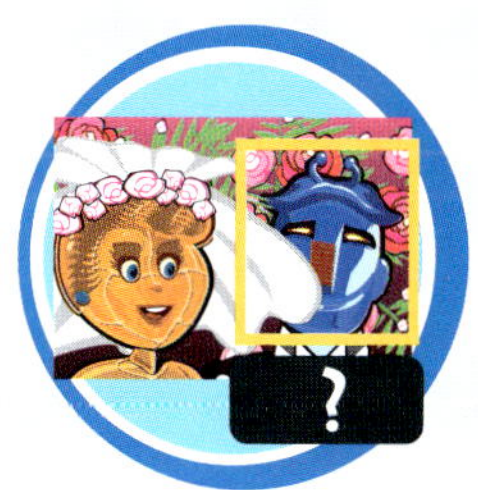

Find Images Using Tags

As you begin to scroll through your photos, the facial recognition software in your computer starts to pick up faces in your photos. With every new face that you tag, it becomes easier to identify the person and then just put that name with the photo.

Finding the photos of the people you are looking for is very easy, especially after you have begun the process and tagged people right from the start.

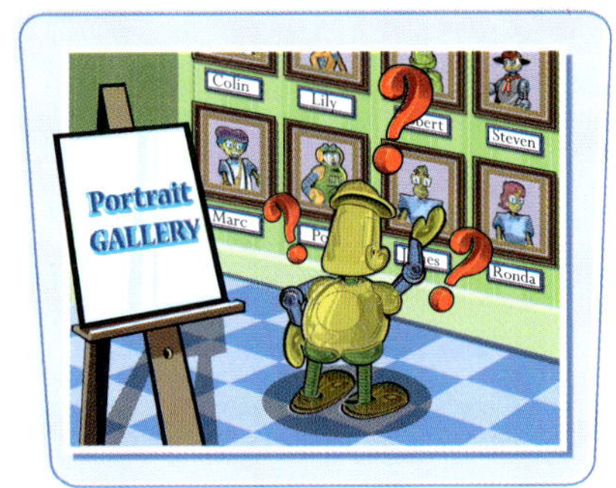

Find Images Using Tags

Using Tags to Find Images in Windows Live Photo Gallery

1. Click **Identify**.
2. Click the tagging square on that person's face.

   The Tag Someone menu opens.
3. Click the name of someone on the list if you have already put his or her name in.

- If it is a new face, type the name and then click **Add new person**.

4. Click the **Arrange by** drop-down menu and click **person**.

- All the people that you have tagged are shown under a headline with their name.

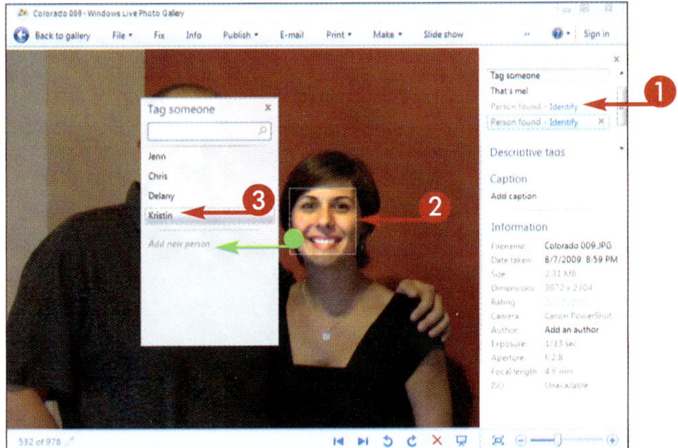

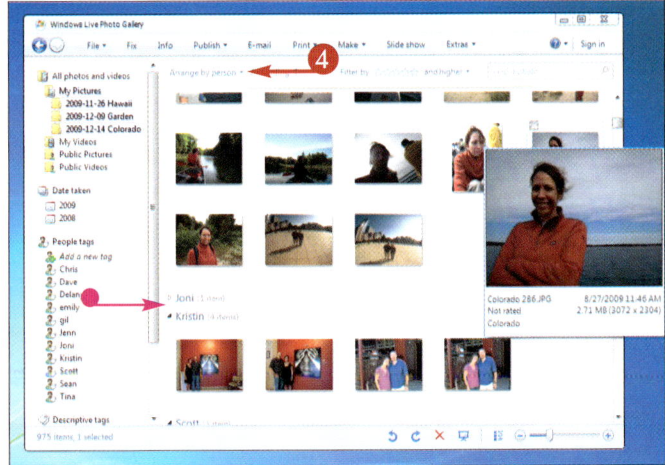

Using Faces to Find Images in iPhoto

1. Click **Faces**.

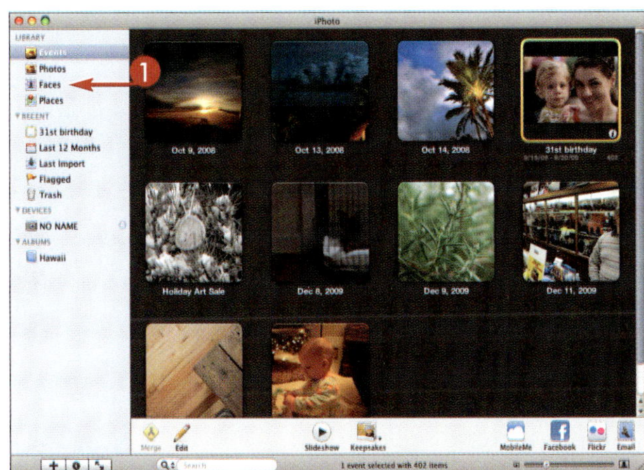

Find the person that you are looking for on the corkboard.

2. Click a face to get to the photos of that person.

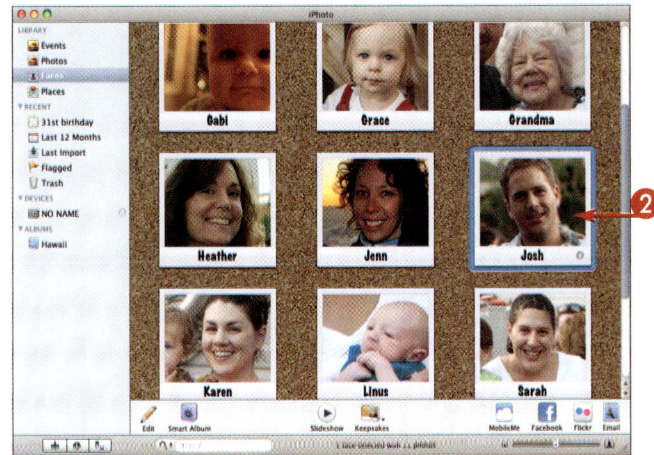

Are there other ways to add information in the Tags field?

You can enlarge the Details pane with a right-click on an empty section of the pane; click **Size** and then **Large**. At that point you can see many fields where you can add or edit data for each photo, such as Title, Subject, Rating, Comments, and Authors.

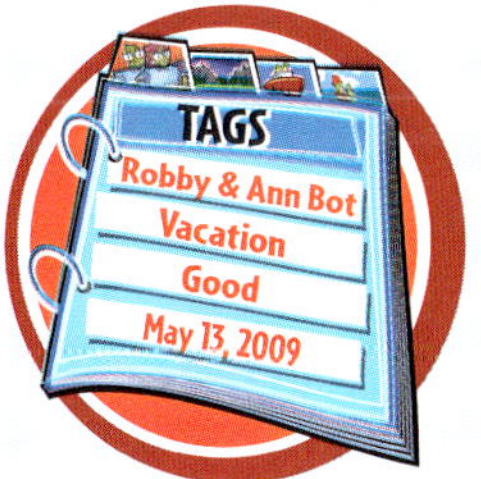

Use Tags to Sort

After you have done any tagging and starring of your photos, sorting through and arranging your favorite photos in any particular folder is easy. This keeps your favorite photos right at the top, or allows you to find what you are looking for easily.

If you are looking for someone, but there are still too many photos of that person, use your tags and sorting tools to find your dates.

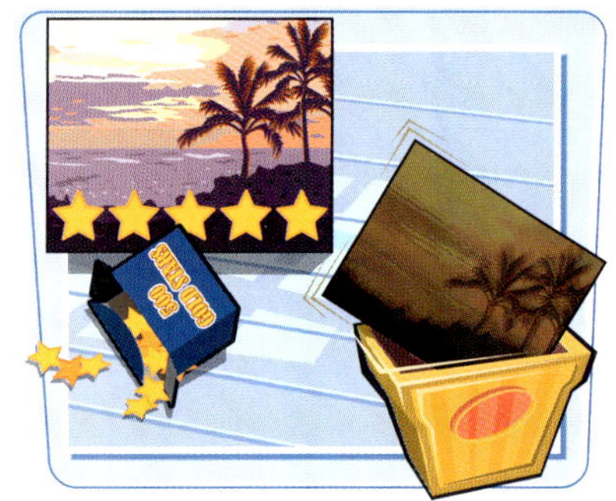

Use Tags to Sort

Use Tags to Sort in Windows Live Photo Gallery

1. Click a person's name.
2. Click the **Arrange by** drop-down menu and click **date**.

- This opens all the photos of the person you selected arranged by month.

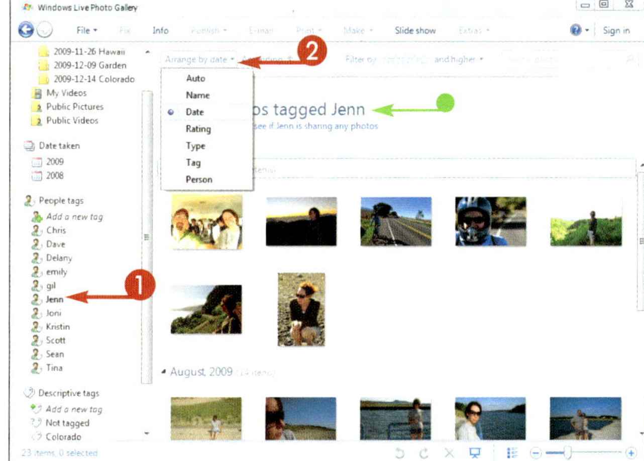

3. Click the triangle next to each month to collapse unused months.
4. Position your mouse over the photo that you think you are looking for to make a larger thumbnail.

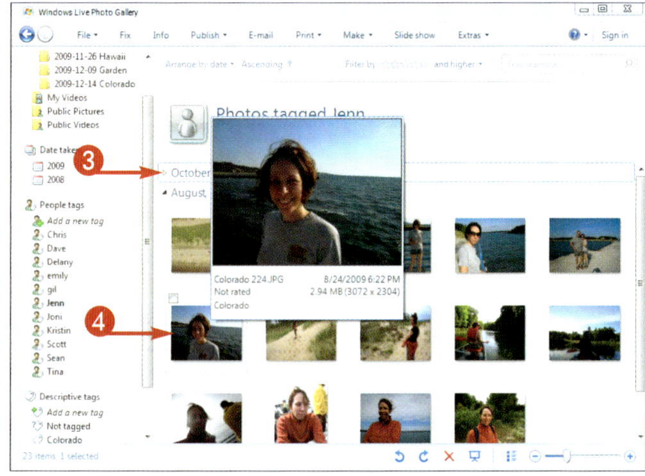

Use Tags to Sort in iPhoto

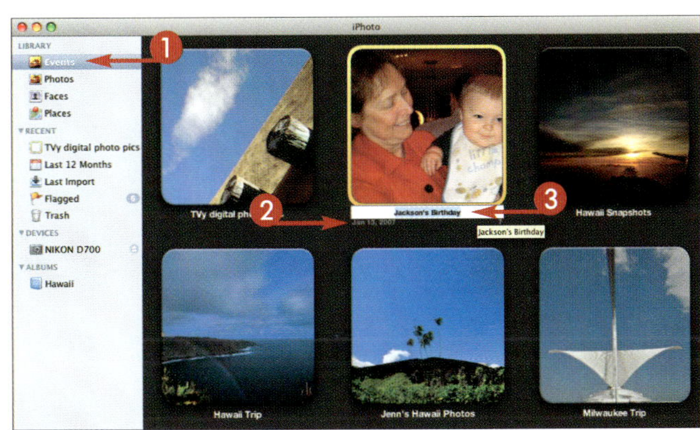

1. Click **Events**.
2. iPhoto initially sorts your photos by the date they were uploaded. Click the date below the photo.
3. Rename that event to a more descriptive title.

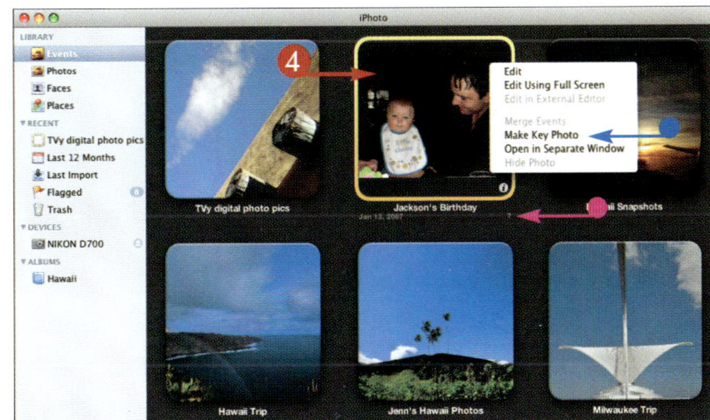

4. Click your event.

- You can see the date and how many photos are in the event.

5. Position your mouse over the Key photo for that event.
6. By simply dragging your mouse over that Key photo you can quickly see all the images in that event's album.

- You can choose another photo as your Key photo. Click and drag your mouse on the event. When you see the photo that you want for that event, Control+click it and click **Make Key Photo** from the menu that appears.

This all seems like so much sorting and tagging and starring. Why should I do this?

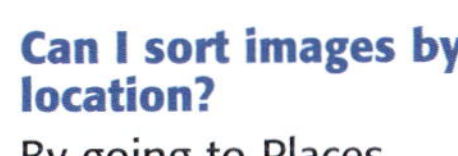

It really does not take long before you will have many, many photos on your computer — and hence many folders. Taking a few minutes when you import your images will save you countless hours when you are looking for things later. The more you do now, the easier it will be in the future.

Can I sort images by location?

By going to Places, iPhoto allows you to use a GPS-enabled camera to locate where you have taken photos. Places is a very easy, menu-driven way to log all your travels and sort your photos by location.